HOW DID LIFE END UP WITH US?

SS O'CONNOR

First published in Great Britain by Otium Press 2022

www.otiumpress.com

Text copyright: © SS O'Connor 2023

The moral right of the author has been asserted

A CIP catalogue record for this book is available from the British Library

ISBN 978-1-7391559-0-2

Cover and end papers: Details from Agave Americana by Bruce McLean.
Copyright, the artist. Published by CCA Galleries, London and printed by Coriander Studios.
Reproduced by kind permission of Bruce McLean and the CCA Galleries, September, 2022

Book design and art direction: Ash Gibson
Photo editor: Cat Costelloe

Type set in Adobe Garamond, Brandon Grotesque and NY Irvin.

Printed and bound in the UK by The Pureprint Group

OTIUM PRESS

Grand Union Studios, 332 Ladbroke Grove, London, W10 5AD

info @otiumpress.com

For Geoff Culmer

The Secrets of Life Quartet

The Secrets of Life:
From Big Bang to Trump

BOOK ONE

HOW DID LIFE END UP WITH US?

SS O'CONNOR

OTIUM PRESS

Life? Just another circus?

INTRODUCTION

A few years ago I was inching my car through the carbon trap of a Piccadilly traffic jam, when I heard the radio interviewer stammering slightly as he attempted to summarise his guest's scientific insights.

'So… what you're saying is XXXX.'

There was a long silence. Had the reception failed? Had the man taken offence and walked off in a huff? But eventually there came the rumble of a chuckle, and then a voice heavy with amused self-mockery.

'Yeeeees. But I'd have taken thirty pages to say it.'

Ha, I thought, raising a fist in mute solidarity. How I admired the great expert for refusing to take himself too seriously. It's not something you hear that often. We live in a world in which knowledge is power, and it's rare to find someone who's willing to take people *out* of a problem rather than showing how clever they are by taking them ever deeper into it. But I was also nodding in appreciation towards the presenter for having the courage to reduce his guest's tricky concepts down to a bite-sized chunk.

But why just thirty, I thought? What about three hundred? After all, how often does one read a book, only to later see a reviewer manage to parcel it all up into just a few sentences? And aren't they generally fairly accurate at getting to the essence of what it's about?

And, after all, in a parallel universe in which the radio existed in Victorian times, wouldn't the presenter have been reflecting the bewilderment of his listeners if he'd been interviewing Charles Darwin after the publication of *On the Origin of Species*?

Perhaps he'd also have tried to sum up what his crazy, beardy guest had just told him about how evolution explained the extraordinary complexities of Nature.

Presenter: 'So, what you're saying is… there's only one general law which leads to the advancement of all organic things, namely: multiply, vary, let the strongest live and the weakest die.'

Darwin: 'That's right. You've expressed it perfectly. In fact, if you don't mind, I think I'll use those exact words from now on.'

In rather the same way, don't most of us rely on distilled bits of experience to decide on what we're going to do? We might respect people who write tracts of philosophy or scholarship - but how often do we actually employ these deep thoughts to guide our actions? Don't we usually just blunder about, using half truths and the inherited lessons of our pasts, each of us probably as baffled as the next man when we try to navigate our way through life? Isn't this how we beat on, our boats against the current?

Yet trying to boil things down is what I've spent my life doing. In my case I was generally analysing corporate operations and then trying to come up with strategies that might make a difference to a company. But sitting in the car that day I wondered if I couldn't have a stab at doing the same thing with what the great men tell us about how life arose - and how it works.

If there really is a long view, I thought, then would it be possible to reduce the research and theories down to a readable narrative? Was it really true, for example, that the same forces had been endlessly shaping evolution, ever since self-replicating cells had somehow kicked off? And if one looked closely enough, could this tell us something about how our complicated world had come about? Maybe even how we humans work?

Why not give it a go? I knew very little about anything, of course, but it seemed to me that a lack of knowledge might actually have a few advantages. First, by being ignorant I could make the kind of generalisations that most academics wouldn't. I didn't need to get tangled up in the weeds any more than the radio man had.

Secondly, unlike the scientists who usually write these books, I'd have no scholarly colleagues keen to jump on my neck if I got things wrong. The only person I had to please was myself. I was the one who was most interested, and most driven by EM Forster's terrific line that: 'How do I know what I think until I see what I say?'

Not only could I cherry pick the bits I wanted to thread the story together, but because I was writing without any academic standing, I could always just sit on the fence when it came to describing the inevitable controversies and spats.

And since I was only an amateur, a storyteller, unlike them I wouldn't be burdened with having to justify everything with a mass of proofs, nuanced opinions, references, case histories, indices and footnotes*.

Instead I could simply explain how things seemed to me. Who knows, I thought, because I was a blank slate I might even be able to understand the general reader's need for clarity and simplicity rather more than an expert would.

Something I discovered pretty quickly was that there weren't actually many 'secrets' at all. And if there were, they were generally hiding in plain sight. In fact, the opposite seemed to be true, and I found that most aspects of life had been pulled apart quite a few times. Instead of mysteries and dark corners, there were explanations and theories galore if one read enough. This all added up to me rather liking the irony of using such a self-regarding title as *The Secrets of Life*.

So what did I find? Did I arrive at a 'so what you're saying is...' conclusion? Yes, I certainly did, it was something that kept me cheered through the long slog of writing. It was a realisation that so appealed to the optimist in me that I began to think of the books as an opportunity to give a boost to all those downbeat people one meets who see nothing but darkness, destruction, confusion and decline in the world.

It was that cooperation has been at the heart of all progress in life. It's the force that built everything we know about, and it's been behind all the major evolutionary steps and transmissions that have made our world. It's what holds everything together - so central to life that we humans are like every other organism in even being living and breathing examples of it. Cooperation was what assembled our raw material - our very cells - and it was what then made them somehow get together and specialise their functions to construct our bodies.

And if one looks at modern life, the logic of cooperation is all around us, shaping the ways we behave, making our societies ever more robust, increasingly undermining the bad guys, and carrying us humans to ever greater heights of achievement. How wonderful.

---

* Except this one. If I ever came to a place where I had to ascribe a gender, I was in two minds about whether to use 'his' or 'her'. There were good arguments for each. I decided to let fate choose, and tossed a coin. It came down for 'his'.

When Douglas Adams was writing *The Hitchhiker's Guide to the Galaxy*, he described how a gigantic supercomputer called Deep Thought had been set to calculate the solution to the Ultimate Question of Life, the Universe, and Everything. It ran for 7.5 million years before finally announcing that the answer was 42. The only problem was that by then nobody was too sure what the question had been.

I think I discovered it as I wrote these books. For me it could only be 'what do you get in life when you add fifteen to fifteen?'

SS O'Connor,
London, June 2022

Luca? The Daddy of us all?

CHAPTER ONE

THE SECRETS OF LIFE? HOW CAN ONE CLAIM ANYTHING SO IDIOTICALLY SIMPLISTIC WHEN THERE'S SUCH A BEWILDERING VARIETY OF ORGANISMS ON EARTH? IF THEY'RE ALL SO DIFFERENT, HOW CAN THEY SHARE THE SAME SECRETS?

Here's an extraordinary thought.

You and me, the Archbishop of Canterbury, koala bears, fungi, cockroaches, oxeye daisies, grass snakes, *E. coli*, Lombardy poplars, cuttlefish, ferns, Lady Gaga, dragonflies… in fact, everything that's around today, every single member of the millions of species on earth from aardvarks to the *Zygopetalum* orchid, can all be defined in the same way.

None of *our* ancestors failed to reproduce.

We're the successful ones. We are the ones whose forebears didn't get eaten, or found environmental conditions impossible, or died in infancy, or dried out, or got trodden on or, for whatever reason, weren't able to pass their genes on.

If we're alive, it's because our ancestors bred successfully. None of them died celibate. They and their offspring could be said to have made the right *decisions* about how to survive. And since evolutionary biologists are fairly confident that 99.9% of all the species that have ever existed would later become extinct, that tells you something about how successful we all are - and also the burn-out rate in life.

We humans think of decisions as conscious steps. For us, they're part of an active process. We *take* decisions by weighing up various factors and then making our choices on what we think is the best thing to do. Other organisms don't do that. Their life 'decisions' are blind; their changes are due to things about which they're unaware, the results of genetic changes, and the way these act on the environment and other external forces.

Their survival prospects are then down to how they behave when they're competing against the millions of other things that are equally out for themselves - all of which are also changing the whole time. What we now see around us on earth is the response to those 'decisions' - the result of trillions and trillions of them, made by millions and millions of organisms over billions and billions of years.

This isn't to say that we're all the result of *continuously* correct choices. Quite the opposite, in fact. Entire groups of things must have looked like they were terrific successes when they were alive - the age of dinosaurs, for example, lasted over seven hundred times longer than *Homo sapiens* has - but that didn't stop the huge majority of them from going extinct in a blink.

On the other hand, many organisms might have been pretty obscure and insignificant in their day, but they progressed largely by the accidental mechanism of mutations - slowly and gradually it's true, but by fortuitously doing the right things, in the right way, at the right time. As the games developer, Ken Levine, says in *BioShock*: 'We all make choices, but in the end our choices make us.'

Humans, actually, got where they are in the same way. We may have evolved from primates most recently, but they themselves had evolved from things like tree shrews and lemurs, and before that from mice-like creatures, and before those from egg-laying mammals, not unlike the modern-day platypus, and before that from reptiles, before that fish, then sea urchins and before them, sponges and comb jellies... and that's only in the last 20% or so of the time that life's existed on earth. Before that we were all just single celled microorganisms like bacteria and protozoa.

This doesn't mean we progressed in an unbroken, linear way. There would have been many strange developments, wrong decisions and extinctions of evolutionary branches along the course of the journey. But the process that led to us would have come from one of the successful mutations that somehow worked. It seems to me that this realisation is rather comforting - to know, for example, that we share something like 70% of our DNA with slime moulds - because even if an environmental catastrophe swept everything away, complex life would probably build back eventually. Would it lead to us again? Maybe. Maybe not.

Ultimately, we and everything else go back to the same seminal moment when a collection of chemicals somehow fired up and created life - what Charles Darwin called 'three or four cells floating in a pool of warm water'. Evolutionary biologists are rather less lyrical when they say we're all descended from Luca… no, not a legendary Italian superlover, but the Last Universal Common Ancestor - the daddy cell from which everything's come down.

But although we might all originate from the same beginning point of life, species have been splitting and diverging ever since, branching and branching, finding different ways of existing, making their blind decisions about how they'll respond to what's around them.

'All species on earth are related to one another like

cousins and distant kin on a vast family tree of life.'

Abhijit Naskar, *Homo: A Brief History of Consciousness*

And every single one of them, wherever it is, is doing everything it can to survive. Why's this so necessary? It's because, programmed into an organism's genes and behaviour, even within its very chemistry, is the knowledge that its future is balanced on a knife edge. One calamity and it's all over: if creatures as advanced and diverse as the dinosaurs can be snuffed out almost overnight, then so can anything.

From the moment that our Luca somehow sparked into life, every organism that's ever lived has been involved in a gigantic struggle for existence, for survival and for success. And this means it's been engaged in the same endless search to find the best way to do this, to find the best *strategies* to keep going, to produce the next generation, to beat the competition… in other words, to win.

And where there's a need for strategies, they'll be implemented by decisions - decisions about what to do and how to behave. Should one stay small or grow big? Live in water or air? Swim, fly, walk or all of these? Be plants or animals or something else? Be single or multi-celled, hot or cold blooded, simple or complex? And many, many other questions. You get the point… ever since life began, organisms have been creating survival strategies and this has led to a staggering variety in their choices about how they might prosper.

How do these decisions come about? If we know anything about evolution, it's that the process doesn't plan forward. Evolution stems from genetic mutations and some of these changes turn out to be good for a species' future - but some can be bad, and some just don't seem to make any difference. The living things we can see, and the incredible intricacies of their forms and life cycles, made good ones - for the time being anyway - because they're currently alive and therefore haven't become extinct.

> **'A wrong decision taken at the right time is better**
> **than a right decision taken at the wrong time.'**
> **Pearl Zhu, *Decision Master***

However, while the genetic mistakes that lead to mutations may shape how organisms run as living machines, they're also helping to make decisions about how things should *behave*: how they should act and respond to other forms of life around them. That's because, if they make the right choices, their behaviour might lead to an advantage over others that are also trying to survive. But, how?

A good question. If everything is instructed by its genes to survive, why do so many organisms make decisions that appear to be completely baffling - and sometimes even counterproductive to their success?

Why, for example, do so many species on earth choose to be parasitic, when crippling or even killing their hosts must logically endanger their own lives? Why do so many things choose to cooperate when you'd have thought that everything in Nature is programmed to fight? Why would organisms decide to live in weird arrangements with other species in ways that expose them to constant danger? Why, for instance, would a bird choose to run the risk of living off the food that's stuck in a crocodile's teeth?

Is it mad?

                                      The Secrets of Life - Book One

Even more extraordinary, why do organisms sometimes sacrifice themselves in a world in which their hardwiring should make staying alive long enough to reproduce their only objective? What kinds of sacrifice? Committing suicide, for example, so that others in their group can survive. Or calling out a warning when they spot a predator, even though doing this might give their own position away and lead to them being killed?

And perhaps among the most bewildering of the behavioural phenomena is why, when passing on one's genes is the sole function of a species' success, do members of some colonies reject this compulsion and deliberately choose to be sterile? Even Darwin was stumped by this.

'You can't begin to understand biology, you can't understand life, unless you understand what it's all there for, how it arose - and that means evolution.'
Richard Dawkins, *The Selfish Gene*

Like every species in the evolutionary superstew, we humans, just as much as the most basic or complex of organisms, are evidence of some kind of extraordinary strategic success, passed down and refined over countless generations.

At the very core of us all are mechanisms that recognise the future is uncertain, and that there's no such thing as a master key that will continue to work in a world in which the lock keeps changing. It's the requirements of an unstable environment, and the constantly shifting challenges from other species - don't forget they're evolving too - that demand endless new ways of surviving.

Just as other organisms have their strategies, so do we humans… but ours lead to decisions that are made far more quickly than theirs. And ours come from rational processes: we employ knowledge, we learn, we copy, we tell each other things, and the information we arrive at shapes how we think and how we act. Information becomes part of our belief systems, part of our hardwiring, and along with our genetic inheritance it all adds up to the reasons we behave in the ways that we do.

But are we alone in taking just a few moments to make decisions that can change ourselves - rather than the aeons that other life forms do? Astonishingly, the answer is no. We share this ability with our ultimate ancestors - single-celled creatures such as bacteria. Like ourselves, bacteria can adapt in incredibly short time periods without waiting for the genetic changes that shape other organisms, and which are then passed on vertically, from parent to offspring. How odd, then, that just about everything in life's journey between us and them chose to evolve so slowly. Why's that?

These books are about these decisions: whether they're deliberate or accidental, how they get made, what the processes are that lead to them and, incredibly, how the decision-making mechanisms of all living things conform to the same logic, and to the same set of rules.

What I hope to show is that while it's revealing when human behaviour is explained by comparing ourselves to plants and animals, it's the reverse that can be even more fascinating.

Because we arrive at our choices so quickly - all the time trying to come out on top - we actually show up how everything else makes its decisions, rather as if we were lab rats. Look closely at us, will be among the books' conclusions, and you'll see how everything from the most basic of single-celled life forms to complicated things like elephants make their own life decisions.

'There is grandeur in this view of life, with its several powers, having been originally breathed into a few forms or into one; and that, whilst this planet has gone cycling on according to the fixed law of gravity, from so simple a beginning endless forms most beautiful and wonderful have been, and are being, evolved.'
Charles Dawin, *On the Origin of Species*

What's so enthralling in looking at these analogies is that scientists from a spread of disciplines have now developed the ability to explore what previous generations couldn't. That's because, in the last fifty years or so, they've developed computer programmes that can investigate how decision-making has a logic, and researchers have now been able to reveal what approaches get the best results. And, in doing so, this research has exposed the most extraordinary similarities between how different organisms do this - and therefore arrive at what it takes to win.

What does 'win' mean? It means survival. Because surviving this far against life's terrible odds suggests that the strategies living things have evolved are the successful ones. But why is this constant struggle so necessary? Why can't everything just carry on forever without the need for constant change? And why did they have to evolve into such an astounding diversity of life forms?

Well, the answers emerge along the way of a long, long story.

So, where to begin? Well, how about… at the beginning?

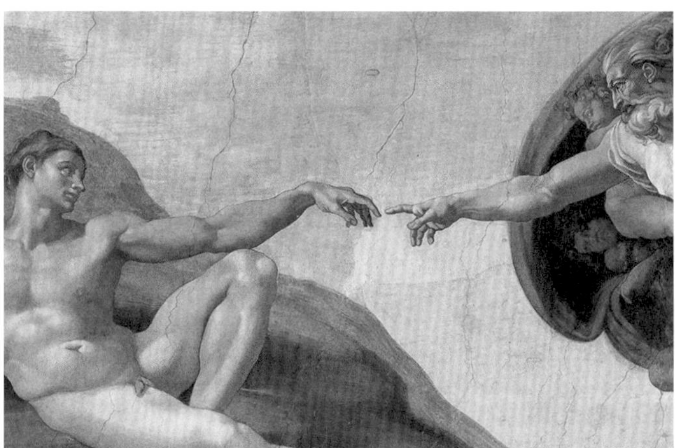

'Off you go Adam... but do watch out for the Laws of Thermodynamics!'

THE BEGINNING? WHY, WHAT HAPPENED IN THE BEGINNING? AND WHY DID IT MAKE US ALL MARCH TO THE *SAME* DRUMBEAT?

13.8 billion years ago and… bang.

In fact, lower-case letters probably don't do it the dramatic justice it deserves. It was rather more of a Big Bang!

(Low groans all round: 'Please, do we really have to go back *that* far?')

Yes, we do, because in less time than it takes for the lights to change and the Uber driver behind you to blow his horn, the split-second explosion that gave birth to the Universe laid down some iron laws that have shaped every aspect of our lives and survival strategies ever since.

Woah. That's a pretty big claim - so what happened? And what's an iron law anyway?

Well, the mind-boggling bit is that although life wasn't going to arise on earth for another ten billion years, when it did come it was going to have to conform to the rules that were set down all that time ago. And we've been following them ever since.

First, because we're spinning round in space, anything that wants to live on planets like ours is going to need a structure that will resist being crushed by gravity. Then, because we're circling the Sun, we spend some of our time not facing it, so we have days and nights, light and dark, and different organisms will be suited to these changing conditions. Then again, planets are spherical and for us on earth this means that parts of it will be closer to the Sun's heat than others, and some organisms will therefore be better suited to higher or lower temperatures.

These sorts of things are fairly obvious when we look around us. But what might be less well known are the laws that were going to decide on how life forms should behave. How should organisms coexist? Would they continuously fight, or would they get along? Why would some things eat each other, and others didn't? Why were some organisms able to survive alone and others evolved to live in highly complex communities? What made these things happen?

Oddly enough, it was only in the last couple of centuries that scientists began to see that questions like these were going to be answered by understanding what the linkage was between 'heat', and what they called 'work'. By heat they meant the energy that's stored in things, and by work, the order this energy could create. Eventually a number of conclusions to this connection were formulated as the Laws of Thermodynamics - and to appreciate how everything depends on them, one needs to know a bit about what heat means, and therefore what happened at Big Bang.

It seems that the pre-Bang universe was a minute ball of incredibly concentrated matter that in the 10^{-37} of a second that the Bang took, there wasn't an explosion that spread out from a single point like a bomb going off. It was, rather, something that occurred everywhere. And this blew space out like a colossal balloon. Because the resulting expansion was of space itself, it all happened faster than the speed of light. (I know, it makes one's head hurt.)

'In the beginning, nearly fourteen billion years ago, all the space, all the matter and all the energy of the known universe was contained in a volume less than a trillionth the size of the full stop that ends this sentence.'
Neil deGrasse Tyson, *Astrophysics for People in a Hurry*

What's slightly simpler to understand, however, is that a primordial plasma of high energy protons was thrown off at incredible heat - hotter than the centre of any star - and it's from this that all matter ever since then has originated.

After an estimated 400,000 or so years, the resulting plasma soup had cooled enough for electrons to combine with nuclei to form neutral atoms of hydrogen, a smaller quantity of helium and some lithium. Gases began to condense under the force of gravity, and it was this process that then slowly formed the galaxies and planets of our current universe.

That's the background, but what's critical to the story of life is accepting the mind-blowing fact that all the energy in the Universe that's ever been - and ever will be - was released at the moment of Big Bang. From that instant on, energy could neither be created nor destroyed. This is what the 1ˢᵗ Law of Thermodynamics says, and the implication from it is that the *total energy in the Universe, since then and forever, will always remain the same.*

While energy can't be destroyed, however, it can be transferred from one object to another and from one form to another - from heat to light to sound, for example - and, most importantly, to do work, to make things move, drive a machine and so on. But how?

Well, back to heat. Heat is energy. When something's hot it has a lot of energy, when it's cold it has less. At absolute zero it has virtually none. Food might be the fuel that makes us work but it's measured in calories… units of heat. Sometimes an object has no temperature, but its heat is still potentially obtainable, in that it's stored up in matter waiting to be released - like coal, for instance.

How is heat energy generated? It comes from the atoms and molecules that are inside matter jumping up and down and bashing into each other. It's therefore everywhere around us as anything with mass and volume, such as gases, liquids and solids, are forms of matter and they all contain the heat energy that's created by the particles that it's made of, vibrating and banging together. Apparently the relationship between them is roughly what $E=mc^2$ means.

The hotter something is, the more its particles are colliding, the more energy it has - and the more it can transfer that energy to matter with slower-moving particles. What happens is that this transference process makes particles move further apart and given enough heat they'll eventually break away from each other. That's how solids become liquids, liquids become gases and how, finally, gases become plasma when matter's atomic structure is broken up.

It may sound theoretical to talk of this one-way process of heat energy transfer, but behind the science it's pretty easy to see the ice melt in a drink, or for one's tea to get cold. Like everything else, both end up in an evening-out process with the surrounding temperature. This mingling means they arrive at a state of 'thermal equilibrium'.

Where the principle of thermodynamics is evident is when heat is used to make something work. As an example, say you have an old-fashioned engine. In it, heat released from something like coal turns water into steam. This in turn drives a piston that makes the air molecules in a cylinder become compressed and choo choo, a rod moves. In this way, heat's been turned into work, one form of energy has been transferred into another, and before long you've got the Industrial Revolution.

This little model is called a 'closed system' in that something goes in at one end and something different comes out at the other. And it perfectly illustrates what leads to the 2nd Law of Thermodynamics: the law that's going to crop up a lot in this story because it's what lies behind the strategies of all living things.

What does this mean? Well, in the engine illustration, as in *all* heat to work transference, the process is inefficient. In the piston example, the air molecules in the cylinder won't all be lining up in the right direction; some will be smashing into the side of the tube rather than driving the rod, and this means energy is bound to seep away from the system. The metal gets warm with friction, the engine might make a clanking noise, start to glow and so on. This is all evidence of energy being transferred - to heat, to sound, to light - but it's also showing that energy is being lost in the process because it's not doing any work.

This lost energy is called *entropy* and it's the reason why no machine - or any other kind of energy transference process - is ever 100% efficient. It is, if you like, the natural world making 1+1 = 1.9, rather than 2.

But while the 1st Law is correct in that energy has neither been created nor destroyed, you might well ask what happens to the 'disorder', the wasted energy? Surely that's now gone and the 1st Law is therefore nonsense? If it isn't, then where does this energy end up?

The answer is that it dissipates into the vastness of the atmosphere and becomes useless. This is rather like putting a drop of boiling water into the Arctic Ocean. The effect is negligible even though the frozen sea has theoretically been infinitesimally warmed. In exactly the same way the machine's lost energy is entropic because it goes into the enormity of space, and this means that its effects are gone forever.

So, this is what the 2nd Law of Thermodynamics says: the entropy in a closed system will increase over time - it will never go down - and will continue to do so until it reaches equilibrium. And equilibrium is bound to lead to a grinding halt, because that's when the heat energy's all been used up, and no more work can be extracted.

But, if that's the case, why doesn't it mean that the Earth will use up its stores of energy and everything will come to an end? It's because we don't live in a closed system. Instead, we survive because we're part of an 'open system', with the Sun pouring down its energy on us every day - far more than we need if we could only harness it efficiently.

In fact, although it's coming to us from 93 million miles away, so much of its energy is reaching the Earth that if you estimate the entire world's *annual* consumption needs at 500 exajoules, the Sun provides the equivalent amount every ninety minutes.

Life feeds off this energy. Plants absorb it through photosynthesis to create energy-rich chemicals. Animals, in turn, get energy from eating them, or each other. Plants, trees and living things die and fall to the ground, compressing themselves to become useful for work but now as fuels: gas, oil and coal. One form of energy, the Sun, has been transferred into others. As Galileo so charmingly put it: 'The Sun, with all those planets revolving around it and dependent on it, can still ripen a bunch of grapes as if it had nothing else in the Universe to do'.

All these life processes are fighting the 2nd Law, slowing down the trend of ever-increasing disorder. In a cascade of chemical reactions, life is sucking out everything it can from solar energy, while the entropic process is discarding what's lost into the atmosphere as low-quality heat.

In exactly the same way, scientists discovered that the energy inherent in an atom could be released if the large nucleus can be made to split into two smaller nuclei. This allows neutrons to be liberated and with this 'exothermic' reaction comes a massive amount of energy. More obviously for us, besides solar power, we have other natural energy available from the vast resources of the wind and the gravitational forces that create tidal power.

'Thermodynamics… is the only physical theory of universal content which I am convinced… will never be overthrown'
Albert Einstein

What's critical to understanding all this is to recognise that heat can only go in one direction: from something giving energy to something collecting it - passing from a hotter to a cooler object. This process means that as heat becomes more disordered - less concentrated - more energy has been seeping away entropically and is lost into the surroundings.

The consequence of this inevitable outcome is that as work is done, the total entropy of the Universe is *always* increasing. And, because this means that everything will keep getting colder, the ultimate upshot is that eventually there will no longer be heat available to produce work. This is a kind of unscientific way of describing the 3rd Law.

Now, hold onto your hats, because this all leads to a chilling, inescapable conclusion. It is the inevitable outcome that, just like the working of the steam engine, the energy in the Universe is gradually being used up as it passes from hot to cooler objects, and this will ultimately end up with what scientists call the Heat Death of the Universe. This is when maximum entropy is reached, or when, as everything is now the same temperature, no more work can be extracted. As the Austrian physicist Erwin Schrodinger so cheerfully observed, this is when: '… the whole system fades away into a dead, inert lump of matter'.

This, incidentally, is called the Zeroth Law of Thermodynamics (apparently it was only recognised after 1, 2 and 3 were formulated and the brainboxes couldn't be bothered to renumber them.) When this zeroth event happens, many astrophysicists

**Flanders and Swann performing
'First and Second Law'**

**'You can't pass heat from the cooler to the hotter
Try if you like but you'd far better notter'**

**'Heat is work and work's a curse
And all the heat in the Universe
Is gonna cooool down 'cos it can't increase
Then there'll be no more work and
there'll be perfect peace
Really?
Yeah, that's entropy, man!**

believe the Universe will collapse back on itself, shrinking to a point as increasingly enormous black holes scrunch everything up through gravity in a process that astronomers call the Big Crunch.

Is this as depressing as it sounds? Possibly not. To get to where we are today, the Universe has been going for about 13.8 billion years, and at the very least there's another twenty billion or so to go before this entropic end game is reached. Even this is in doubt, with some people suggesting there could be trillions more years yet. Whenever it turns out to be, it's certainly far beyond the point at which our own Sun's energy is expected to run out, and for it to collapse in on itself.

If you take an even longer view, quite a few people believe that a process of renewal then starts off again. They say that the Universe's energy that's all been sucked up and concentrated then combines to explode in another Big Bang and the cycle is repeated.

Who knows, maybe it's all happened a number of times already? Certainly this was the view of the Nobel laureate, Sir Roger Penrose who, together with Stephen Hawking, theorised that an earlier universe existed before the Big Bang and, indeed, has left evidence of itself behind in the form of 'dead' black holes from which all the radiation has leaked away.

> **'The Big Bang was not the beginning. There was something before**
> **the Big Bang and that something is what we will have in our future.**
> **We have a universe that expands and expands, and all mass**
> **decays away, and in this crazy theory of mine, that the remote**
> **future becomes the Big Bang of another aeon.'**
> **Sir Roger Penrose, *The Guardian***

Perhaps there were other people, rather like me, struggling with exactly these concepts fifty billion years ago. And others will be doing it fifty billion from now. Poor saps.

Now these Laws are so incontrovertible, and form such controlling principles in our lives, that they're defined as 'iron' because they're absolutely central to everything that happens. But they're pretty tricky stuff and apologies if it's taken some time to try and explain them.

You'd probably agree with the German physicist Arnold Summerfeld who said: 'Thermodynamics is a funny subject. The first time you go through it, you don't understand it at all. The second time you go through it, you think you understand it, except for one or two small points. The third time you go through it, you know you don't understand it, but by this time you're so used to it, it doesn't bother you anymore.' I know the feeling.

'How many educated people could describe the 2nd Law of Thermodynamics?
Yet (it's) the scientific equivalent of 'have you read a work of Shakespeare?''
CP Snow

Complicated as the implications are, the conclusion that matters for the story of life is fairly simple: it is that everything, everywhere, at all times, is endlessly falling apart. All matter is becoming entropic or, as scientists say, 'is tending to chaos'. This may be the macro picture but we also see micro versions of it all around us. Everywhere we look, things are ageing and decaying, withering - and *dying*. As Woody Allen so pithily summed it up in *Husbands and Wives*: 'It's the Second Law of Thermodynamics: sooner or later everything turns to shit.'

What does this all add up to? And what does it mean for the secrets of life?

Well, first, at the most profound of levels, if life is about getting energy from somewhere, then the most successful things like compounds, chemical structures, cells, organisms and so on, must be those that have strategies to extract the most order from the system before it dissipates. And, therefore, they've evolved to somehow arrange themselves to get that energy most efficiently, even if it means fighting for it.

In the natural world, of course, organisms are getting their ordered energy from what's around them. Plants get it from the Sun, and then herbivores take it on and, frequently, are then eaten themselves in the great cascade of energy transfer known as the food chain. No wonder so many people view life as 'red in tooth and claw'.

But, secondly, if the great realisation is that everything's falling apart and dying, what's also clear is that Nature's response is inevitable: *every living thing is trying to beat the 2nd Law*. At base, all that matters is survival - and that means staying alive long enough to pass on one's genes, of doing anything one can to resist entropy, and being utterly ruthless in going about it. This is why we have to recognise that the survival instinct goes far deeper than we might imagine, and is at the root of everything a life form does. It's woven into every decision, present in chemical make-ups, apparent in functions, and always, *always* it's evident in the way things deal with what's around them.

Look closely at life and you have to conclude that the only reason organisms have to keep going is to survive long enough to produce a new generation. Unlike us, other living things don't have retirement, the garden, or a glass of wine in front of the telly. More obviously than us, they seem to 'recognise' that holding back the 2nd Law is a constant effort, and that the compulsion for survival is the motor that drives it all.

The profound requirement for everything to pass on their genes is what Darwin's 'fitness' means. The better an organism is at it, the more genes that get out into the gene pool, the greater the chances are of its survival. And the best at doing it are 'the fittest'.

**'Thermodynamics correctly interpreted does not
just allow Darwinian evolution, it favours it.'
Ludwig Boltzmann, *Theoretical Physics and Philosophical Problems***

This elemental survival compulsion is deep in the cells of every life form, in its biochemistry and in its genes. It's nothing to do with the organism, but everything to do with the internal mechanics of reproduction. Richard Dawkins describes it succinctly: 'We are all just survival machines - robot vehicles blindly programmed to preserve the selfish molecules known as genes. They are the replicators, and we are the survival machines.'

'Passing something on' to conserve life is the essential motor force in all genes. And if the organism is threatened, then the gene isn't above ditching its 'robot' carrier… because the survival of life matters more to it than the survival of the organism. This is what leads the building blocks of life at a cellular level to combine and give life to things but, also, for organisms to then combine themselves into more and more complex structures, into colonies and, from there, into sophisticated societies. This is the never-ending struggle to protect successful species against the disintegration that comes from entropic forces.

**'The paradox that immediately bothers everyone who learns about
the 2nd Law is this: If systems tend to become more disordered, why, then,
do we see so much order around us? It seems to conflict with our
"creation myth": In the beginning, there was a Big Bang ... no one
is saying that the 2nd Law of Thermodynamics is wrong, just
that there is a contrapuntal process organising things at a higher level.'
J. Doyne Farmer, *The Third Culture***

As the great Robert Wright puts it in his masterpiece, *Nonzero: The Logic of Human*

Destiny: 'The growth of an organism creates new order and structure. But on balance, says the 2nd Law, the organism has to consume more order than it creates. And so it does. The key to staying alive is to hang on to the order and expel the disorder'. What he's implying, of course, is that living things not only have to do this… but have to do it in competition with everything else that's trying to survive as well.

How does this work? Well, take the story of two men out hunting in the wilds. An angry bear spots them and charges. They're running madly for their lives when one suddenly stops and sits down to take off his boots. Then he starts putting on a pair of trainers.

'Why are you doing that?' shouts the other. 'You can't outrun a bear you know, even in those.'

'No', the man replies, tightening the laces, 'but I can outrun you.'

So yes, life may be a fight that everything will eventually lose… and, as for species, don't forget the horrible proof that 99.9% of them have become extinct. But this doesn't mean that the instinct to survive, in some form or another, isn't making the gene keep looking for ways to adapt to changing conditions. And it's this that helps organisms succeed, even if the competition doesn't.

There's a hoary old question that philosophy lecturers like firing at their students that asks: 'What is the problem that life is trying to solve?' A pretty good answer must be that if the 2nd Law is insisting that everything is falling apart, eroding and dissipating energy, then life on earth is about producing an opposite force.

And it does this by constantly creating order… by finding a winning strategy to do it, by beating the odds, beating the competition, cooperating with other things if this is going to help its ambitions, and by endlessly trying to succeed, entrench and then prosper - if only for what, in evolutionary terms, might appear to be a very short time.

'Why the awe for the second law? The second law defines the ultimate purpose of life, mind, and humans striving: to deploy energy and information to fight back the tide of entropy and carve out refuges of beneficial order. Under appreciation of the inherent tendency towards disorder, and a failure to appreciate the precious niches of order we carve out, are a major source of human folly.'
Steven Pinker, *This Idea is Brilliant*

Personally, I find it rather comforting to know that however many individuals and species face the inevitability of death and extinction, new ones are always coming along. Life may be all about reproducing and dying… but life goes on because life has evolved to counter the 2nd Law.

Is this drumbeat heard in humans as well? It is indeed, although we have layered so much on top of our base drives that one has to listen very hard to hear it. And, of course, we don't see the process working because the time frames in evolution are so unimaginably long.

But we come from the same stuff as everything else does and we, too, live in a constantly shifting world of threats, mutations and environmental change that's leading to success for some species and failure for others.

If it's all about survival, though, how does this come about? More to the point, where does life come from anyway?

Perhaps if we knew more about how things got here, it would tell us something about who we humans are, why we came along - and where everything is going.

You think the world is going to pot now?
You should have seen it when it first started.

CHAPTER THREE

LIFE? WHAT IS IT ANYWAY?
AND HOW DID IT START?
ISN'T IT ALL A BIT OF A MYSTERY?

The Universe was already in late middle age when its latest offspring first started to emerge about 4.5 billion years ago.

The new planet was ours, and like most of the others around us, the Earth probably originated after a massive supernova explosion had occurred somewhere in the galaxy, causing a vast cloud of space dust to blow out and then to collapse in on itself.

Gravity would have made the rotation of this colossal mass increase, and as in all solar systems, it then flattened out into a disc. The Sun - over a million times larger than the Earth - was at the centre of this swirling constellation, and the planets within it then materialised as dust particles fused together into enormous rocks, gases and ice.

Perhaps the weirdest thing about what was to become our home was how unpromising it would have seemed. If it was found by a space probe today, the TV newsreader would probably announce its discovery with a smile of enthusiasm before dropping gear to sorrowful gloom: '… unfortunately, scientists believe that what they have named 'the Earth' doesn't have the conditions to support life. It has a violent climate with scorching surface temperatures and, sadly, neither water nor oxygen.'

So what went right?

Well, for the first seven hundred million years or so, not much. Most of that time saw a wildly troubled childhood that's become labelled as the Hadean Period, named after Hades… Hell!

And so it seemed: fire and brimstone conditions, an atmosphere largely made up of sulphur, molten rocks bubbling up, screamingly high temperatures, forks of lightning, dust storms and constant eruptions. The Earth's crust hadn't yet formed, and there'd have been endless landslides with heavier iron atoms sinking down to become the planet's core, and lighter atoms like silica and hydrogen rising up to the surface. Once there, the hydrogen and other gases that were emerging like carbon dioxide, methane and nitrogen would have been evaporated away into space by the high temperature.

If that wasn't bad enough, around 3.8 billion years ago the young planet came under a relentless pounding from asteroids and meteorites in a process called the Late Heavy Bombardment. These huge rocks were sometimes miles wide and rained down onto the molten surface. One particular bully, probably around the size of Mars, even whacked a huge chunk out, and this then sailed off into orbit to become the Moon.

'All of recorded human history is much less than 4.5 billion minutes.
And yet… Earth has been around for more than 4.5 billion years.'
Robert Hazen, *The Story of Earth*

As so often happens, however, when things couldn't get much worse, they got better. The assaults took a break, the exterior began cooling, and it actually turned out that there'd been some benefits along with the blows. One great advantage came with what's been called the Wet Planet Theory. Although it's a disputed idea, particularly recently, many scientists believe that water arrived here in the form of icy comets that condensed in the heat to form vast oceans.

Another benefit was that large quantities of complex carbon and nitrogen chemicals probably also turned up from within the meteorites. Carbon is critical to life, but physicists have always had trouble in understanding its origin. While it was present within the core as the planet settled, they think it would either have stayed down there, because it bonded so readily with iron, or boiled away if it rose to the surface.

What's now widely believed is that these volatile elements came as side effects of the bombardments once the Earth's core had finished forming. Why did this matter? It's because they're both critical to life, and carbon particularly so, as it bonds with hydrogen to form long chains of molecules called hydrocarbons. These produce the central differences between inorganic chemistry - which means a bunch of elements - and organic chemistry, which is carbon based, and is what we're made of.

Why was this so important? It was absolutely critical because hydrocarbons are what form the Swiss Army knife at the core of life. They're the central element of the proteins, nucleic acids and lipids that are themselves the basic building blocks that lead to everything else.

Appreciating this makes one realise that whatever else humans might be, we, along with everything else on earth, started as space dust. As the 1st Law of Thermodynamics predicts, energy has been transferred; the atoms may have fallen apart yet they've recombined - and things are going on forever. The great astronomer, Carl Sagan, summed it up when he wrote: 'The cosmos is within us. We are made of star stuff.'

What's fascinating about all this is the way that even *before* life somehow sparked off, the very chemicals that were to make it all possible were showing how things benefit from cooperating: how their problems of instability could be overcome by getting together and merging with other elements, then organising themselves into ever more complex molecules. And it was from here that they could then move on to bewilderingly complicated compounds. If this shows anything, it is that even at this most basic and profound level, every step of the evolutionary process has always been about challenging the 2nd Law - acting to produce order from disorder, and creating integrity and structure out of its very precariousness.

How does this happen? First, one should start with atoms - things that can't be reduced any further. All of them have a nucleus and a unique number of particles that whizz about in orbits around it. But atoms are naturally unstable, and they want to bond with other things to get over their instability. They do this by sharing some of their particles - particularly electrically charged ones called electrons - with another atom. It's in this way that they form molecules, the smallest unit of a chemical compound.

This is essentially how chemistry works - it rearranges electrons. The great advantage of the process is that when they come together to form a molecule, the new configuration has a lower total energy than the two separate atoms. The 1st Law of Thermodynamics then comes into play, and there's now energy left over. This liberated energy is available to do other things… and the process so necessary for life is then underway.

Some atoms, like oxygen, are very active in trying to combine with others. Some are more picky. So how do things get together? They do it by following strict rules depending on the atomic structure of their elements. And the bonds themselves also differ; sometimes they're strong, sometimes weak. As an example, a simple compound like a water molecule has two atoms of hydrogen which bond with one atom of oxygen. The famous H_2O.

But add another element to make something more complicated like the ascorbic acid of Vitamin C, and you'd need six atoms of carbon to bond with eight atoms of hydrogen and, now, six atoms of oxygen. Then again, table sugar uses the same ingredients, but in a different recipe: $C_{12} H_{22} O_{11}$. And grain alcohol is similar but also quite different: $C_2 H_5 OH$.

Nonetheless, how did this chemistry all mix together to make life get going?

Nobody knows.

Of course there are plenty of theories, but they really all boil down to two main ones that depend on the answer to which came first - the chicken or the egg? This may seem a silly question but it's relevant to theorising how - if random chemistry had somehow managed to throw up the miracle of a functioning process called 'life' - how could the trick then be *replicated*? Did it keep recurring, or was there some kind of system that kept it going? This led to the great scientific battle between the 'genes first' or the 'metabolism first' hypotheses.

This argument was neatly illustrated by the famous Herbert Simon parable of an assiduous watchmaker. Simon, a Nobel laureate economist, told the story of a man trying to assemble a complicated timepiece with a thousand different bits. He could either put the watch together, a piece at a time, or he could make chunks of it into a sort of sub-assembly process, before he then slotted these larger elements together. The latter was the more secure of the two ways, Simon said, because if the watchmaker happened to be interrupted for some reason, he wouldn't have to start again entirely from scratch.

Simon's view was that this option was far more efficient, and that its logic gave an insight into the origins of early life. It suggested that once stable things like amino acids and small biomolecules called nucleotides had been formed, they could then be assembled into more complex structures in a way that a random combination of individual molecules could not.

Under this theory, the 'primordial soup' would be rich in chemical building blocks which could then form increasingly complex molecules like proteins and nucleic acids in shallow water at the edge of a puddle. The potential for merging these elements would become catalysed by ultraviolet light from the Sun, or electrical charges from lightning, and as the pool kept filling up and drying out, a kind of cooking process would take place that could create biological molecules. This theory says that basic life forms would therefore keep being generated until a chemical mechanism evolved that could churn out copies of itself.

Scientists got very excited in the1950s by experiments that seemed to replicate this process in the lab. After the encouragement of early success, however, there were then endless failures. Even for its biggest fans, it was hard not to conclude that the odds on amino acids spontaneously combining to form cells - and then to keep duplicating the process - were staggeringly long odds.

The other theory claims that the very first life molecules would have carried genetic information themselves - and were therefore self-replicating from the very start. The argument goes that these molecules were a basic form of genetic material called ribonucleic acid. Better known as RNA, this later evolved into the mechanism that DNA uses as a messenger to pass on instructions for controlling the synthesis of proteins. This is what gives scientists their ditty that the gene flow of existence is that 'DNA makes RNA makes proteins'.

This theory still doesn't explain how an incredibly complex molecule like RNA might have ever arisen. Many scientists now think that the odds against such a thing happening spontaneously are astronomical, and that smaller and less complex molecules would surely have come first that eventually led to the far more complicated RNA arising. Isn't this the precise description of Simon's watchmaking technique?

Who knows which is right? Incidentally, there's another theory altogether called panspermia, which says that life came here pretty much fully formed from outer space. This suggests that microbial life drifts through space, and could have reached the Earth in the form of virus-laden comets that crashed onto its surface.

The theory has its critics but also its many adherents, largely based on its originator, Sir Fred Hoyle's famous assertion that otherwise: '… a superintellect has monkeyed with physics, as well as with chemistry and biology' to create life. And that the random emergence of even the simplest cell without panspermia would be like: '… a tornado sweeping through a junkyard and leaving behind a fully assembled Boeing 747.'

Panspermia is no longer such a barmy idea as people first thought. Stephen Hawking gave it particular emphasis when he said: 'Life could spread from planet to planet or from stellar system to stellar system, carried on meteors', and it's now known that bacteria survived for up to three years on the outside of the International Space Station. Bacterial groups were found there in which the ones on the surface of the colony had died and formed a protective layer that allowed the remaining microbes inside to stay alive.

Whatever it was that stimulated a bunch of chemicals to somehow function in a self-supporting way... how did cellular life then follow? That's a good question because whatever method built the large molecules of proteins and nucleic acids that got things going, there was still the gigantic next step of forming individuals that are enclosed by a membrane. This had to be done so the cell could keep its internal conditions separate and protected from the external environment. Phew.

However, a few hundred million years is a long time, and what emerged about 3.8 billion years ago to start the process of making our world was a kind of 'special forces' bacterium that could exist - even seemed to thrive on - incredibly tough and extreme conditions. These earliest of 'extremophiles' are what have laid a claim to being how life somehow spluttered into action, and so became our Luca.

This is all pretty recent thinking. In fact, it was only in the late 1970s that the scientists trying to understand how amino acids could club together and then somehow survive on little more than hydrogen and carbon dioxide, discovered this whole new domain of uber-hard microorganisms. They were similar to bacteria in being single-celled, but radically different in their molecular structure. They were termed *archaea*, and since then, they've come to be seen as an entirely different domain of life forms.

Both they and bacteria are collectively known as prokaryotes (which means that they're just jelly-like stuff, without a kernel, or nucleus) and the gel on the inside is held together by a membrane that regulates which chemicals can go in and out. In this way the proteins inside the cell are protected from their hostile surroundings and a little island of order is therefore created in a sea of disorder and chaos.

These membranes are fantastically clever and let the molecules inside them provide the energy to make proteins. They're also telling the cell what's going on outside, both in the environment and in the surrounding cells. This is vital because the cell has to be able to respond to dangers like toxins or environmental changes such as sudden droughts, or a changing pH balance. Once it comes under these kinds of threats, it'll take action either by reproducing itself by splitting into two, or by shutting itself down.

The stuff inside the cell is called cytoplasm and it's largely the same in both archaea and bacteria. What makes the two life forms different, however, has led to a lot of scientific argument, largely about the nature of their membranes and their biochemistry. Nonetheless, the net result as Ed Yong summarises in his book, *I Contain Multitudes* is that: '... archaea are as different from bacteria in biochemistry as PCs are from the Mac operating system.'

But it's what makes them the same that's even more interesting. This is because these earliest of prokaryotes could live without oxygen - in places like the boiling water of deep-sea thermal vents (where some scientists even think life itself might have first started) - and by managing to survive anaerobically like this, they were somehow sucking energy out of the other things they found around them.

More importantly, those that were out on the Earth's surface found a way of taking in the Sun's energy through photosynthesis, and then releasing oxygen as a waste product. Now we were off. This was the starting pistol for our world. Why was that? It's because oxygen is one of the most reactive elements, and it now began to form compounds with many of the other things around it - silicon, iron, copper - and this process led to hundreds of new minerals being created. Simmer this for tens of millions of years and you've got an oxygenated planet with a huge range of really useful minerals.

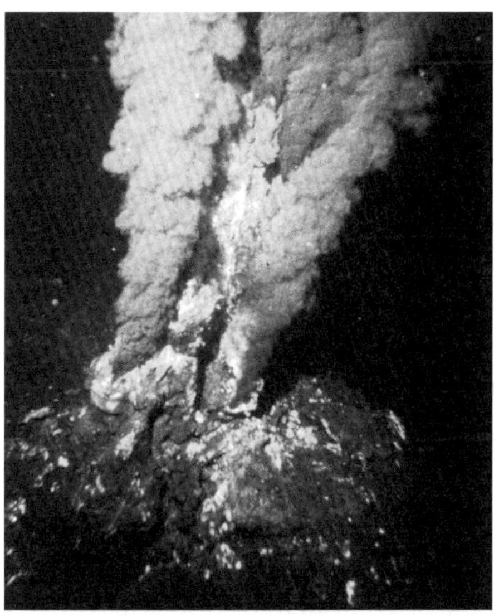

Scalding hot and no oxygen... can this
really be where it all began?

Astonishingly, scientists think that archaea have stayed virtually unchanged since they first emerged all those billions of years ago. Different species have been found that are capable of living in incredibly hostile environments. Acid springs, the searing heat of volcanoes, radioactive waste, even Chipping Norton; it's all the same to them.

And if anything could be said to be resisting the 2nd Law of Thermodynamics, it's bacterial life together with their tiny prokaryotic archaea cousins. This is because, out of the collapse and entropy that comes to all living things, these minute things found they could produce order out of decay by converting the vital elements of carbon, nitrogen, sulphur and phosphorus into the compounds that are critical to life - and then returning them in an ordered form again by decomposing their organic bodies.

Of course, archaea are little known compared to bacteria - or 'little sticks' as the Greek origin has it. Indeed, we hardly ever think about the place any of them have in our lives, and yet they're always around us - and within us. If we ever do wonder what they're up to we might shudder, usually equating them with disease and illness. Yet they're not only everywhere, but they're arguably even more critical to life on earth than anything that's ever come after them.

And for things that are so small as to usually be invisible, they have an impressive presence. Put them all together, for instance, and prokaryotes have the greatest collective mass of all the living things on earth. As for our relationship with them, while it's reckoned we might have something like a hundred trillion cells in our bodies, some scientists believe that there could be as many as *ten times* this number of prokaryotic life forms on us, and in us, cooperating with our organs, and carrying out an untold number of vital functions that help to keep us going.

'… more bacteria live and work in one linear centimetre of

your lower colon that all the humans who have ever lived.

That's what going on in your digestive tract right now.

Are we in charge, or are we simply hosts for bacteria?'

Neil deGrasse Tyson, *Space Chronicles*

Perhaps what's most humbling about all this is that just as everything has come from them, so it could return. All plant and animal life began as these minute things, and if complex life disappeared, they'd simply carry on and, no doubt, start the process of evolution all over again.

Prokaryotes are central to everyday life. In fact, they're arguably more important now than they've ever been. But what's plain from looking at these early steps of theirs is that even at this point, when life was still embryonic, two principles had emerged that laid down how things were going to unfold in the story of life.

'Microbes have always been part of our ecology.

We evolved among them. Also, we evolved from them.'

Ed Yong, *I Contain Multitudes*

The first was the realisation of just how much change comes about from things cooperating. Atoms had combined synergistically to form molecules, molecules then cooperated to create compounds, and compounds found that by getting together in certain ways they could somehow spark off life. From the very earliest organisms onwards, this power of cooperation - *of making 1+1 = 3* - is arguably the most vital of all the forces in life. As Martin Nowak puts it in *SuperCooperators*: 'Cooperation at the molecular level may even be older than life itself.'

The second great insight came when biologists saw how third parties, outside sources, could be the catalyst for creating change. The Earth, for example, may have been the victim of meteorite bombardments, but the early chemistry could never have happened without the elements they brought supplementing and combining with the ones that were already here. This ability to use 'outsourcing', together with things cooperating for their greater good - instead of simply competing - are themes that will constantly crop up as the creation of more complex organisms and colonies unfolds.

So now life's been established. Yes, it's basic, there are only microbes, but at least it's now got a finger hold on survival.

But how did it keep going? How did these simple things replicate? If they copied themselves by using DNA, then what is DNA? And where did this extraordinary mechanism come from?

Salvador Dali painted 'Galacidalacidesoxyribonucleicacid' when he heard about Crick and Watson's discovery of the structure of DNA. He said: 'This is, for me, the real proof of the existence of God.'

CHAPTER FOUR

DNA? WE ALL KNOW WHAT THAT'S SUPPOSED TO DO... WHY SHOULD IT BE SO INTERESTING?

When I was a small boy, my mother used to be troubled by the television.

'How do they get the little men in there?' she'd laugh, and then invariably add: '…but seriously, how does it *work*?' On and on this would go until we children would snap in irritation.

'Mum, why can't you press the button like everyone else and just enjoy it?'

DNA's a bit like that, isn't it? No doubt everyone would agree that it's extremely complicated science - but who cares? It obviously works. It makes us look like our parents and policemen seem to think it nails criminals. Why worry after that?

Yet, in many people's opinion, it's worth putting a bit of time into appreciating it not only to be staggered at the elegance of its operation, but also to see it as the start of the decision-making processes that are so critical to the survival game. Or, to put it in terms of thermodynamics, to see what the mechanisms are that create enough order to hold back the inevitable outcome of the 2nd Law.

What exactly is DNA? Well, it's a molecule that carries genetic information, a nucleic acid - a substance that works together with proteins and carbohydrates to make up the three cornerstones of life. It's the way that every living thing, from the smallest microbe to the largest whale, passes itself on. And has done so ever since the earliest life forms emerged.

Whatever the organism's size or complexity, DNA is the biological agency needed for creating just a single cell, and it's from this tiny start point that everything then grows. The cell divides, then divides again, and keeps this up until the organism is built. It's how life creates new life and, in that sense, DNA is what drives the process that led to us all being descended from Luca, the original cell.

We humans are like other creatures in having DNA in the nucleus of just about every one of the cells in our bodies, and it's this that carries the code to make a new version of itself. In this sense, it's understandable why evolutionary biologists like the gag that, actually, we're all just 'DNA's way of being carried around so it can make more DNA.'

Unbelievably, in spite of us humans having something like a hundred trillion cells, nearly every one of them has the same DNA in its nucleus. It sits there in a thread-like structure called a chromosome, and this is constructed of what's known as chromatin - something that's made up of the DNA molecule and a string of proteins stuck together on it like a bead bracelet.

In a staggering feat of engineering all this fits snugly into the cell, in spite of the length of the chromosome being about a thousand times longer than the nucleus is wide. But by curling itself up into incredibly tight spirals, the molecule manages to shrink itself down into a minute apparatus that represents no more than 1% of the cell's weight. Yet if you managed to unwind the DNA's structure, and stretched out the complete molecular linkage into a straight line, it would be over two metres long.

Even though we might conclude that it's tiny, the strands of DNA are actually immense structures in the molecular world. In fact, it's widely regarded as a complex polymer in that it's composed of smaller molecular units that are chained together in a specific order.

DNA stands for the mouthful of deoxyribonucleic acid, and it's famously strung into a double helix like a twisted, spirally ladder. The outer 'uprights' of the ladder are built from chains of ribose which is a kind of sugar. The 'rungs' of the ladder are constructed from pairs of chemicals called nucleotide bases, or bases for short, and they're complex acids that contain nitrogen built around rings of carbon.

There are four types of base (adenine, cytosine, thymine and guanine) that pair up in DNA and the order of these bases creates a four-symbol code: ACTG. It's these symbols that write out a series of sentences in the DNA, and it's this that makes up the book of life.

It sounds pretty simplistic to describe it like this, but there are over three billion pairs of these bases lined up to create the human genome. Science writers like to make a visual mind-blower out of this by equating it with the written word. One example of doing this is to say that if you saw the unique sentences our genes are making, typed out on paper, the result would appear as the equivalent of two hundred copies of *War and Peace*. And that's going on in nearly every one of our hundred trillion cells. That makes the code pretty long, you might think, and yet many plants and animals - including some types of amoebas - have even longer genomes.

Genes are in small segments of the DNA strands, and each chromosome has thousands of genes. How many? Well, oddly enough, far fewer than you'd think, with most geneticists concluding that we humans would only have about 20,000. This is a bit weird as even the potato is thought to have more.

But 20,000 seems to be enough, and what happens in the process of reproducing itself is that DNA gets RNA to go off with the coded messages needed to make certain amino acids. These, in turn, all link together to make the proteins that are the chemical foundations of the new life that's being generated. If this was happening to us, our individual traits arise from which proteins are switched on or off in a process known as 'gene expression'.

Now DNA is a doubled-up molecule, so the precious genetic code is kept protected in the heart of the double helix. When it's time to pass on its information, an enzyme (a chemical catalyst that's released in the body) 'unzips' the DNA molecule into separate single strands of nucleotide chains. When each strand's been separated, these then act as templates to grow back their missing mirror copy, and this process instantly creates two identical DNA molecules where there had only previously been one.

Human DNA is packaged up into 23 pairs of chromosomes - 46 in all - in which the DNA is coiled up, and coiled again around a scaffold of proteins. Most of the time chromosomes are too slender and diffuse to be seen under a microscope. Instead, their presence is revealed by a faint colouring, or chromatin, in the nucleus - hence the term chromosome - although most of us might picture them as the ragged X shapes that are seen in medical and genetic scans. This is the form they take when they're tightened up even further during cell division, and the X shows the chromosome has just copied itself into a set of duplicates that are poised to split apart and head off to populate the nuclei of two fresh cells.

It's quite often said that chromosomes are like decks of cards, and genes are the cards. It doesn't matter how many decks there are as long as all the cards are in the deck. This means that not everything has the same number of chromosomes as us.

Roundworms, for example, have only two, while hermit crabs have 254, and there's even a species of fern that has 1260.

Why is it that virtually every one of our trillions of cells contains DNA? Surely it's only needed to make your children inherit those fine features of yours? Not so. It's because our bodies are 24 hour factories that contain a never-ending production line of cells that are dying and being replaced with new ones. And they all need DNA to tell them what to produce.

Our cells do this by dividing in the way that bacteria do - in a process called *mitosis* that means one cell splits into two, with each new one getting a copy of all 46 chromosomes. To do this, the chromosomes first make clones of themselves after which the cell then divides down the middle.

These body cells are known as somatic, yet the DNA in them carries our entire genome. This is what contains the instructions to tell each one of them how to become replicas of what was there before. And therefore what specialisation they'll have - liver cells, brain cells and so on. Astonishingly, human beings have about 230 different types of highly specialised cells within us, all cooperating to build a functioning body as a gigantic collaborative exercise. If cells haven't yet received their orders about what they're going to be when they grow up, they're known as stem cells.

**'Chromosomes are communities of genes whose fortunes
are intertwined. By linking with others to coordinate replication, each gene
ensures that all the daughter cells acquire a full complement of
cooperative genes. In this way, selfish interests promote cooperation.'**
Martin Nowak, *SuperCooperators*

In us, in our bodies, this amazingly complicated process of renewal is happening during every single moment of our lives… and replacing our bodies at a rate of something like 300 billion cells a day. After about seven years, we've just about rebuilt ourselves. No wonder we're always exhausted.

Why do cells do this? First, of course, we grow when we're children and the process to do this is by cell division. Later, when we're fully made, one of the reasons biologists think organisms are in a state of constant renewal is as a way of evading parasites - a throwback to our bacterial heritage and to the endless need to stay one step ahead of things that are trying to live off us.

Some cellular renewal is simply replacing what was there before to keep us healthy

- skin cells, for example, are continuously being replaced at an incredible lick: as many as 40,000 every minute. Others, like brain and nerve cells, are also being remade, but at a lower rate.

Cells regulate their renewal mechanism by communicating through a kind of signalling system which is used to tell each other when they should start dividing. But it's also vital that they're able to stop the process once this has happened. If something goes wrong - and they don't - rampant cell division can lead to harmful growths and cancers.

Besides somatic cells, organisms also have things called sex cells that are quite different in the way they work. In humans, instead of having 46 chromosomes, these cells only have 23, and that's because one of them is going to fuse together with somebody else's sex cell during fertilisation and the two lots of 23 will end up as the 46 needed at the start of new life.

And it's this combination that will make an entirely new individual in a kind of double mitosis - a process called *meiosis*. What kind of individual? Well, a muddled one - one with a mixture of the two parents, because the new life's genes will come from 44 chromosomes that contain nearly all of the DNA's coded information.

The process is rather like shuffling two suits of cards so that the numbers all end up being in the right order, but the suits are a mix. Instead of just a few cards, though, the complex information present in the chromosomes means there'll be untold millions of possible combinations.

Nonetheless, the DNA you get from your two parents is delivered in a 50-50 split - just as they received exactly the same proportions from their own parents. This means, of course, that you get a quarter of your grandparents' code, an eighth of your great-grandparents and so on.

But if I said 44, then where are the other two chromosomes, the missing ones from the 46? They're what decide your sex. These are the famous X and Y - women get one X from each parent but men get one X - and only they also get a Y from their fathers. (For some reason, whenever one reads about this, the writer always seems to delight in saying how biologically feeble this Y chromosome is, and how little presence it has in our total DNA. Not very butch.

Not only that, but evolutionary biologists reckon that something like 97% of the genes that were once on the Y chromosome have been lost in the last three hundred million years, one consequence of which is to have made women genetically closer to chimpanzees than men are. Bizarre.)

Why don't we all end up as an exact mix of our parents though? Why does it seem like a lottery whether some children look more like one parent than the other, or get features that don't seem to be in an equal mix? Or inherit the intelligence of one but not the other? Or other characteristics - or maybe not?

It's because our parents' DNA gets shuffled when the sperm is transferred to the egg. But it's not a precise process, and bits of our inheritance could be more like that of the mother or the father - although it tends to be somewhere in between. Additionally, after fertilisation, the new genetic individual is working with a double set of each gene which contains a version from the mother and another from the father. These versions are called alleles.

Taking the gene for eye colour as an example: a child might inherit the allele for brown eyes from the mother and blue eyes from the father. In the simplest cases one allele is dominant over the other (the recessive gene), and so the child in this example 'expresses' the brown allele and has brown eyes. In reality the dominance of genes is much more tangled and complex, but the major point is that the recombination and shuffling of genes during sexual reproduction creates a never-ending supply of genetic diversity and unique individuals.

In mechanical terms, what happens is that a small portion of each chromosome breaks off and attaches itself to another chromosome. This is called 'genetic recombination' and it's why siblings from the same two parents can often look so very different to one another.

Staggeringly complex though all this is, the end result of the 23 chromosomes from the father's sex cells mixing with the mother's 23 is… just one cell. One master cell. And it's from this that further cells will come, and which will then keep dividing and dividing until you end up with 'you' - and at every division the DNA plans are copied at breakneck speed with hardly ever a mistake.

'An irrefutable proof that such single celled primaeval ancestors really existed as the direct ancestors of Man is furnished according to the fundamental law of biogeny… that the human egg is nothing more than a simple cell.'

Ernst Haeckel, *The History of Creation*

Hardly ever a mistake… *but they do occur.*

But before seeing what the consequences of these mistakes are… it might be worth going back to why the DNA molecule is shaped like a double helix. First, recall that the molecule is two metres of genetic instructions packed into a nucleus so small that it can't be seen. How to do it? By scrunching it up in the most efficient way possible. As an analogy, think of trying to shove a long rope into a glass. It wouldn't fit if you just dropped it in. But if you wound it round and round and then pushed it flat, the now ordered shape would fill the space more efficiently - and without any gaps.

Secondly, the spiral shape is chemistry's way of protecting the bits in the middle. These are the sugar molecules and, like sugar in tea, they dissolve in water. Since the cell's cytoplasm is mainly water that could be a problem. But what DNA does to protect these precious molecules is to wind itself up so unbelievably tightly that the nucleotide strands on the outside are now squeezed together so closely that they stop water from getting inside.

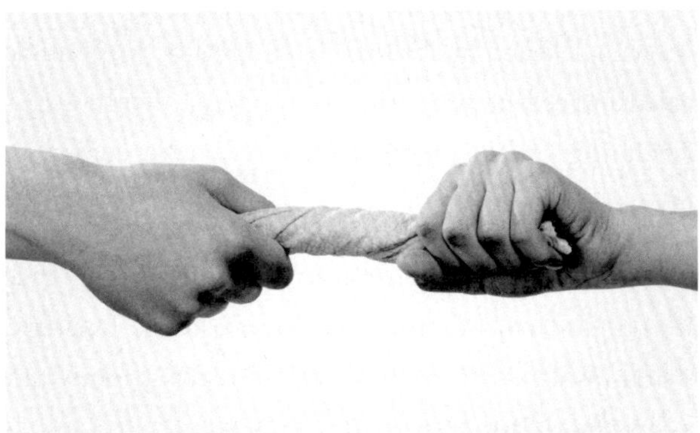

The DNA helix, wet on the outside but dry on the inside

Now, although making the DNA molecule into a helix was a stroke of sublime evolutionary genius, the shape creates a problem when it's being 'unzipped' for replication. This is because, if you can imagine the two strands of a twisted rope being pulled apart, the bit that's left unseparated gets increasingly tangled because a twist is added to it for every twist that's pulled out.

How does the creative powerhouse that is microbiology solve this? By having another enzyme come along periodically that chops the now separated strands of DNA off, releasing the tension in what remains. (Incidentally, this process can now be replicated in the lab in a process known as 'gene editing'. Essentially, scientists can snip out a length of an organism's DNA and insert a new gene, eliminating some of the most lethal diseases or altering the organism's traits in some way. In doing this the process is behaving as Nature does, but with more direction.)

Now not only is this untangling procedure happening at unreal speeds, but there's also a completely different biological process going on that's *repairing* any errors that might crop up. And it's this procedure that brings about mutations (either naturally occurring or artificially introduced through editing) to be inserted into the new strands of DNA.

As if all this wasn't incredible enough, it also turns out that only something like 2% of our DNA actually codes. Much of the rest is known as 'junk DNA', and while its purpose is thought to be largely structural, holding the whole thing together, it also plays a role in deciding how the body's cells divide, and therefore why some people develop particular traits, or are at greater risk of certain diseases.

So… our DNA is two metres long, with each chromosome strand a thousand times longer than the width of the cell's nucleus, only 2% of it is needed, it's only 1% of a cell's weight, it's in a hundred trillion different places in our bodies and millions are replacing themselves within us every second.

I don't know about you, but I find the sheer beauty of all this, the way that the biochemistry of DNA has evolved to solve coding problems, engineering problems and chemical problems and yet to operate at an incredible pace to replicate itself while keeping mistakes to a minimum, makes me slack mouthed in amazement. If you'd put a hundred of the world's cleverest men and women in a room for a year and told them to come up with a solution to the problems and opportunities of inheritance, they would never have managed to design anything like this.

It's hardly surprising that some people see the hand of God in it all. Others see tens of millions of years of endless trial and error… of chemical experimentation and continuous evolution that's essentially trying to preserve life. How's it doing that? By helping things survive through passing on the order needed to hold back the chaos predicted by the 2nd Law of Thermodynamics.

The brilliant research scientists who first realised how the molecular structure must be ordered won the Nobel Prize for their work. In 1953, James Watson and Francis Crick were at the Cavendish Laboratory in Cambridge when they came to interpret the X-ray diffraction images of the DNA molecule that another genius called Rosalind Franklin had managed to photograph.

You'd have to be made of stone to be unmoved by Watson's account of the point at which the realisation of the mechanism came to them. In his book *The Double Helix*, he describes how he and Crick were so mad with excitement that they had to find people to celebrate with. And so they left their lab and tumbled out of the freezing cold that dank, February day into the warm fug of their local pub, The Eagle, and blurted out to everyone within hearing distance that they'd found 'the secret of life'. In true British style, one of the most seminal lunchtimes in the history of scientific discovery is celebrated by… the pub's beer. Eagle's DNA bitter. Very well regarded it is too.

Once microbiologists had seen how the structural trick worked, they began to peel back the deeper mysteries of inheritance, and in doing so they became increasingly intrigued by the gene itself. Here was a product of biochemistry, the result of a bunch of original elements mixing together and somehow creating self-sustaining molecules.

So far, so mechanical. And yet if one gave it a personality, the gene almost seemed to possess a higher intelligence, apparently less concerned with where it was in the present than where it was going, its eyes seemingly focused more sharply on the future.

If it's impossible to see the inevitable outcome of the 2nd Law as anything but bleak, then one can only be cheered by the undying tenacity of the gene. What became clear as intensive studies of DNA unfolded was that at every step in the existence of life, the gene had evolved to extract the greatest possible order out of the conditions that faced it. At the same time, however, it was always laying the foundations for the next generation. By doing this, it is forever acting to secure the best chance of new things then passing on the baton of life itself… again and again.

> **'Just as the constant increase of entropy is the basic law of the universe, so it is the basic law of life to be ever more highly structured and to struggle against entropy.'**
> **Vaclav Havel**

Whenever I think of the gene, I'm always reminded of the clichéd scene in so many outer space movies. The forces of the Master are usually being overwhelmed and his faithful lieutenant comes to tell him that defeat is inevitable.

'Send in the Invincibles', the Master orders brusquely, 'and tell them to defend the ship to the last man!'

'Yes, sir!' replies the aide.

'And have the men prepare my escape pod.'

Where's the parallel? Richard Dawkins explains it in *The Selfish Gene* when he writes about how genes get into their escape pods when death seems inevitable: 'We can expect to live a few more decades', he says. 'But the genes in the world have an expectation of life that must be measured not in decades but in thousands of millions of years. The genes are not destroyed by crossing over, they merely change partners and march on. That is their business. They are the replicators, and we are their survival machines. When we have served our purpose we are cast aside. The genes are denizens of geological time: genes are forever.'

'You are a side effect… of an evolutionary process that cares little
for individual lives. You are a failed experiment in mutations.'
John Green, *The Fault in our Stars*

But hang on a minute. 'They are the replicators', Professor Dawkins says, but where's the replication? If DNA is so sublime in its copying brilliance - and the gene is so precise about passing on the parents' code - then how come everything in life started out as the same cell all those billions of years ago, and yet have ended up so completely different to one another? How is it that some organisms are nettles and others are parrots?

The reason for this diversity goes back to the mistakes we're told are bound to happen during the reproduction process. But if there are so many random errors, then how can they be helping the decision-making process?

If the argument is that different life forms are the result of decisions about what they're going to be, and how they're going to behave, then the replication process doesn't seem to be foolproof at all.

What's going on?

How mutations work

IF DNA IS SO GREAT AT PASSING ON GENES, THEN WHERE'S THE REPLICATION? WHY ISN'T EVERYTHING THE SAME INSTEAD OF BEING SO OBVIOUSLY DIFFERENT?

OK, let's say you're a tennis nut. In fact, you're such a knowledgeable fan that you even occasionally have a punt on the outcome of a match. The Wimbledon tournament is coming up, and as usual you're excited at the prospect of watching some fabulous games, perhaps getting to see an outsider knock out one of the seeds. Maybe you'll even be going online and placing one or two bets with your favourite gambling company?

But before play gets under way, you receive a strange email. It comes from an outfit you've never heard of, but it grabs your attention. In a short and punchy message the company says that it's come up with a method of forecasting the results of matches… *with 100% accuracy*. The sender claims to use a mixture of insider information on the players' form, then to weigh up environmental factors and, last, to apply a black-box algorithm that they've developed over many years.

And, the note claims, they're never wrong.

The email then predicts who is going to win the first match. You take no notice - it has to be nonsense. But after the game is over you get a follow-up email. 'See', it says, 'we were right.' As it happens, they were.

Now the company predicts the result for the second match. But then comes the dangled hook… 'you'll see just how accurate we are about this one too. And if you want to know who'll win match 3, then send $20 now!'

You still ignore them. But match 2 produces an extraordinary result as a no-hoper journeyman beats one of the hot favourites. And this weird outfit got the result right. Then the third email comes. 'Surprised?' it says. 'We told you we were never wrong.

Here is who's going to win match 3. And, if you want to know who'll win match 4, then send $30'.

This goes on… and on. Every time they email you they've predicted the outcome with a really creepy accuracy - even if it was highly unlikely. But now, with each new forecast they make, the price you have to pay for information about the following match goes up.

You started by dismissing the whole thing, but now you're really interested. You wait to see if their new forecast is accurate. It is. And, after each prediction you've been sent has been bang on for an incredible seven times in a row, you break - and send off money for their next forecast. When it arrives you have an enormous bet on it and, who knows, you might even win. Or lose.

Of course, it's all been a fraud. But how does it work?

It couldn't be simpler. First, the swindlers bought a colossal list of worldwide email addresses. Say it's a hundred million. They then created a simple programme in which people on one half of the list are told that Player A is going to win, and the other half are told that it will be Player B. If Player A wins, then an email goes to the fifty million who had been given the right result. The programme again splits the sample and, once more, the half that received the correct outcome then gets the next prediction.

By the time you've been taken in at match 7, the list is down to a couple of million people. But like you, everybody who's come this far now thinks the tipsters really are infallible. They'd been accurate about their prediction every time they wrote… and with a track record like that, lots of people would be willing to pay for the result of the next match. It's a nice little earner for the bad guys - and one that's been used a number of times with horribly successful results.

What's the point of the story though? It's because it isn't a bad illustration of how mutation theory works.

Just like the Wimbledon swindle, evolution is a numbers game. Its underlying approach is that waste doesn't matter, only that something wins in the end. In the same way that one's led to think that the scam's prediction history is credible, so one can look at the wonders of life on earth and find it impossible to believe that it wasn't all planned.

Indeed, to many people, the unbelievable diversity and complexity of life forms they can see supports a theory that's become known as Intelligent Design… 'intelligent' in that it appears to regard present day organisms as the result of a long process of refinement by an outside agent, usually God. In many ways, it's a seductive idea.

To others, the current state of the world's life forms, and the interaction between the different species, can be explained by scientific laws. To this latter group, as with the fraud, we're all the product of continuous sample splitting that's led to living things changing as the impact of mutations takes effect over unimaginably long periods.

'Accepting trial and error means accepting error.'
Tim Harford, *Adapt: Why Success Always Starts with Failure*

Just like the tennis trickery, mutations have only two outcomes for change: they either win or lose, making something better suited to its environment, or less so. In the language of evolutionary biologists, this acts to make its 'fitness' stronger or weaker - fitness being the measure of an organism's success in getting more or less of its genes out into the gene pool. Those most suited to their environments win, their genes increase and so do their chances of reproducing… which is what 'survival of the fittest' means.

Survival of the fittest has nothing to do with cross country running and masses of push-ups. In fact, it's nothing to do with the organism at all, other than it has traits that might be appropriate to its surroundings - and this means it will be pumping out more genes than the competition. This is like the man leaving his friend behind when they were running away from the bear. The organism can survive while others can't. I think I mentioned before that there's actually a third outcome possible with mutations, which is that any alteration has a neutral effect which therefore doesn't in any way impact on the organism's survival chances.

'It all boils down to how fit you are. Not so much whether you can run a marathon or how much you can lift, but how many children you can produce that are yours. The more kids you have that are genetically yours, the more copies of your genes there will be in the following gene pool.'
Adrian Raine, *The Anatomy of Violence*

How do mutations come about? They're the result of *mistakes* occurring as the DNA carries out the replication process. They arise because something has gone wrong in the genetic coding that's being passed down to the next generation. But surely, you'd think, this kind of bodged outcome should be impossible when everything we know about how DNA works points to the molecule's incredible efficiency? If it's so staggeringly brilliant, why doesn't DNA perform with greater accuracy? And if it's developed so many extraordinary ways of solving problems, why hasn't it overcome the obvious issue of how to fix any miscoding that might be occurring?

Evolutionary biologists think there's only one answer possible for the way errors get through. *It's because it suits it.* Or, more accurately, it suits the genes that sit on it. This is because being part of a flawed process is as good for the gene's objectives as Wimbledon is for the fraudster.

Why? How can this possibly be the case when everything in life is trying to instil order and certainty? How can Nature have developed a system that actively encourages mistakes - some of which might even threaten an organism's survival?

It's because the gene doesn't care if things go wrong. (I know, it sounds as if one's investing a collection of chemical compounds with the intelligence and self-awareness to arrive at a strategy. But even if it isn't sentient… what other conclusion can there be?) Just as Luca, the Last Universal Common Ancestor, had a way of replicating itself and establishing life on earth, so the gene has been the driver of a strategy of change - because any change is good for it, good for the survival of something, *anything*, as long as whatever happens keeps life going, keeps extracting order from disorder, and keeps reproducing itself.

'There is an unbroken thread that stretches from those first cells to us.'
Carl Sagan, *The Dragons of Eden*

As Richard Dawkins says about the function of the gene: '… that is its business'. That is how it works. And what a brilliantly clever system it is. If you have a world like ours in which everything is in a state of constant change, where there's a never-ending struggle to overcome collapse, in which the gene's experienced things like the air changing from sulphur to oxygen, of temperatures moving from blisteringly hot to freezing cold, of the Earth's surface fluctuating between being mainly land or mainly water, of soils becoming acid or alkaline, of sudden mass extinctions that wipe out vast numbers of species… then the gene's job is to hedge its bets, to encourage *diversity*, and to get as many different living things out into the world as it can.

That's the way it builds safety nets under life - so that there are as many chances of something surviving as possible.

The American chemical engineer and Nobel laureate, Frances Arnold summed up the process like this: 'The fuel for evolution is diversity, with natural selection leading to continuous adaptations and improvements in Nature's handiwork.' While the gene's function is to make this happen, there is no need for it to care what results from its actions. It doesn't take sides, it doesn't mind what survives or goes extinct, or wins or loses… just as long as *life* somehow keeps going in one way or another. Because if life carries on… then it's doing its job.

'The essence of life is statistical improbability on a colossal scale.'
Richard Dawkins, *The Blind Watchmaker*

How does this come about? What was the initial process that somehow managed what could otherwise be a chaotic free-for-all? Early life forms like bacteria give a clue to the answers, and because their direct descendants are easily studied, scientists can be fairly certain about how they evolved.

First, the binary fission of bacterial cells splitting into two by making copies of themselves would have meant that while prokaryote life had the world to themselves, any change would have happened extremely slowly. Because bacteria reproduce asexually, and therefore pass on the vast majority of their genetic material to the next generation, Professor Dawkins has likened their evolutionary progress to making a photocopy of a photocopy, and then repeating that process a hundred times. The hundredth would be very similar to the first, its original ancestor, but it still wouldn't be exactly the same.

'Nothing is more conservative than a bacterium.'
Nick Lane, *Life Ascending: The Ten Great Inventions of Evolution*

At some point, for example, early prokaryotes evolved enough to develop a kind of tail called a flagellum that waves around to push themselves forward. Like other organisms, they also became incredibly specialised in their functions and their ecological niches, and this resulted in untold numbers of microbial species co-existing with one another and frequently working together.

Unseen by us and largely ignored, this seething bacterial world is more numerous, more vital to life's future, and when they're all combined, add up to a greater biomass than all the other organisms on the visible planet. In many ways this diversity and scale isn't that odd either, because for the great majority of the time there's been life on earth, there were *only* prokaryotes. And, of course, their presence continues to this day.

But change was slow, very slow, and evolution was only to accelerate when sexual reproduction came along. When this happened, the action of sex cells fusing together and meshing their chromosomes meant that complex chemical processes were unleashed that wildly increased the chances of mistakes occurring - and provoking change from one generation to the next. Not only this, but while bacteria and archaea continued to be tiny, the more complex organisms that came after them evolved into a far broader range of sizes and physical characteristics.

It's hardly surprising that the fusing process in sexual reproduction leads to errors - just look at the speed with which it takes place. During the first few minutes of the process, the smallest cell in the body, the sperm cell, manages to get through the membrane of an ovum - the biggest cell in the body, some 85,000 times larger than it is.

The DNA in this fused cell then embarks on unzipping and making copies of itself in a huge number of different places, creating something like ten billion proteins at a rate of more than 100,000 chemical reactions a second. No wonder things can go wrong. But having things go wrong is exactly what suits life's search for diversity. As the American physician Lewis Thomas put it: 'The capacity to blunder *slightly* is the real marvel of DNA. Without this special attribute, we would still be anaerobic bacteria.'

How does this process result in inherited characteristics - and the 'decisions' that lead to things like us? It's because the traits that decide how organisms grow and eventually turn out are controlled by genes. They act together to create the genome. Now, this genome might be the total of all the instructions it receives, but the reason that the same recipes don't all cook the same pie is that the demands coming from what's happening in the environment are critical too. This combination of the structural and behavioural aspects of an organism - the observable results - is known as a phenotype, a word that sums up what 'shows'.

This means that many of the characteristics a thing displays aren't inherited whole, but are due to the interaction of the genotype (the mechanical side) together with the organism's surroundings. This is a critical distinction because it's the organism in its entirety that contributes to the next generation. What this means is that natural selection is affected by the addition of the genetic structure of the population, but also indirectly affected by the contribution of phenotypes.

As an example, someone's much-admired suntan is the result of an ability to go brown, together with the sunlight the person had been exposed to. But suntans aren't then passed on to one's children - although the ability to tan easily might be. This is a trivial illustration, but traits that give an organism an advantage over its competitors certainly aren't. And it's the organism's enhanced ability to survive and reproduce that leads directly to its 'fitness'.

Does this mean that the inheritance of characteristics is random? One school of thought says it is, and that the process simply chucks a lot of genes together into a shaker and an unknown cocktail comes out. But many other theories say that genetics can't just be this open to chance, and that the process of what you get from either your mother or father isn't simply a roll of the gene expression dice.

What has now largely been accepted is that there's something called 'gene drive' which describes the mechanisms that favour a specific gene. Because of this, instead of a gene just having a 50-50 likelihood of being passed from parent to offspring, gene drive gives it a far higher chance of becoming a trait that will be inherited - or not. This is partly due to dominant and recessive genes and is to some degree where the idea of genetic decision-making arises.

Mark Stevenson sums up the process in *An Optimist's Tour of the Future*: 'If a gene is a recipe for a protein, then 'gene expression' is the number of helpings - and just as is the case with food, too much or too little of something can be bad for you. Nature and nurture. Genes and gene expression, entwined like a couple doing the tango, an intricate dance of life where you cannot understand or appreciate one without the other.'

Research into this relationship has opened up a whole new field of science in which geneticists are now carrying out DNA editing operations to manipulate gene expression, and by doing this to create genetically modified organisms. Not unreasonably, this has led to questions as to why, if the process can be carried out artificially, might there not be a similar process in Nature that would make the organism look as if it was making a choice, arriving at a decision that would impact its future?

This argument is strengthened by the presence of genes called mutators that influence the rate of copying errors. Quite how they work is still open to debate, but it's clear that if there's a mutation that acts to the advantage of an organism's fitness, then the mutated gene can spread through the gene pool and ensure that the advantage multiplies by making those particular genes more numerous.

Breakthroughs in genetics all seem a bit like climbing in a mountain range. You reach the top of one exhausting peak only to see another, even higher and more challenging in the distance. In the same way, just as scientists seem to be arriving at a set of established scientific laws, another research programme comes along with further discoveries that raise the bar of knowledge yet again.

'How the Elephant Got His Trunk'. No, it didn't.

Wasn't it all easier in the old days, before new discoveries kicked off all manner of tricky questions? Surely it had to have been back when the accepted belief was that God alone decreed the position of living things in an ordered Universe. But when the great scientific uprising of the Enlightenment came along, a surprisingly large number of people started to believe that organisms had evolved from previous generations.

Possibly the most influential of these was a French biologist called John-Baptiste Lamarck who hypothesised that an organism could be altered by a process that passed on characteristics it had acquired *during its lifetime*. This meant that a horse had horse ancestors, even if they'd looked very different, and that progress had come about because of environmental pressures. Kipling's *Just So Stories* about how animals ended up looking the way they do was an amusing version of this idea, but very much reflected the Lamarckian views of the recent past.

Environmental impact was the key difference between these theories and Darwinism's later theory of natural selection. Lamarckian thinking held that an organism's surroundings led directly to changes. Natural selection, on the other hand, said that variations made organisms more or less *fitted* for the environment they found themselves in. Both mutations and changing environmental conditions were kinds of

     The Secrets of Life - Book One

accidental incidents, but when they combined then life flowed. The more suited things were, the better they reproduced, the fitter they became, and the more they flourished.

Amazingly enough, Charles Darwin's own grandfather, Erasmus, was one of the people who thought that environmental stimuli led to improvements being inherited by successive generations. When Darwin, the grandson, first published his ideas he rebutted this thinking, even though he had no idea about genes or genetics, and certainly couldn't have known anything about the mathematics of dominant and recessive traits.

While his theories were becoming widely accepted, the idea of inherited characteristics arising from the environment during an organism's lifetime was blown out of the water. But he had his own problems too. In particular, many of the early readers of *On the Origin of Species* would have found his natural selection theory full of holes, because not only did it appear to question God's role, but it also left itself open to some serious counter-arguments.

The battle of ideas:

'Improvements are inherited by successive generations'
Erasmus Darwin, 1796.

'One general law, leading to the advancement of all organic
things, namely: multiply, vary, let the strongest live and the weakest die.'
Charles Darwin, 1859

Darwin didn't help himself by being feeble at finding answers to these questions, frequently pleading with people that they had to look at the big picture and not to pick holes in it. In many ways, he was right, because before investigations of the underlying microbiology and genetics came along, it was impossible to appreciate the reasons for evolutionary strategies.

Since Darwin's time, however, modern evolutionary synthesis has connected the mutations so necessary for natural selection, together with the mechanism of DNA, into a unified theory of genetic inheritance. As the theories unfolded, people's eyes were opened to an understanding of the interaction between the genotype and the phenotype.

These recent insights have led to a far more detailed explanation of the biological relationships from genes to species, grouped under the gaily termed description of 'evo-devo'. This describes the exploration of how changes between generations (evolution) act on patterns of change within individual organisms (development).

While it's all pretty new stuff, the latest science is now principally focused on finding out what makes certain genes get switched on or off by environmental stimuli - and how this happens. Why does this matter? It's because it governs the process of making different things have different forms, and the great surprise that's come out of evo-devo is the discovery of how small a percentage of genes control the changes that take place in the embryo - and just how ancient those genes are.

Oddly enough, just as microbiologists have been getting to grips with the underlying mechanics of genetics, the Lamarckian idea that organisms can pass on traits they've acquired in their lifetimes seems to be making a comeback. At its heart is the observation that living things can, in some way, select the characteristics that are inherited, and that these then allow them to have a degree of control over their own destiny. This therefore appears to contribute to them making decisions about where they're going.

Does this fit in with Darwinian thinking? No, it certainly doesn't, and in fact it could be said to run counter to the core mechanism that he'd proposed about how random variation acts with the environment to produce selective pressures. In spite of this, the idea is not only very intriguing, but it's one that seems to be supported by experience and observation.

This 'neo-Lamarckian' concept is known as epigenetics ('in addition to genetics') and at its centre is the idea that changes to the chemical structures that control the shape and activity of a chromosome can be inherited. However, these chemicals are *not* changing the DNA sequence, or genome, that produces the genotype, but they *do* promote the expression of some genes and the inhibition of others.

The precise chemical make-up of these chromosome structures (the epigenome) appears to be influenced by environmental factors. In this way, the effect of a period of hardship or plenty experienced by the parents (and even grandparents) can be seen in the next generation, even though these offspring might by then be living in completely different conditions.

What does this mean? It's another way of recognising that the mechanisms that regulate genes to control protein synthesis - turn them on or off and therefore shape the phenotype - arise from the presence of environmental pressures that are coming down on the organism. The implication is that instead of changes lasting just for the organism's life, and then being reset by each new generation, epigenetics says that some of the effects of the stimuli can be passed down.

The geneticist and broadcaster, Adam Rutherford, gives an example of this in his wonderful book, *A Brief History Of Everyone Who Ever Lived*. In it he describes how the Dutch endured such terrible starvation towards the end of the Second World War that the period became known as the *Hongerwinter*. Because of the severity of this dreadful experience, he says, the effects not only damaged the health of the survivors, but epigenetically also damaged their children's and even their grandchildren's health as well.

'Epigenetics refers to changes in gene expression - how genes function. We often conceive of genes as fixed and static, but they are much more changeable then commonly believed. True, the underlying structure of the DNA - the nucleotide sequence - remains relatively fixed. But the chromatin proteins that DNA wraps itself around may be altered by the amino acids that make up these proteins. Proteins can be turned on - or turned off - by the environment. That alters how the DNA is transcribed and how the genetic material is activated.'

Adrain Raine, *The Anatomy of Violence*

Natural selection would argue that the genotype shouldn't have been altered by an experience like this. The theory would claim that even though an individual might be harmed during his lifetime by going hungry there should, theoretically, have been nothing to stop that person from having robust children. Observation of examples such as this would suggest otherwise.

The most favoured explanation for this outcome suggests that epigenetic inheritance generally seems to be the result of chronic stress. No one's quite sure how it works, although there's a great deal of research currently going into understanding its mechanism.

So what underlies all this? What makes environmental conditions have consequences that shape the hardwiring of an organism's behaviour? While different genetic theories may differ or overlap, what's not open to argument is that *something* is happening to set the survival strategies in living things, and that this is what drives their decisions about how they will behave.

The gene is very clearly the motor force behind all this. But, you might well ask, what are its aims? Perhaps if we understood its strategy better, we'd see how it affects what it travels around in, its vehicles - organisms - and that includes us.

In which case, what is it trying to achieve?

'Let me introduce our Investment Director, Gene.'

CAN THE GENE REALLY BE SAID TO HAVE A STRATEGY FOR THE FUTURE? AND, IF SO, HOW DOES THIS AFFECT ITS 'VEHICLES' - LIVING THINGS - WHICH WOULD INCLUDE US?

A very grand investment banker friend of mine once told me about the kind of work his firm did for their 'ultra, ultra high net worth' clients. These people, he said, were generally little known to the general public and that they liked it that way, typically keeping their cards close to their chests and using their 'family offices' to invest their colossal fortunes.

But although they kept a low profile and often assumed admirably modest lifestyles, they were all extremely keen not to lose their places among the smelliest of the world's stinking rich. If anything, he said, many of them often secretly wished they could rise above their peers and become widely known as the outright winners of the 'who's the richest' game.

My pal described how the bank was largely responsible for laying out 'what if' scenarios that speculated on the potential for serious political and economic disruptions in the world. These and other trends were then factored in to refine what long-term investments the family might make.

Interestingly, most of these clients of his worked to a very distant horizon of human progress, and were pretty phlegmatic about shocks and fluctuations along the way. Their visions stretched out over the generations yet to come, and they knew that no one could get things right all the time. This meant that they'd accept reversals as long as their great fortunes were preserved and grown in the long run.

'Calling someone who trades actively in the market an investor is like calling someone who repeatedly engages in one-night stands a romantic.'
Warren Buffet

One thing they seemed to share, and my friend smiled as he said this, was that they'd all have a fully fueled and staffed private jet available wherever they went. After all, what was the point of all that money and planning if they weren't able to get out at a moment's notice if trouble blew up?

Now, imagine *you've* been hired by the richest of these families to head up their investment strategy. They've given you a one sentence brief and will then leave you to get on with your job. The sentence? 'We don't mind if our money goes down, but whatever happens… make sure we'll always be the wealthiest people on the planet.'

What do you do? Of course, you wildly diversify your investments. Into everything. You recognise that the world's an uncertain place, and therefore that you need to have your fingers in lots of pies if you're to grow the pot. And you will also need a spread of assets if you're to plan for the worst.

Very quickly you also ditch your conscience… you figure that if you're to survive and come out ahead you can't afford to be too precious about judgments on whether the people you're dealing with are good or bad. Or whether your investments are ethical or unsavoury.

There are also a couple of other things you work out. The first is that you don't mind investing in competing companies. 'Let them fight it out', is your maxim, 'the winner will be all the stronger for the struggle. And if it wins then it could have the market to itself.'

The second is that you love backing new ideas: inventions that solve problems, innovations in the way services get delivered, even disruptive technologies that create whole new areas of business, many of which will generate completely different kinds of consumers.

Of course there are failures and blown investments along the way, but you find that over the long term you come out well in front by finding and backing some big winners. Better by far, you reason, to help build Amazon and Apple than to just sit on your shares in old technologies like the Metropolitan Gas and Coke Company and the United Candles Corporation.

But rather than letting them fight to the death, one of the things that pleases you most is when you see your companies helping each other. Above all, you love to watch them merge, or agree to work together in ways that add profitable new ventures and services. Encouraging them to make 1+1=3, and so create entirely new opportunities, has to be good business, you feel.

Some of your friends say you've become ruthless and selfish in how you're behaving. But you argue that you're doing the job you were hired to do, focusing solely on meeting the family's objectives and making sure their fortune doesn't go up in smoke. Whatever happens, you're determined to see it grow in scale for future generations.

Then, one day, the worst of the worst all comes at once: a series of gigantic meteorites destroy much of the American continent, volcanic eruptions are triggered around the globe, and tsunamis wipe out vast swathes of Asia and the Pacific region. In the chaotic conditions that follow, a dreadful, virulent pandemic sweeps through country after country. 90% of the world's population is believed to have died, the entire financial system collapses, power delivery fails everywhere, and the rule of law barely applies.

How's your fund now?

Ironically, it's never been in better shape. Of course, the great majority of the companies you'd invested in are now worthless. But some of your less adventurous ideas have suddenly come good. Gold had returned nothing for years, but it now becomes the only universally accepted currency. And you have lots of it.

Guns are needed to keep order and your factories are the major producers; your security services become critical as a temporary police force, and your pharmaceutical labs boom with the need for medicines. Before long, your power, construction and communications companies dominate the post-crash world and have entire niches to themselves.

How bizarre, you muse in your fortified office, that the fortune might now only be a fraction of what it once was… but the proportion you hold of the world's wealth has actually increased.

Not only does the state of the family fortune make its members comparatively richer than they've ever been, but you're now able to shape the post-apocalyptic world by rebuilding it in a way that suits your fund. In many instances, you're one of the few sources of money able to invest at this most critical of times. Now you can make sure that your grip tightens on the globe's institutions, and your future investments will put you at the forefront of the new business landscape.

But what, you must be thinking, is this rambling fantasy all about?

Quite simply, I can't think of a better analogy for imagining how the gene works. From its role in replicating the chemicals that somehow kept the earliest flickerings of life going, it's been its job to behave exactly like the fund manager, investing in layer after layer of diversity as its strategy for reducing the risk of death and destruction.

In doing this it has created more and more species with more and more odd qualities that will ensure that *something* survives a changing world - and particularly organisms that will get life through a sweeping catastrophe. As it does this, the gene is behaving in a way that's been described as 'selfish', because it's focused to the exclusion of everything else on doing its job, of holding back the inevitable disorder of entropic forces, and becoming in the process… *immortal.*

Has it succeeded? Yes, brilliantly. Although genes are only a few molecules sitting on a strand of DNA, they behave as if they're the puppet masters of life. But it would be a mistake to think that. They don't pull an organism's strings any more than your investment manager shapes a company's strategy. Organisations wouldn't grow without money, but investors don't actually run the companies. The gene doesn't plan forward any more than money has an entirely predictable effect. It may support and encourage innovation, but it doesn't create it.

The business analogy might also continue by saying that a company's production lines, raw materials, patents, buildings and other background things like these can be handed over from one lot of managers to another. These solid facts are rather like the genotype passing down characteristics to the next generation. But these are only part of the story - in commercial life it's what the management then does with these tools that makes the difference.

Just as a company's products and brands, image, pricing, packaging, ethical culture, presentation and propositions are what a consumer sees, so an organism's outward face is its phenotype - an expression of its genes as well as the influence the environment's making, and the interactions between the two. In this way, not everything with the same genotype will look or act in the same way, because appearance and behaviour are modified by the environmental or developmental conditions that come to bear on an organism.

Successful brands also depend on other things like good distribution, advertising, PR and marketing strategies. In the same way, phenotypes depend on extensions of themselves to maximise their chances. So, for example, the design details of a bird's nest, or a beehive, are said to be 'extended phenotypes' because these structures play a major role in helping the life form prosper as a species out in a competitive world. In short, the distinction between the genotype and the phenotype is between an organism's heredity and what that heredity produces.

By these means the gene has influence beyond the genotype by being carried around in organisms - vehicles - and in doing so, genes reach out to manipulate the world outside, sitting at the hub of a circle of radiating spokes of extended phenotypic power. No wonder there isn't a key that will work for long in a world like this. The biosphere's lock keeps changing as everything in life is constantly affected by a colossal web of influences, orchestrated by the countless number of genes that are sitting in millions and millions of different organisms, all similarly struggling and challenging for survival.

How does this work? Well, just as the investor's money and the company are mutually dependent, so are the gene and the organism. Genes work by controlling protein synthesis and while this is the core activity in building the next generation's embryos, it's a slow process. It needs vehicles to carry it around that will decide on its own behaviour, because that's the way they're both going to survive. So, if gene expression helps a living thing to do this - and it then successfully reproduces - this will help the gene's own future. By being replicated, the gene is, in turn, of further benefit to its vehicle.

The result of this mutually beneficial dance is that the evolutionary process is selecting from competing phenotypes by altering the success of the underlying genes. By doing this, it's spreading the resulting mutated instructions out to help its offspring prosper. One might conclude that here are the gene's decision-making activities at their most evident. This is how the gene and its robot carriers travel down their evolutionary paths, and life ends up with organisms becoming so completely different.

What are the gene and its vehicles aiming for? As Greta Garbo famously said, they want to be left alone. Their objective is to arrive at a strategy that can't be bettered by any deviant individual, to be safe from outside threats and, therefore, to have 'won'. The trouble, of course, is that however hard genes might try to achieve this, any victory is likely to be short-lived.

'Owing to this struggle for life, any variation, however slight and from whatever cause proceeding, if it be in any degree profitable to an individual of any species, in its infinitely

complex relations to other organic beings and to external nature, will tend to the preservation of that individual, and will generally be inherited by its offspring.'
Charles Dawin, *On the Origin of Species*

Why's that? It's because something will always come along that will change the game, usually in the shape of a critical shift in environmental conditions. Nothing lasts forever. As the wag said: 'Life is just one damn thing after another' and even though the time frames can be staggeringly long, this is never truer than in evolution.

And so, just as the investor can use his private jet to get out of trouble if it flares up in a country, so the gene ultimately doesn't care if it has to ditch a species. It only uses a particular vehicle while environmental conditions suit it, and it's always prepared to leave it to die or go extinct if something else is better for its prospects. In this sense (however repugnant it appears to us with our self-directed view of existence) one is forced to accept the gene's eye point of view that life is only about one thing… and that is survival. Nothing else.

'We all come from a single source. Everything that lives has its genetic code written in the same language. Unity is diversity.'
Krista Tippet, *Becoming Wise*

Looking at the life cycles of plants and animals and, particularly, insects, it's almost incredible how creative, how subtle and how unbelievably clever most survival strategies are. But, also, just how precarious their hold on life so frequently is. Once an organism has reproduced, the gene really has no further need for it.

And so, in a sense, death could be described as a life strategy because the gene's compulsion to be immortal wants to clear out old life so that the new offspring have the best chances of inheriting mutations. This is because the process might then lead to a more secure niche - and therefore to a greater likelihood of something surviving.

Oddly enough, this evolutionary process doesn't always appear to move along at the same pace. One theory holds that there seem to be periods of conservation and then bursts of rapid change. Another suggests that there's a more continuous process of evolution, but that this gradual rate can fluctuate over time. This schism has led to evolutionary biologists teasing each other about whether they're 'creeps' or 'jerks'.

Both schools of thought would agree, however, that the most notable period of change came with what's known as the Cambrian Explosion, a time when exaggerated speciation took place around 535 million years ago. It only lasted for about twenty million years, but it resulted in the appearance of large numbers of new animal species. Quite why it flared up is open to speculation.

But if we return to the investment analogy, have there ever been global catastrophes that the gene, too, has had to face? Yes, indeed, there've been exact parallels to the story's crash, and each time they've occurred the gene's chances paradoxically flourished - and novelty erupted.

This is because environmental conditions change so radically at a time like this that entirely new biosystems trigger surges in innovation and decision-making. From these colossal reboots, wholly new types of living things, and quite different kinds of behaviour, can send life forms careering down completely fresh paths.

'It turns out that Darwin... was wrong in one key respect: evolution does not always plod along at a snail's pace. When natural selection is strong - as occurs when conditions change - evolution can rip along at light speed.'
Jonathan Losos, *Improbable Destinies: Fate, Chance and the Future of Evolution*

When they research these periods of rebirth, scientists can only guess at what must have happened before the start of what they can see in the fossil record - something that only began with the Cambrian Explosion. Of course, life had been in existence for three billion years by this point, and there would unquestionably have been countless global extinctions before this, but earlier life forms left no trace of these behind. It was only when organisms became durable enough to imprint the evidence of their existence that palaeontologists could interpret what must have happened.

What emerges from their digs and rock bashing are records that show that somewhere between five and twenty mass extinctions - depending on the definition - would have taken place between then and now. And each one of these brought with it a fundamental change to the dynamics of living things.

Most extinction events seem to have been caused by such wild swings in the Earth's atmosphere and global temperatures that they affected sea levels and salinity. The first of the really serious, recent ones arrived about 440 million years ago, and was probably due to widespread glaciations that locked up so much water that sea levels plummeted, and shallow-dwelling creatures were wiped out. In all, some 70% of marine life perished.

Another, about 380 million years ago, was due to volcanism and annihilated 75% of species over a twenty-year period, including all the proto-amphibians.

The big one, known as the 'Great Dying' came 130 million years after this, possibly triggered by immense volcanic eruptions in Siberia, and is estimated to have driven 96% of marine life, and three out of every four land species to extinction. This means that only a handful of things remained to become our new common ancestors.

Two hundred million years ago saw a further one that killed off the early forms of mammals and 80% of all the other species, probably due to asteroid impacts. And then the most recent, and most famous, was about 65 million years ago when the dinosaurs, flying reptiles and most birds were wiped out as volcanic blasts spewed so much ash up into the atmosphere that the Sun was obliterated.

'Put crudely, adaptations evolve most strongly when the going gets tough.'
Daniel E. Lieberman, ***The Story of the Human Body: Evolution, Health, and Disease***

One of the great debates is what would have happened if these events hadn't come along. Would the species alive at that point have kept diversifying and endlessly continuing to branch? Some researchers suggest they would have done so. Others argue that each taxonomic group has its limits and that once it reaches a certain size, it stops growing. Many others believe we'd have ended up with more biodiversity than the world has ever seen.

Rather more sombrely, quite a few evolutionary biologists think that we're living through another mass extinction today, largely due to human activity. Maybe we are - although the evidence for this remains thin. While there have been a number of land animal species that have ceased to exist within the last 50,000 years, the profound implications of man's arrival on earth probably haven't yet been bottomed out.

The pessimists all assume that we're doomed, but then again the environmental future is unpredictable. What comes next probably can't be extrapolated from where we are now, any more than an ancient scientist could ever have guessed that a few tiny rodents would become the ancestors for such a sophisticated species as us humans.

Even though much of the thinking is fairly recent, and still open to differences of opinion, most environmental biologists now support the 'gene-based theory of evolution' together with its core belief that it's not the organism that's driving life on earth, but the gene.

What isn't in any doubt is that the replication process behind all evolutionary change stems from the actions of the gene leading on to mutational errors. Because this process is capable of generating vast numbers of copies that can give rise to varieties, each of which differs greatly from one another, it's this above all that drives change. Previous theories assumed that the underlying force stemmed from species acting for their own good. Now the great majority of scientists are convinced that behind all change is the gene.

The old thinking led people to view speciation as being part of a 'Tree of Life', with its implication that innovation branches out from a solid trunk, deeply embedded and secure. Now we know that life began as Luca, just one cell, and since then the entire mazy progress of creation has branched and branched from this single point, as life found new ways of existing and reproducing. From this ever greater complexity came wholly new mechanisms for survival. Entire sections of a biosystem might be destroyed, but what's left starts again, and new life blooms.

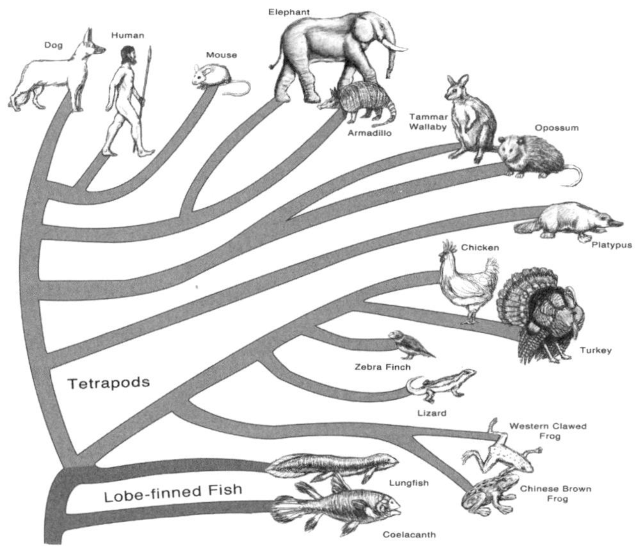

Life doesn't branch from a solid trunk.
Everything comes from a single cell.

I find this picture deeply moving. The idea that a great tree is inviolate is nonsense to anyone who's witnessed the effects of a powerful storm and seen a wonderful, ancient oak lying on the ground with hundreds of years of life lost in an instant. Far rather, for me, is the image of life as one of those extraordinary seaweeds, criss-crossed with interconnecting spores and bladders, that's anchored to an ocean rock with a minute holdfast. It may wildly jerk about in violent seas - but it's flexible and bends rather than breaks. Sections rip off and regrow. Only very rarely, though, does it lose its grip.

Why has this gene-based solution arisen? Why does the gene hold all the cards in this way? It's because nothing ever stays alive for long. Everything dies, and all species will eventually become extinct. Conditions change and even the best designed and most robust will either decline or be forced to change.

Of course it doesn't look that way from our standpoint, but then *Homo sapiens* has only been here for the fluttering of an eyelash, a couple of hundred thousand years at the most if you include our original ancestors. Even the longest-lived species, however, champion stayers that are still with us today like the alligator gar or the coelacanth, have only been around for some three hundred million years or so. This might be over a thousand times longer than us hominids, but it's still less than ten percent of the time that the gene's been seeing different life forms come and go.

It's worth repeating that of all the five billion species that are estimated to have existed over the lifetime of the Earth, 99.9% are reckoned to have gone extinct. Some lasted a long time, some came and went in a flash.

How many species make up our world now? Almost incredibly, nobody seems to be sure. One credible source postulates 15 million - of which only two million are currently known to science.

Others confidently state that there are 8.7 million, of which 1.7 million have been identified and named. Some biologists have even speculated that if one works backwards from how many base pairs are available on DNA molecules, there could be as many as tens of billions of species around the globe, most of which would be microorganisms.

Whatever it might be, it's a very big number. But the only thing everyone can be quite certain of is that ever since life began, the gene has been the constant companion and partner of every single one of them. Of course it also partnered those that have been lost, doubtless helping them before this wherever they could. Nonetheless, the gene wouldn't be the gene if it hadn't been prepared to jump ship for a better vehicle when circumstances changed.

'Biological diversity is the key to the maintenance of life as we know it.'
EO Wilson, *Storm Over The Amazon*

Along the 3.8 billion years since life began, the gene's 'learnt' more than a few tricks about how to maximise its chances of survival. And it's this drive that leads to one last parallel with our mythical investor. This is because, just as it suits markets to have companies and products compete - fighting to be the best and constantly improving to do so - so the gene thrives when species are challenged. It's this process that leads living things to adapt and change, using their mutations as the mechanism to do so.

But there's also a better method that both the investor and the gene discovered, and that's to let things cooperate, to form associations that work together for the good of both groups. In many ways this is the gene at its most focussed, encouraging an organism to adapt its short-term, self-serving aims and to cooperate either within the species, or with others outside it to ensure its future. This is the fund manager caring more about his investments than he does for the people working for the company.

If this approach means sacrificing individual members of a species, then the gene will be ruthless in supporting the strategy. Who should these individuals sacrifice themselves for? Others that will do their job for them, of course, and that means things with a similar set of genes to themselves.

What about us humans? Are we the same as everything else, driven and shaped by our genes? Only up to a point, and this is what makes us both so revealing, yet also so elusive. Of course we're made of the same chemistry and elements as other things, the same kind of cells, and the same genetic mechanisms to reproduce.

But uniquely among organisms, we've grown highly developed brains that took us on to higher intelligence, to consciousness, language, culture and an ability to imagine the future. And it's these abilities that have allowed us, as Richard Dawkins says, to have '… evolved to the point where we are capable of rebelling against our selfish genes.'

> **'Perhaps our greatest distinction as a species is our capacity, unique among animals, to make counter-evolutionary choices.'**
> **Jared Diamond, *Why Is Sex Fun?***

The qualities we developed over the incredible speed of our evolution as a species (nothing else would come near us) have made us into the reasoning, sentient, aware and sophisticated bunch we are, capable of judgement, self-knowledge and free will. But it's these very qualities that have also left us so often in conflict with the far deeper drives we have in us, in which the lessons of our genes and our heredity are demanding to be heard. The results of this conflict are frequently painful. We may think we know what we want, but the price of going against our inherent tendencies can be high.

Like everything before us we, too, are forever running up the down escalator of entropic forces and we, too, are programmed to put survival first. Like all other things, we too wish to be secure, to prosper and, above all, to win. Perhaps it doesn't feel like this, but we have to accept it. And as these books will try and explore, it may be worth investigating the different ways in which we achieve this.

Among other things, we appear to have developed the tools for manipulating our genes - opening the gate to creating our own genetic mutations. This may allow us to dominate the diseases and ageing processes that most fundamentally affect us, even arguably controlling the pace of our own evolution. But who's to say where this will end up?

Among the most widely quoted examples of how extreme the rebellion against our genetic inheritance can be, we can even decide for ourselves whether we want to reproduce or not. Since passing on one's genes has been the key compulsion of every living thing on the planet from the moment that life first began, contradicting this drive suggests either that the reproductive imperative is less powerful than biologists have believed, or that humans are able to resist even the most profound of the gene's demands.

Never before in the history of the Earth has there been an organism like us. It's the way we arrive at our life choices, and the processes we use, that makes us so fascinating to evolutionary biologists. Because scientists can examine how we weigh up our decisions and then manage to execute them so quickly, they've come to see us as central to their understanding of how organisms in the natural world also make their choices.

But humans and other advanced beings arrived very late in the history of the Earth. For *over two billion years* life only consisted of single-celled prokaryotes - bacteria and archaea - for whom there was virtually no decision-making to be done as they split themselves asexually into two clones. So why weren't their genes just happy to let them continue doing that? After all, creating exact copies was plainly a very successful strategy for making the gene immortal - as well as being much easier to control than having a world of complex life forms.

Since that's the case, why did evolution change a winning team?

And possibly more to the point, how did this change end up with us?

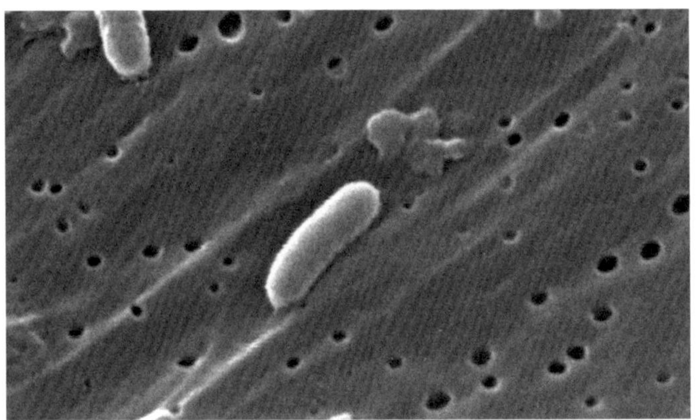

One's a bacterium and the other's an archeum... spot the difference.

CHAPTER SEVEN

PROKARYOTES WERE OUR ANCESTORS. SO, WHAT HAPPENED FOR THE TWO BILLION YEARS WHEN THEY WERE THE ONLY LIFE FORMS ON THE PLANET? AND SINCE THEY STILL EXIST, WHAT CAN WE LEARN FROM THEM?

If life on earth started about 3.8 billion years ago - 700 million years or so after the planet was first formed - then, for a huge chunk of our history, colonies of single-celled organisms were all there was… in fact, for getting on for the great majority of the time.

The cry goes up… boring! What have bacteria got to do with us humans?

The answer is quite a lot, really, as these minute life forms have always acted out existences that aren't so very different to our own. If we look at how they've evolved in their vast parallel existence, we get fascinating insights into why we behave in the ways we do, and how the same survival ideas progressed from prokaryotes to work equally well in multi-celled organisms. This shouldn't really surprise us. Not only is everything that's alive today a descendant of theirs, just as they are themselves descendents of Luca, but because their lives are still so closely entwined with ours, they continue to exert a huge influence over so many of the things we do.

What did these ancestors of ours look like? Unsurprisingly, they probably looked exactly as bacteria and archaea do today - flexible bags of gloopy stuff called a cytoplasm that contain enzymes and salts, and with specialist areas called ribosomes that control the protein production for the cell's energy source.

On the outside, holding all this together, there are membranes that cleverly regulate what chemical substances go in and out, so that the cell can survive to be largely independent of its environment. At one end of the membrane there are frequently one or more flagella that act like screws or propellers in the way they drive the cell forward. These tail mechanisms are probably the result of an early example of evolutionary progress as, at some point, they must have mutated from the prokaryote's own proteins.

But while it might sound as if these little things are all very similar, so tiny as to be invisible to the eye and simple in their structures, this shorthand couldn't be less true. Their cell walls can differ greatly, altering their biochemistry, and they come in a wide range of shapes, from spheres to rods to spirals. Scientists think that, incredibly, there could be millions of different species out there - of which they reckon they've probably only discovered a minute proportion, possibly even less than 1%.

They're everywhere: maybe a million in a millilitre of water, 40 million in a gram of soil, up to 100 million on your toothbrush. Nice. This ubiquity makes their numbers utterly staggering - biologists have reckoned there might be as many as 5 x 10^{30} of them on the planet, which is a lot of zeros, and roughly a billion times more than there are stars in the observable Universe.

And even though they're impossible to see, there are so many of them, and they occupy so many different niches, that if you put them all together their total weight would almost certainly be greater than all the plants and animals on earth put together.

Just like the single-celled organisms that emerged from the original chemistry set of life, some prokaryotes still survive solely on a diet of sulphur. This allows them to thrive in the scalding waters of hydrothermal vents in the deepest oceans, living off the echoes of a once molten planet. Others appear to be happy with their niches in the frozen wastes of polar ice caps, the extreme salinity of the Dead Sea, or even the hostile alkalinity of caustic soda lakes. These 'extremophiles' are found pretty well everywhere, from communities in dark underground caves to colonies being blown about by the winds that move the highest clouds.

'Bacterial cells are incredibly small… (yet) each is in effect a veritable micro-miniaturised factory containing thousands of exquisitely designed pieces of intricate molecular machinery, made up altogether of one hundred thousand million atoms, far more complicated than any machine built by man and absolutely without parallel in the modern world.
Michael Denton, *Evolution*

Bacteria and archaea didn't die out once more complex and sophisticated life forms came along. Instead, many of them simply adapted and integrated themselves into the new organisms that had evolved from them. And they then developed central roles in how these things existed. Others went on as they'd done in the past, leading independent lives and continuing their original roles.

In doing this they remain critical to life today by recycling elements such as carbon, nitrogen and sulphur that are so crucial throughout the biosphere. They enrich the soil and water, and some even take energy directly from the Sun through photosynthesis. And by degrading organic materials into sugars, proteins and fats, they wring every last iota of energy out of the inevitable decay of life, ultimately returning this disorder to the soil as ordered material. Without them life would have no defence against the crushing inevitability of entropic forces.

They've managed to adapt so well to a changing world that they'll survive on pretty well anything. Scientists have even found some that 'eat' the chemicals found in rocks. Different species will coexist with each other and with other organisms: many have formed symbiotic associations with both plants and animals, becoming a necessary part of the host organism's functions and benefiting from both their food and their waste.

What about us? Do we share our lives with them? Yes, of course, and most people would accept that they ride along with us as part of our existence. But if you don't like to think about this too much, then look away now!

It's believed that prokaryotes embrace us in truly gigantic numbers. There could be as many as 10,000 different species sharing their lives with ours - forty times the number of cell types in our bodies - and between them they could have some eight million genes, each of which is coding for proteins. This means that there are likely to be roughly four hundred times as many microbial genes at work within us as there are human genes. Add this all up and we're hardly human - numerically speaking - as our own bodies theoretically constitute under 1% of what's going on.

In spite of probably being unaware how intertwined our lives are, it's not surprising that many people think of microbes as alien and creepy, instinctively believing that they bring disease and decay to our lives, and preferring to ignore them at best, or to demonise them at worst.

Why should we feel that? Is it because we have so little control over their presence that we imagine microbial life as an existential threat? Or perhaps it's because humans fall victim to bacterial illnesses so frequently that the received wisdom is that they're always harmful? So widespread must this belief be, and so deep does it lie in us, that there are entire industries devoted to eliminating them.

But the fact is that we're a vast menagerie of bacteria, archaea and tiny fungi, living on us and in us, coexisting with each other and with our own cells in a colossal cooperative relationship that regulates our metabolism and runs many of our critical functions.

Put together, our prokaryote partners behave like another organ, as important to us as a stomach or a lung, and their trillions of individual bodies are working as a unified mass that's running many of our functions, and protecting us from a wide range of dangerous hazards.

Oddly enough, we emerge as new-born babies without any bacterial life on us at all. But from the instant of our birth we begin to build what's known as our microbiome, a vast symbiotic other world that's critically important to our well-being. This isn't fully mature until we're about three years old, and is largely established by our mother's bacteria, usually through her breast milk.

In fact, recent analyses have led scientists to think of this milk as having a key significance to the biome's own development as much as it is to the baby's nourishment.

**'We leave the womb without a single microbe. As we pass
through the mother's birth canal, we begin to attract entire
colonies of bacteria. By the time a child can crawl, he has been
blanketed by an enormous, unseen cloud of microorganisms…'
Michael Specter, *The New Yorker***

Ed Yong describes this happening in *I Contain Multitudes*, when he observes: 'Every mammal mother feeds her baby by literally dissolving her own body to make a white fluid that she then secretes. The ingredients of the fluid have been tweaked and perfected through two hundred million years of evolution to provide all the nutrients that infants need. These ingredients include complex sugars… but babies cannot digest them! Why hasn't natural selection stopped such a wasteful practice? Because it turns out that the sugar is passed to the stomach and the small intestine unharmed, and lands in the large intestine where most of our bacteria live. What scientists are now thinking is that milk isn't food for babies at all… but food for microbes.'

The majority of the thousands of different species of bacteria within us are found principally in our intestinal tract. There they work tirelessly to release nutrients, break down toxins and enable us to produce vital vitamins and minerals. And what a task it is. Yet hardly any of the cells in our stomach last for long as the lining is constantly being hosed down with highly concentrated hydrochloric acid, and this means it has to remake itself every few days.

Our microbiomes never rest. Instead, they're in a constant state of change as all the different species in them are competing and cooperating, interacting with each other and with our own bodies, developing and running the intricate networks of our nerves and fibres. We depend on them for our growth and for our wellbeing. Perhaps most importantly, our immune system hinges on bacteria to distinguish between non-harmful organisms, and what could turn out to be dangerous, disease bearing germs.

So central is the microbiome to our lives that biologists reckon the untold trillions of prokaryotes within us share the work of making our bodies function, and collectively make up something like 3% of our body weight.

Are they a threat to us? In general, no, quite the opposite, and the vast majority of the species are quite harmless. On the other hand, there might be a hundred or so rogue types called pathogens which can cause infectious diseases. The good bacteria in our microbiome help to protect us from these baddies by smothering them to death, or by killing them off with antimicrobial chemicals. The balance between doing this, and letting beneficial bacteria thrive, is of central importance to our health.

Many biologists now believe that the emphasis in modern life towards extreme cleanliness, as well as the widespread use of antibiotics, may actually have reduced the power of our microbiomes, and that this has very likely contributed to diminishing the efficiency of our immune systems. It's even thought that it's led to the increase in conditions such as diabetes, celiac disease, osteoarthritis, food allergies and depression.

The ways in which the two worlds in our bodies coexist remain largely a mystery. In particular, there are many questions over how this microbial partner of ours fits in with the gene-based theory of evolution. Yet if the bacterial genotype follows the example of the multicellular world, then it's almost certainly having a role in our development.

Some scientists even go so far as to say that our microbiomes are as much an extended phenotype to us as a nest is to a bird, in that it's shaped by genes to encourage certain bacteria to grow. It may be outside its owner's control, in other words, but it's playing as big a part in an organism's existence as any other phenotypic extension.

'When we eat, so do they. When we travel, they come along.
When we die, they consume us. Every one of us is a zoo in our

For these and other reasons, researchers are becoming increasingly interested in what a healthy gut microbiome should look like. It's known, for example, that a well-balanced relationship in our intestines between our own cells and microbial life plays a major role in our metabolism, our cardiac health and the immune system as a whole.

Even our moods, personality and energy levels are influenced - although the mechanisms for this are still little known. It's even reckoned that our mental health can be affected, and clinicians have begun to reveal the communication networks that link the gastrointestinal tract to our central nervous systems. They term this the 'gut/brain axis' and it's now thought to be a key component to us having a balanced outlook, and therefore to the way it influences aspects of our human interactions.

In particular, some scientists have recently been spotting that their Alzheimer's patients display markedly different microbiomes to healthy people. Other studies have come to the same conclusions about schizophrenia sufferers and depressives. In all these poor people there tend to be substantially increased levels of inflammation in the body. These inflammatory processes are then somehow thought to impact the brain through the blood supply, or even to help rogue proteins travel through the nerves connecting the gut to the brain.

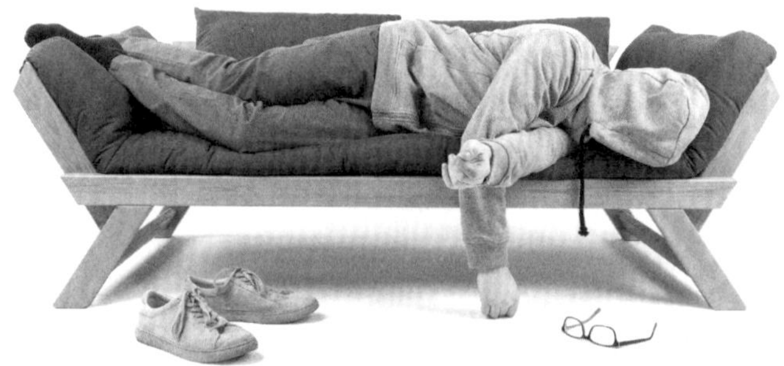

'I'm afraid Michael won't be in today, he's suffering
from a hango..., I mean gut/brain linkage.'

The relationship between these two areas is easily illustrated when the composition of our internal microbiome is somehow damaged in such a way that it provokes an inflammation of the gut lining. When this happens, the injured area can allow bacteria to pass through the lining in what's known as 'leaky gut' syndrome, and this can then stimulate an immune response.

Recent studies have shown that any sort of stress can change the gut environment detrimentally. Too much alcohol, for instance, can produce a temporary illustration. Anyone who's suffered the physical side effects and psychological confusion that can come after a night on the toot might begin to agree that the gut/brain linkage isn't just a myth.

The reverse is also true, and a healthy microbiome can help our social behaviour and cooperative instincts. If you want to achieve this, it turns out rather boringly that your mother was right, and that sleep, weight, exercise and healthy things like fruit and vegetables all lead to a gold star biome. Grrr.

> **'Every day we live and every meal we eat we influence the great**
> **microbial organ inside us - for better or worse.'**
> **Giulia Enders, *Gut: The Inside Story of our Body's Most Underrated Organ***

One thing that was previously not thought to be in doubt was that the brain was a bacteria-free, sterile organ. That's because there's something called a blood-brain barrier that should keep microbes out. But recently, clinical researchers have begun to realise that this protection system is breached more frequently than they'd previously believed.

The meningitis pathogen, for example, had always been known to get through somehow, but now researchers are beginning to think that the brains of otherwise normal patients might also contain live invaders. Not only that, but recent research suggests that healthy bacteria can also sometimes be present in there, even though what they're up to is yet to be understood.

What are the insights into how life works that these smallest and earliest organisms give us? What do they illustrate about the decision-making processes in life that have ended up with us having such a bewildering variety of different things on earth?

It seems that there are three great lessons.

The first, mildly depressing realisation is that from the dawn of life right down to the biosphere we inhabit today… wherever there's something alive, there's also something else trying to live off it. Yes, parasitism existed in microbial colonies right from the very beginning.

What happened? Well, single celled organisms reproduce through a process called binary fission that's a lot like the mitosis procedure that divides our body cells. Essentially the cell splits into two clones, and each new cell gets the same DNA that was in the original.

But DNA in prokaryotes isn't stored in the complicated way that it is in ourselves. Rather, it sits in a single circular plasmid that, together with some proteins and RNA molecules, make up what's known as the cell's nucleoid.

Of course, microbial life only rarely leaves clues to tell scientists about the past, but they're pretty sure that what must have happened was that bits of DNA somehow broke off and floated clear of this reproductive process at about the same time that self-replicating molecules first occurred.

These stray bits of DNA then became independent in the sense that they were separated from the cells, but then had to find host organisms to invade for their survival. Opinion therefore differs among biologists as to whether these orphans can even be described as life forms at all since they can only exist by living off other things.

Early scientists weren't in much doubt about it. When they first saw that their very existence was parasitic, and that they could only survive by infecting their hosts, they named them after the Latin word for poisons: viruses.

Being only a molecule, viruses are obviously much smaller than other microbes. And although they're just particles of DNA, they are wrapped up in protein coats that give them their shape and this, in turn, is usually surrounded by a fat membrane. Viruses are normally not attached to anything, but simply float around looking for things to grab hold of. Once they've latched onto a microbe, they invade it and become known as bacteriophages, or just phages.

They manage this by coming up alongside a bacterium and throwing out fibrous grappling hooks to hang on and then inject DNA into it, rather like a mosquito sticking its proboscis through your skin. Once these viruses have parasitised the cell, the imported DNA turns its host into a production line for untold numbers of new phages. These then erupt out of the host bacterium rather like that terrifying creature in *Alien*, and then rampage off to find other poor microbes to invade. No wonder viral illnesses can blow up so quickly.

'Every person is a collective, a vast and complex gathering of interdependent life. Any description of 'human' must acknowledge these intimate strangers. Our bond with microbes is such that they are not so much riders, parasites, and assistants as part human. And we, it's becoming increasingly clear, may need to begin thinking of ourselves as part microbe.'

Guy P. Harrison, *At Least Know This: Essential Science to Enhance Your Life*

I suppose in the pantheon of the scary, bad guys in our bodies we'd instinctively rank viruses even higher than bacterial pathogens, and certainly up beyond microbes in general. But it's not as simple as that because it turns out that certain bacteria can actually store the viral DNA code in their own chemistry as a way of defending themselves against the invaders - just as a vaccine can immunise an organism.

It also seems that a few viruses can do good work, some of the time, and can even be beneficial for our health by keeping otherwise dangerous pathogens in check.

How do our bodies control all this? Like other organisms we use that odd gooey, unattractive stuff called mucus. Microbes live on it and off it - it provides nutrients - and it turns out that organisms can unconsciously change its composition and use it as a kind of control mechanism. When they do this, it seems they're employing it rather like a traffic light system that allows certain kinds of viral phages to wipe out nasty bacteria, but also to keep others at bay.

In this way, mucus is being used to regulate viruses by letting them stick to it. The deal is that, in return, they're allowed access to bacterial hosts. Research shows that the more viruses animals have in their mucus, the greater is the likelihood of phages finding bacterial victims. So neat is this balance that it really looks as if the strange arrangement was the origin of our immune systems.

But nothing's straightforward in the microbial world: good bacteria can turn bad, bad can turn good, viruses can threaten or assist our health, and outside factors from our own bodies and the environment like sleep, temperature and the time of day can all change the situation in a blink.

The MRSA superbug, for instance, a nailed-on killer if ever there was one, can be found in the nasal passages of roughly a third of the population. Are carriers therefore about to die? Or are the bacteria, as biologists tell us, being good partners by acting to keep pathogens out?

Another example is a species of bacteria called *Escherichia coli* (E. coli), two words that usually strike terror in the breast of any alert Health and Safety Officer. However, they're actually beneficial normally, living in our intestines and helping our digestion process. But some are pathogenic and, if they escape from their gut home, they can frequently carry their poor victims off to a better world.

In rather the same way, bacteria and fungi on our skin are wholly beneficial - but if they leave the surface and enter through an open wound, they can cause big trouble.

What does this all add up to? Does the microbial world make *Game of Thrones* look like a meeting of the Mothers' Union? Is it a lawless, dystopian power struggle typified by disloyalty and ruthlessness? It may look that way, but biologists refute this with one telling question: 'if that's the case, why does nothing ever win?' It's a good question, because if these tiny life forms have the capacity to be so powerful and potentially deadly, then why doesn't something sweep the competition away and bring any semblance of cooperation to an end?

Instead of this, there's an undoubted order in microbial societies, even though there are no rules or policing. Their huge numbers appear to form largely balanced groups not unlike our own human societies, with a range of specific jobs being carried out for the good of the whole.

But once this cohesion is challenged by tiny versions of cheats, rogues and defectors, the community starts acting in its own best interests. When this happens, it displays self-regulating mechanisms that restore order and the kind of symbioses that lead to mutual gains. In fact, just as we do in our own communities.

The second great lesson that provides insights for our existence also stems from a pretty good question: 'If prokaryotes reproduce by dividing themselves and making exact copies, then why don't individuals live forever?' After all, if each new offspring gets 100% of the parent's genes in asexual reproduction, then surely what they're doing is making fresh copies of themselves.

To this you might add other questions that our own experience of them would throw up: 'And if they just make clones of themselves, why do we have to keep chasing after them with new antibiotics? Why aren't they sitting ducks once we know where they are? How come they can change so fast and make themselves resistant?'

The fascinating answer to this is that microbes employ the same techniques to wriggle out of trouble that built life in the first place. That's because, just as elements, compounds and molecules developed through outsourcing and collaboration, so prokaryotic life forms do exactly the same thing. Even at this elemental level of life, these microorganisms are using cooperative mechanisms that allow them to change and respond to threats when they're under attack.

And they manage this by altering their biochemistry at lightning speed by swapping genetic material between themselves.

What they're able to do is exchange their DNA, either by floating bits across from one bacterium to another, rather like their version of sex, or by picking up free-floating DNA from the environment. This is material that might, perhaps, have been left behind by dying bacteria. Sometimes they even use viruses to transfer DNA between themselves - turning the relationship round and employing the dreaded parasites as instruments for their own ends.

By having all these tricks available to them, they can import alien DNA when they come under pressure. What this means is that it's possible for them to mutate at incredible speed, sometimes beneficially for themselves and sometimes, more importantly for our bodies, of benefit to their environment - us.

But doesn't this evolutionary process take a long time? After all, mutations can take millennia to have an effect in other organisms. And aren't mutations rare anyway?

They are, but these DNA swapping tactics mean that microbes don't need the thousands of generations it can take in other organisms. Because the bacterial reproduction rate is extremely rapid - a new generation in only a few minutes - they can allow different mutations to be unleashed until they find one that works for them.

Instead of the usual way an adaptation occurs - by taking place slowly and vertically, from parent to offspring - this genetic exchange process in bacteria is known as Horizontal Gene Transfer, because genes are moving across between members of the *same* generation. In doing this, they're acting out the forces of natural selection because they're getting the fittest genes out into the gene pool in the same way that other organisms do … but they're doing it at blinding speed.

Recognise this? Doesn't it sound pretty similar to the way we human beings work? Unlike other poor creatures that can be written off by a sudden change to their environments, or from a competitive species invading their space, we have the ability to analyse threats and then take immediate actions to respond. We don't have to change through mutations. Instead, we can defend ourselves at huge speed, using outsourced weapons, making alliances, moving away from trouble or somehow altering ourselves. And now it turns out that our ultimate forebears could, and still can, do exactly these things as well.

But perhaps the third and last great insight that comes from looking at prokaryote behaviour is even more extraordinary. It turns out that bacteria have another way of fighting off the existential threat of killer phage attacks. What they do is form up in front of the invading viruses like an army of crazed Spartans… and destroy themselves! Not just one or two of them either: biologists reckon that as much as 10% of a colony might wipe themselves out in this way.

Why do they do this? How can it help? What happens is that their suicides create a sort of soggy trench of dead bodies that makes it impossible for the raiders to get through - because there's now a kind of firebreak between the living bacteria and the invaders.

There's also another great legacy left behind by their sacrifice. Not only do they protect the colony, but when their tiny corpses collapse they release precious nitrogen that's then used to enhance the future prospects of the ones they're leaving behind.

Bacteriologists have discovered that the genetic mechanism for this activity uses messenger RNA to order the cells' protein to begin the death process. But what they've also identified is that the chemical for this is actually a 'quorum sensing molecule' that originates from *outside* the bacterium itself. What does this mean? It suggests, almost incredibly, that there's a sort of collective intelligence at work, a monitoring system within the community that drives individual behaviour… 'Bandits at four o'clock! Tell the boys to kill themselves.'

'Every suicide is a solution to a problem'
Jean Baechler, *Suicides*

Isn't this astonishing? What's obvious is that these little things are sacrificing themselves for the colony's well-being, and therefore acting for the survival of their genes. But surely this goes against life's imperative to fight the 2nd Law of Thermodynamics, as well as the central principle of natural selection?

Why's that? It's because if everything's programmed to do whatever it takes to keep going - to get their genes out into the gene pool and therefore increase fitness - then this suicide lark would seem to be self-defeating. Surely logic dictates that, over time, a colony would be diminished by losing the selfless genes that make them behave like this in the first place?

Evolutionary biologists would tell us to think again because, at base, what we're witnessing is something that's cascaded down the long history of life, from these earliest living things to every organism that's ever come after them. It passes through the evolutionary story like a connecting thread, linking each development in turn, until it ends up resonating in every aspect of our own human conduct, every argument about morality, and every decision we make about how to behave.

It's doing nothing less than highlighting the great conundrum of life: *should one be selfish and win by fighting others… and beating them? Or is it a more profitable strategy to win by helping one's community - by being cooperative - and so win by being part of a winning team?*

What conclusions are we to make from these ancestors of ours? Some of them are trying to build, others are attempting to live parasitically, everything is constantly fighting to defend itself, some employ cooperation as a defence mechanism, some gain from outsourcing - using things other than their own resources - while some insist on the success of the group at the expense of the individual. All these and more could be human issues. In coming up with these solutions, prokaryotes seem to have always been laying down the behavioural templates for what was to come after them.

Since this seems to be the case, perhaps if we look at the great journey of life we'll be able to see if the same themes and lessons are passed down through the extraordinary diversity that evolution was to throw up?

And, if so, what does this mean?

You wouldn't have thought so, but you're looking at how life first discovered the benefits that come with the division of labour.

CHAPTER EIGHT

HOW DID LIFE SPEND SO LONG AS SINGLE CELLS, AND THEN SOMEHOW PROGRESS TO END UP WITH ORGANISMS LIKE US? AND WHY DID CERTAIN CHANGES SEEM TO WORK, AND OTHERS DIDN'T?

The great construction project that's arrived at life as we now know it was put together by the evolutionary process to end up rather like one of those impressive skyscrapers one sees, its steel and glass gleaming in the sunshine, apparently an effortless outcome of technology's aim to produce user comfort.

Only rarely does one think about the years of investment and forethought it must have taken to put it all in place, let alone the time-consuming, old-fashioned slog and muscle that was needed to lay the foundations and erect it.

In the same way, sophisticated life forms look so planned, so natural and so organised that it's easy to forget that they, too, had to spend millions of years digging the trenches and putting in their footings. This progress was painfully slow, and things only seemed to inch forward over the first few billion years of our history.

Nor was this the only impediment. There must have been any number of ways that prokaryote life would have tried to anchor their futures in hostile environments, yet they must have experienced multiple failures as they did so. No doubt the vast majority of ideas that evolved simply ran into the sand.

But some things did work. And if the aeons that make up life's journey show anything, it's that any success early organisms had in these experiments arose from the underlying motivation to resist the Laws of Thermodynamics. This was because life had to find ways of transferring energy efficiently, and therefore had to create order within the ocean of disorder that surrounded it.

So, what were the foundation stones that the skyscrapers of later sophisticated life forms used to build on?

Prokaryotes themselves were obviously the great breakthrough. Once they'd established themselves, the different species found they could keep refining their biochemistry and behaviour in ways that allowed them to live off whatever energy the planet or its atmosphere was generating. Arguably the most successful of these employed whatever was in the greatest abundance: the water that was so prevalent, carbon… and the Sun's energy. Mixing these together was how photosynthesis came about.

How did this originate? Plainly these early microorganisms found a way of using the magnesium-rich chemicals in their bodies to absorb the red and blue photons of sunshine. The chemical in question is called chlorophyll, which is famously green because it rejects the green light, and instead reflects it back, making it visible to us. In fact, if photosynthesis was more efficient, then the leaves of plants would look black.

Next, prokaryote life used this bottled-up light energy to manufacture sugars (simple carbohydrates) from carbon dioxide and water, two raw ingredients that have always been readily available in the environment. Bingo, another kind of outsourcing had worked: energy from space had been transferred to energy on earth - and prokaryotic life forms began to flourish.

The early atmosphere was ideal for this process. It had lots of sulphur, nitrogen, carbon dioxide - and water vapour. The Sun's energy was used to split this vapour into hydrogen and oxygen - and the oxygen released by the process formed ozone. This then filtered the Sun's rays, and so shielded the young planet from harmful ultraviolet radiation.

Everything might have been working fine but progress was slow. With such a narrow base to rely on, prokaryotes were still constantly threatened by sudden environmental change. This meant that although they emerged as long ago as 3.8 billion years, it wasn't to be for another five hundred million years or so until another major innovation made conditions easier for them.

What happened was that these cells must have begun using the proteins in their membranes as a way of protecting themselves against environmental damage, because at some point individuals began to develop a kind of basic signalling mechanism from one cell to another. And they used this to warn their neighbours if there were dangers occurring in their surroundings.

From here it was a short step - well, OK, maybe a few hundred million years - for mutational change to allow bacteria to excrete a sugary protein that had the effect of gumming the membranes of the neighbouring cells together. Now, instead of just being individual life forms, they were bundling themselves up and building colossal colonies. This process led to great mats of joined-up cells called cyanobacteria - and by combining in this way they found they could release a certain amount of *surplus energy*.

Why surplus? Why would that happen?

It came about because instead of each cell having to do everything it needed to look after itself, this new kind of group endeavour found a way of dividing up the necessary tasks for survival. There were huge benefits to this, not least of which were that the colony somehow designated those on the outside of the group to do the job of protecting the rest of them from atmospheric toxins.

In this way, elaborate structures of cells were gradually being put together in which microscopic organisms were working as a team, providing a means of giving individuals the shelter and protection they needed to exist in the harsh environments that surrounded them.

In short, life had discovered that cooperation could succeed for the benefit of all parties.

> **'From simple cells to supersocial animals like us, the story of life on earth is the story**
> **of increasingly complex cooperation. Cooperation is why we're here,**
> **and yet, at the same time, maintaining cooperation is our greatest challenge.**
> **Morality is the human brain's answer to this challenge.'**
> **Joshua D. Greene, *Moral Tribes: Emotion, Reason, and the***
> ***Gap Between Us and Them***

Once prokaryotes had stumbled on this sticking-their-membranes-together dodge, cyanobacteria (so-called because of its blue-green colour) began forming vast blankets that lay on the surface of the sea, or over pools, sucking up solar energy and splitting water molecules to make sugars for themselves. And, in the process, expelling oxygen.

As the oxygen levels in the atmosphere rose, so the amount of carbon dioxide dropped, and this caused a climate change that cooled the Earth's surface. A secondary effect of it was that as oxygen created the ozone layer, it filtered out harmful solar rays and this allowed complex biological compounds to be formed. In turn these fed evolutionary experimentation, and so catalysed the production of new life forms.

Amazingly enough, the first cyanobacteria have even left rock-like fossils of themselves. These so-called stromatolites date back billions of years and provide a record of the very first attempts at this collaborative way of living. Some can still be seen in parts of the world as varied as Greenland and Australia and, under analysis, they show up as layered bio-chemical structures of the earliest cyanobacteria mats. These would almost certainly have originated in shallow water, but as they became trapped, they were bound together in perpetuity as their membranes gradually cemented.

So astonishingly profitable did the photosynthesis trick turn out to be that all the plant life that was to come later in the Earth's history is still based on an elaborate joint venture with cyanobacteria inside their structures.

These are now known as chloroplasts, yet they still do what they learnt all those billions of years ago… converting the Sun's energy into nutrients and so serving its host plant. Just as the first mats did, this process continues the ancient work of making our planet inhabitable by sucking up carbon dioxide, fixing nitrogen into ammonia - and then releasing oxygen out as a waste product.

What followed from the extraordinary cyanobacteria breakthrough has become known as The Great Oxygenation Event. And, after it had been working for a mind-boggling 1.2 billion years or so, the Earth ended up with oxygen at a presence of roughly 21% of the atmosphere. The rest was, and still is, mainly nitrogen together with some trace gases, carbon dioxide and water vapour.

This atmosphere may have taken a long time to develop, but it's what has given us the relatively benign conditions that we and every other living thing now experience. How does it stay that way? It's because the gases that are given off are retained by gravity, and the resulting atmosphere protects life by creating enough pressure to keep water in its liquid form. This warms the Earth's surface through heat retention, and absorbs ultraviolet solar radiation. It's because of all this that the extremes of temperature that the planet first experienced were largely tamed.

Before oxygen was available in such quantities, life was limited and fragile. But once the atmosphere was established at more or less the current level, it's reckoned the outcome boosted the Earth's biomass by a thousandfold. Hierarchical levels in the food chain multiplied from two tiers to five - some scientists even argue for six - and in many ways, today's complex life forms owe everything to oxygen's ability to form compounds with other elements.

But why is the settled-down oxygen level at 21%?

                                                   The Secrets of Life - Book One

No one's too sure. There's no doubt, however, that the entire global biosphere has grown up around this level. Besides anything else, it has enabled plant life to continue to take in carbon dioxide and to pump out more oxygen. For rather foggy reasons, however, although 21% seems to have won out, there were times when scientists believe the proportion could have been as high as 35%, and even as low as 12%. Instead of this being an insurmountable obstacle to growth, though, these fluctuations are now thought to have acted as stimuli for many of the evolutionary changes that were to take place later.

The build up was also what would lead to the extraordinary mechanism of breathing. The way this works is for organisms to transfer the sucked-in oxygen molecules to its blood cells. Once there, they're picked up by an iron-rich protein molecule called haemoglobin, and this is used to burn food in a slow and controlled way, liberating energy for cells. The waste product of the process is carbon dioxide, which dissolves in the blood as it's transported back to the lungs. And it is from here that it's eventually dispelled back into the atmosphere in the out-breaths.

'Oxygen flooded into the atmosphere as a pollutant, even a poison, until natural selection shaped things to thrive on the stuff and, indeed, suffocate it.'
Richard Dawkins, *The Greatest Show on Earth: The Evidence for Evolution*

And round and round the cycle goes, with some things taking in oxygen and expelling carbon dioxide, and others, like plant life, doing the reverse as photosynthesis takes place. The result is the one we can see - a world with a vast number of symbiotic relationships that keep all living things in balance.

But prokaryotic life was still on a dangerously narrow base in those early days. Diversity was limited and chemical reaction times across the cell were slow. How was the gene doing to broaden its chances of survival?

The answer was to come about 1.8 billion years or so ago - and it was to change everything.

What happened? Well, the metaphor of $1+1=3$ has been used a few times already in this book to describe the way that cooperation acts as the mechanism life uses to find ways around evolutionary cul-de-sacs. From atoms, to molecules, to compounds, and eventually on to cyanobacteria, things that seemed stuck in their development had repeatedly found extraordinary new ways of solving problems by joining up and creating benefits for each other.

Now, almost laughably, the metaphor became literally, as well as figuratively true. That was because it was at this point that *two separate prokaryotes joined up to make a third*. And by getting together they became an entirely new kind of organism.

Although there doesn't seem to be a definitive answer to the question of why this came about (was it aggression, cannibalism, an accident or simply the drive for cooperation?) at some point one of the many kinds of tough extremophile archaea must have eaten a bacterial cell… but instead of it being ingested, they both survived. *In fact, one ended up living inside the other.*

Scientists not only have no definitive idea about how or why this happened, but nor do they know whether it was a single incident, or if it had occurred countless times before the experiment worked. But what they do know is that the biochemistry between the two cells must have somehow gelled - and an entirely new life form was created.

One of the major reasons for the vagueness about all this is because cellular fusing like this has never been seen since in Nature - or in the laboratory. Nonetheless, biologists seem to think that the outcome of the original swallowing manoeuvre was so unlikely that it must have happened billions of times before trial and error made the trick work.

The result of the snaffling, however, was a completely different kind of cell. Whereas prokaryotes were simple mechanisms that had no 'kernel' (or nut), only gel, the new life form was labelled as a 'eukaryote' because one of the two cells now specialised to form the kernel - called a nucleus - while the other became the motor force for the fused entity.

This motor evolved to become a power generating plant for what was now an infinitely more complicated cellular operation. Over time it then evolved further to contain tiny organs called organelles that became collectively known as the cell's mitochondria. So efficient did this engine become that it's reckoned to provide about 90% of the energy needed for a eukaryote cell to function.

This marriage of convenience might have somehow created eukaryotes, but it only went so far. Like all symbioses, the fact that they are phenomenally successful processes never entirely overrides the fact that there'll always be tensions between the parties at the heart of any arrangement. And so, to continue with the marriage metaphor, both families in the eukaryotic wedding also appeared to want to keep their heritage alive. The result of this was a solution in which, astonishingly, both parts of the new cell would keep their individual DNA.

This is a phenomenon that's continued right up to the present day. The nucleus' role is to provide virtually all of the inherited genetic information, while mitochondrial DNA only passes down the female line - and no one seems to be completely certain what it's responsible for. Not much appears to be the best answer, although it's become vital in evolutionary studies, and anthropology, because of its ability to show the relatedness of individuals. But why a father's mitochondrial DNA should get rubbed out from a cell, and not the mother's, remains a subject that's still rich in debate.

Eukaryotic cells may have been an adventure of great mutual risk to the two original prokaryotes, but the merger turned out to have enormous advantages for them both. One now found protection from a hostile environment, while the other had the benefit of harnessing a far more powerful source of energy than it had previously had on its own.

The joint enterprise has led some biologists to describe the nucleus as behaving almost like a brain, in that it runs the cell's operation and 'plans' for the future. Mitochondria, on the other hand, might be said to be in charge of the present, in that it keeps the cell alive by using oxygen to create energy. It also acts like a furnace, extracting energy from glucose and then storing it in something called adenosine triphosphate, which acts as a kind of battery for vital provisions. This energy is then transported around the cell by a molecular structure that's constantly being formed and broken down again in a series of biological reactions.

> **'A eukaryotic cell may be thought of as an empire directed by a republic of sovereign chromosomes in the nucleus. The chromosomes preside over the outlying cytoplasm in which formerly independent and degenerate prokaryotes carry out a variety of specialised service functions.'**
> **Gunther Stent, *Molecular Biology of Bacterial Viruses***

Not surprisingly, many people feel that the sudden jump to eukaryotic cells rather blows a hole in Darwin's belief that evolution is a gradual process in which tiny changes eventually add up to major differences. In this sense, eukaryotes appear to represent a developmental lurch, even though their components had previously been so firmly established as prokaryotic life.

Yet as the American evolutionary theorist, Lynn Margulis, was to describe the incredible length of the process: 'To go from a bacterium to people is less of a step than to go from a mixture of amino acids to a bacterium.'

Alongside this development, though, prokaryotes continued with their independent lives as bacteria and archaea, much as they do today. But the eukaryotic cell they'd created was an infinitely more complex form of life, and it now embarked on exploiting the benefits to be had from dividing up tasks and needs. This was because one of the two conjoined cells was no longer having to devote so much of its DNA to generating energy, and instead this left it free to code protein nano machinery.

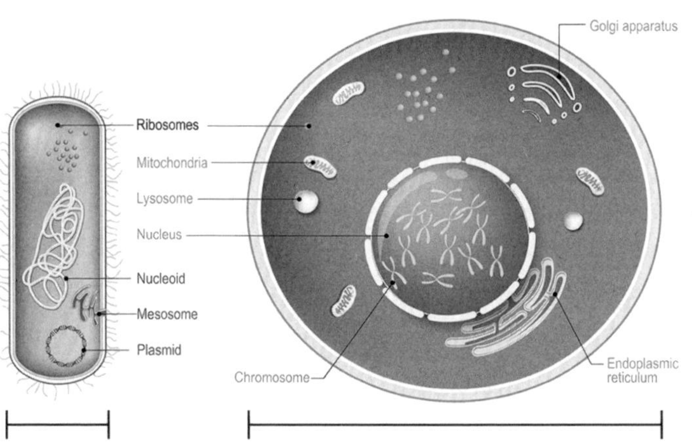

How a bacterium compares with a eukaryote cell.

The other part, the mitochondria, kept the home fires burning. And the resulting symbiosis meant that cells were now able to become far more substantial - up to twenty times bigger - as well as far heavier than prokaryotes were on their own. The result was greater complexity - and vastly more genes.

In his book *What A Wonderful World*, Marcus Chown describes eukaryotes as 'cities in bags' with the nucleus behaving like the government office and the cell's internal substance, or cytoplasm, being like the atmosphere. The mitochondria provides a huge range of services, he says, that have developed astonishingly specialised functions over time - some acting like energy power stations, some like factories for chemicals,

                                   The Secrets of Life - Book One

some like post offices for sending messages around the cell, some handling waste disposal, some guarding what comes in and goes out through the cell's membranes, and some packaging up proteins in different coats depending on what they're going to be delegated to do next.

In short, one of these cells is less like a simple prokaryote, and more like a colony of carefully arranged specialist functions… in fact, rather like our own bodies.

Their new scale and complexity meant that the internal parts now needed protecting, and eukaryotic cells could no longer just be soft little containers like bacteria. They solved this - again like their descendants - by having a kind of skeleton.

But instead of using bones for this, the tiny things employ a network of microtubule scaffolding poles called a cytoskeleton, something that not only gives it a firm structure, but which also allows the mitochondria's organelles to attach themselves in different places, rather as our organs are arranged in specific places in our bodies.

These tubes have the additional function of creating a transportation network that gets proteins around the cell to where they're needed. This is all beginning to look like a rough sketch of the way that advanced organisms would develop their own structures… hardly surprising as everything you can see around you - plants, fungi and animals - are *all* descendants of the first eukaryotic cell.

In other words, it was like a later stage Luca, a more recent common ancestor from which all complex life forms evolved. And with the eukaryote's emergence, an entirely new 'domain' had been introduced to sit alongside bacteria and archaea as one of the three basic divisions that describe all living things.

For a long time these new kinds of cells seemed to show little ambition to push ahead. Instead, they simply aped their prokaryote forebears. This led the period from about 1.8 billion to around 0.8 billion years ago to be labelled 'The Boring Billion' by biologists, because it seems to have been fairly stable in climatic and environmental terms, and without much evolutionary progress.

During this time, however, eukaryotes settled down to create different types of single-celled creatures called protists, and so created a new 'kingdom of primitive forms'. Some of these would later become the protozoa, or 'primitive animals' that remain with us today, both as free-living and parasitic creatures. Historically, these protozoa were regarded as 'one-celled animals', because they often had animal-like behaviour, yet they didn't have a cell wall as plants or algae do.

Protists still coexist with us, just as bacteria do, and they come in a range of sizes from things like amoebas, which are capable of changing their shape and having various ways of getting around, to parasitic spore-forms, and on to paramecium which have a fixed body and a more complex structure. But instead of sharing their lives with us like bacteria, they decided to make their homes instead in a variety of moist habitats such as fresh water, marine environments, and damp soil. Sometimes they even group together to form fungus-like slime moulds.

As they developed over time, eukaryotes now gave the appearance of learning from the past. They, too, repeated the cyanobacteria trick and began to join up with others to form gigantic blooms that lay on water. Again, as with prokaryotes, the group benefits followed.

These ancient, multicellular organisms are called algae and, of course, they're now everywhere, still displaying their ability to generate energy photosynthetically from the Sun. However, they also pushed on and gradually evolved to form cooperative arrangements with other living things. Perhaps the best-known example of this was when they symbiotically joined with fungi to create lichens.

Just as the fictional fund manager would have monitored his investments, so the gene must have learnt from the benefits of these joint ventures. The evolutionary process has always been driven by the gene's 'selfish' compulsion to find the most secure way of living - and merging individual organisms was clearly a fantastic method of increasing life's survival chances, and of widening the diversity of organisms that could carry yet more genes around.

Colonies of symbiotic eukaryotes now began to join up to create a range of organisms. While there were enormous benefits to be had from this, the early results, whether creatures or plant life, were still collections of individual cells that were all doing much the same kind of job. They hadn't yet specialised their functions in other words, and therefore hadn't crossed the crucial next step on the evolutionary ladder towards the multicellularity of more advanced organisms. Only when they did this were they to carry out the highly specific tasks and functions that make up bodies such as our own.

'At the level of their biochemistry, the barrier between bacteria and complex cells barely exists.'
Nick Lane, *The Vital Question: Energy, Evolution, and the Origins of Complex Life*

Like somatic cells, though, these eukaryotic cells reproduced asexually in largely the same way as prokaryotes, splitting themselves into two through mitosis. Great though this method was, it wasn't taking life much further forward because the process only produced exact copies of itself.

The result was that even after hundreds of millions of years of refinement, eukaryotes remained in a kind of evolutionary dead end. In short, all life forms were still faced with the same challenges: first, how to diversify and so reduce the risk of extinction from sudden environmental crises; and secondly, how to get away from the infernal parasites that were constantly trying to live off them, taking their energy as they did so.

Something had to happen if there was to be real change. Something had to accelerate the evolution of diversity.

What could that be?

'Could you just run through that stuff
about slot A and tab B again, please?'

THE JOURNEY CONTINUES. AFTER 90% OF THE EARTH'S STORY, EVOLUTION AND NEW LIFE FORMS BECAME SUPERCHARGED. . . BY THE MARVEL OF SEX. BUT WHY AND HOW DID THAT HAPPEN?

It's probably a cliché to open a chapter on sex with the first lines of Philip Larkin's famous poem, *Annus Mirabilis*. But, why not?

> Sexual intercourse began
> In nineteen sixty three
> (which was rather late for me.)

1963? Perhaps that's not quite right. But, if the joke's wide of the mark, then a later couplet is improbably exact about how early life forms had been created, and then managed to reproduce themselves. Larkin laughs at his own experiences, but in a way that eerily sums up life's long history:

> Up to then there'd only been
> A sort of bargaining.

How odd this is - because a 'sort of bargaining' had been the basis of virtually all the cooperative gains and change that had taken place since the very origins of the planet.

And as for sex, until about 1.2 billion years ago the glacial pace of evolution was constrained because there was still only the 'binary fission' mitosis process available for single-celled things like prokaryotes and eukaryotes to make new versions of themselves.

The great disadvantage of this was that the genetic codes that were already present in the parent would always be locked in. It therefore limited what the next generation could inherit, and meant that the chances of mutations occurring, or real change ever happening, were extremely rare.

But around this time eukaryotes began to take a page out of the bacterial playbook… and they, too, started exchanging DNA between themselves. What brought this on? It was probably for the same reasons that bacteria had defence mechanisms to respond to environmental stresses, or threats such as attacks or overcrowding. Now the same pressures were leading eukaryotes to start rolling the genetic dice as a way of finding beneficial mutations.

So, was sex therefore invented by stress? Theoretically yes. Ha, no doubt Larkin would have liked that.

Quite what the first tentative steps to escape the restrictions of cloning might have been are open to argument. Some scientists think that eukaryotic cells might have copied one of bacteria's favourite tricks of growing an appendage, a pilus, out of its membrane and using this to grab hold of another cell and then to run its DNA out along it. Undoubtedly this has a pleasing similarity to what was to come later.

Many other biologists think this was probably unlikely, given that eukaryotes have very different kinds of membranes to prokaryotes. Instead, most now speculate that the earliest sex experiments would have used viral parasites as messengers for horizontal gene transfers. Or maybe they found other ways of swapping nuclear genomes through cell fusing.

It's even possible that they could have repeated the elaborate assault of the eating-your-neighbour game. Instead of completely digesting the victim, or making it a slave, however, the swallower might somehow have just hung onto the other cell's genome.

But whatever methods were developed, the invention of sexual reproduction was a colossal breakthrough because it brought with it a way of letting advanced cells increase their genetic spread… and suddenly species *diversity* was possible. This was unquestionably a huge step for the gene.

Was having two lots of parent's genes instead of just one bound to be a good idea?

Well, yes, in theory. But there were some big downsides too, because life would now be giving up some of the major benefits that came with the previous methods.

Not least of these was that asexual reproduction was a far faster and more efficient process than having to get two separate partners to find each other, and for them to then need some kind of inducement to mate.

This meant that if the new ways were ever going to be successful, there would have to be some fitness benefits.

As ever, the forces of Nature appeared ambivalent. Life is the ultimate hoarder, always hanging on to what's gone before, even when it sees practical innovations opening up new opportunities. Evolution may be all about the future but the process still hates giving up things that have worked in the past.

Like an elderly man with a garage full of cars he could have traded but never did, the natural world loathes making unnecessary decisions. Instead, it prefers to update and tinker with the old models rather than getting rid of them altogether. You never know, it seems to be saying, they might be useful later. And this frequently turns out to be true as advanced organisms become extinct - and then the basic ones pick up the threads and start evolutionary branching all over again.

In just the same way, the new-fangled sexual reproduction approach was plainly better on some levels than the old, asexual methods. But the two techniques each had their good and bad points, and this made the gene incline towards keeping both ways going.

This remains the case today, even though some eukaryotes such as amoebas continue to employ a hedging strategy in that they're able to swap backwards and forwards between sexual and asexual methods, depending on what the environmental conditions demand.

Sometimes they'll pass on the entirety of their genome by splitting their DNA into two copies through mitosis, in which case they're known as diploid. And at other times they'll use the sexual combination process and end up with only 50% of their genes in the next generation - at which point they're referred to as haploid.

Nonetheless, by the end of the Boring Billion period, about 800 million years ago (and 400 million years or so after cells first started the early experiments with sexual reproduction), the genetic diversity advantages of the new methods were taking life in previously unknown directions.

Why, what was happening?

Well, it was turning out that sexual reproduction was an infinitely more complicated process than simple cell splitting. The major reason for this was because it led to something called recombination in which DNA strands were aligned so that those from the female and the male lines could cross over when they met. But this wasn't a predictable process. Instead, there was a lot of chance involved because a chunk from one parent might pass over to a chunk of the other. And this chunk could also come from different parts of the chromosome.

The result of all this was that completely new nucleotide sequences could now be created that meant offspring would inherit some physical or personality traits - but not others. Or more of some and less of others. But it also meant that, although its DNA might have come from only two parents, the end result was *unique*, in that the progeny would always have new characteristics.

Now this recombination business may have introduced variation but the outcomes were still inherent to the organism. In other words, what the offspring inherited still depended on what was in the parents' genes. However, there was another way in which sex now began to really turbo charge change, and this was because the complications that arose from combining the DNA of two parents in the sex process could lead to vastly *more mistakes*. The opportunities for coding errors ramped up as the fusing process took place - and this led to genes being damaged or somehow altered.

Was this such a bad thing though? Not at all, it turned out, because when these errors were being made, the actual genetic message itself was being modified.

This was how mutations came about. They're random inaccuracies. They're the kind of cock-ups that are bound to happen when highly intricate processes are being carried out at lightning speed. And, just like the tennis fraud, while the results arose by accident… they could be exactly what was needed to solve a problem. If the mutation turned out to be beneficial, then it might introduce precisely the right adaptation for the organism to meet whatever new challenge had suddenly arisen.

Alternatively it could be detrimental, and this would lead to a change that damaged the organism's future. These are what biologists call deleterious mutations… in which case, tough luck.

Or they could lead nowhere, of course, and there would just be a neutral outcome.

'The proof of evolution lies in those adaptations

that arise from improbable foundations.'

The Secrets of Life - Book One

How do these mutations occur? I think I mentioned some time ago that when DNA is unzipping itself to make two copies, there's another chemical process taking place alongside this that's trying to repair any damage to the DNA that could lead to coding errors. The enzyme that's doing this is seeing whether the two complementary strands of DNA on a chromosome are the same, rather like someone at the end of a manufacturing line checking for imperfect products.

If they don't match, the process doesn't care which one is error free and which one isn't - it simply zaps them both. Once they've been blown away, however, there's then a gap, and this is filled by repeating the gene sequence at the same region on the matched chromosome. This all sounds rather technical, but what it amounts to is that bits of DNA are randomly getting crossed over as new cells are being formed.

These mutations really come about because the repair service isn't totally efficient. Why hasn't Nature fixed this though? It's because the outcomes of the system are exactly what the gene would want to happen. In fact, you could almost imagine that this was all part of the gene having a cunning plan, because it meant changes were now random… with the result that these errors would produce novel things in the genetic code.

Even this was only the beginning. Mutations can then begin to pile up on top of other mutations. And any changes that come about can either be helpful or not. If they are - and the altered organism somehow survives because it luckily now turns out to have the right traits to meet new circumstances - then it's in pole position to win. This is how natural selection works. It's how genomes became 'fitter'. If the mutation matched the need, then there were advantageous traits for the future of the organism, and therefore for its genes. If not, then it's Goodnight Vienna.

How can mixing the DNA of two cells potentially make it work better for the next generation? It's because only half of the two cells' genes are passed on in sexual reproduction. Mutants therefore have the opportunity to spread at random. And, if that mutant produces an advantage, then it will increase in prevalence - and the organism and the species will look as if they have made an *evolutionary 'decision'*.

To sum it all up… sexual reproduction leads to variety because errors in the process produce mutations, mutations lead to novelty, novelty leads to diversity, and the new characteristics might be just what's needed to cope with random change. The genius that is the gene wins again. What had originally begun as a survival strategy in single-celled creatures now became the mechanism for accelerated genetic variation - and in doing so the gene had hugely increased the speed of evolution.

No doubt with a little titter, biologists refer to what happened from the point at which sexual reproduction really took off - roughly 800 million to 540 million years ago - as the Big Bang of Sex. A process that had started out with prokaryote cells merging to create a new kind of life form had evolved, over hundreds of millions of years, to eventually produce specialised sex cells. And from there, it progressed to create the different sexes, to eggs and sperm and even, as a consequence of the process, to hermaphrodite versions.

Once the process was refined, marine organisms led the way when they began to spawn vast clouds of reproductive material into the surrounding water in the expectation that some of them would join up and fuse - be fertilised in other words. Many species still use this method.

But the emergence of land animals that came around this time also led to some of the new life forms evolving internal fertilisation methods and this developed the lock and key mechanism so loved by schoolboys. What exactly is it? As the American romance writer, Kresley Cole says in *Dreams of a Dark Warrior*: ‘I can draw you a diagram. Hint: I’m slot B and you’re tab A.’ Incidentally, this matching up process is what defines a species - the slot and the tab only work together if both parties are members of the same species.

Now, was sex a good move for life to adopt? Some people might have thought not. The famously elegant Jackie Onassis would have wrinkled her nose when she said it ‘rumpled the clothes’. But Woody Allen was unequivocally in favour: ‘I don’t know the question, but sex is the answer’.

Was it a good idea biologically? In many ways it wasn’t. For an individual, it could look questionable because sexual reproduction meant that only 50% of one’s genes now went to the next generation instead of 100%. An organism that had arguably been *immortal* while it was passing on all its genes - just making copies of itself - was now embarking on a process that guaranteed its death as a genetic entity.

Asexual reproduction had also been a far faster and more energy efficient way of making new generations. There'd been more assurance it would work as a biological process, and more offspring could be expected as a result.

Now that sex had come along, the only certainty was that less genes would be passed on. There was also the need to find and select a mate to share the process with. This all meant a lot of precious time and energy were being used up on making this come about.

Losing half one's genes, and having to search for a partner, added up to what the great evolutionary biologist John Maynard Smith was to call the 'twofold cost of sex'. Throwing a whole bunch of cards away and getting another lot from someone whose reproductive potential was uncertain made the whole business of breeding go from a one-way bet to a rather unattractive long shot. Maybe the new partner was a dud? Maybe the introduction of their genes would have a bad effect on the next generation, rather than being beneficial?

'The evolution of sex is the hardest problem in evolutionary biology.'
John Maynard Smith, *The Theory of Evolution*

All this unpredictability led to risk. Instead of splitting oneself into two and knowing what the end result would be, an organism was now playing with a new deck of cards every time it reproduced - and possibly not getting the trumps that it wanted.

The fact that one was no longer wholly responsible for how offspring turned out now made finding the right mate a matter of critical importance. What was the gene going to do about it? A lot was the answer, and it now began working at the deepest of levels to extend its influence into organisms' phenotypes, improving them wherever possible and, by doing this, highlighting the importance of getting the mating choice right. This was because the reproductive process was not only playing a genetic role in the decision-making mechanism, but the mate was as well.

To meet the overriding need to make a good choice, highly complex displays and routines started to emerge so that organisms could show each other what great breeding stock they were.

With females this meant that evolutionary pressure began to come down on them to tell potential mates that they had the body shape and other qualities to suggest how healthy their offspring would be. By implication, this was also showing that she'd ensure the progeny grew to adulthood - and so, in turn, that they'd be good reproductive material themselves.

For their part, males began to evolve ever more elaborate signals to point to the kind of qualities their descendents were likely to inherit. To take two famous examples of this, the lion's mane and the peacock's tail are often seen as cumbersome impediments to individuals, but they and others like them were designed to shout out to prospective females how powerful the individuals must be to cope with the handicaps. They're saying 'hey, look at me' in other words, 'see how strong I am.'

But if these are some of the disadvantages of sexual reproduction for the individual vehicle, what were the advantages for the gene?

Well, if its 'job' was to reduce the survival threat to life by equipping organisms to stay alive (and, by extension, to make safer vehicles for itself), then sexual reproduction had to be a fantastic new strategy. For the best part of three billion years, life on earth had only produced prokaryotes and eukaryotes, and any number of parasitic microorganisms that were all trying to live off them.

So far they'd only come up with ways of copying themselves as a means of survival. It was true that horizontal gene transfers meant they had fast ways of adapting to immediate threats, but life was still on a precarious foundation if a major environmental crisis blew up.

Sexual reproduction now began to introduce organisms at a markedly faster rate than evolution had ever managed before. Novelty boomed, and just as the mythical fund manager had concluded, the greater the diversity and the greater the complexity - the less the risk. This all added up to the biosphere becoming increasingly complex, because the more that different things were emerging, the more there'd be challenges from new kinds of competition.

These pressures meant that organisms were being incentivised to get themselves into increasingly defined ecological niches, and towards finding ever more robust defence strategies.

'Benefits to groups can arise as statistical summations of the effects of individual adaptations... As a very general rule, with some important exceptions, the fitness of a group will be high as a result of this sort of summation of the adaptations of its members.'
George Williams, *Adaptation and Natural Selection*

From the Darwinian view of natural selection, though, the resulting 'hybrid vigour' as he called it was more than enough reason to see sex as a critical catalyst for life on earth. The mathematician John von Neumann, writing a century after him, reached the same conclusion when he summed up the underlying advantage of sexual reproduction as: '... organisms having the ability to produce something more complicated than themselves.'

The second great advantage was that if cells were now exchanging genes and creating new types of organisms, then this had to be a fantastic new way of beating off the constant attacks of parasites. These pests had been trying to grab hold of other organisms' energy almost from the first sparks of life, and the endless warfare this involved meant that potential hosts were in a constant, energy-sapping battle to avoid life-threatening invasions.

Now there was a new way for things to escape them - by mutating their way out of trouble. This led the American evolutionary biologist Leigh van Valen to describe the advantage as the 'Red Queen strategy', after the character in *Through the Looking Glass* who tells Alice she has to keep running just to stay in the same place.

Van Valen's view of life was that it was a never-ending arms race between co-evolutionary species: hosts and parasites. Now evolution had come up with a novel way of getting away from the threats… by breaking into a sprint through using sex to accelerate genetic diversity, and so to keep coming up with fresh ways of outwitting the bad guys. For the more advanced life forms that were now emerging, this ability was rather like the way bacteria escape viral parasites through swapping their genes. In using sexual reproduction, multicellular organisms found they could achieve the same result.

> **'Reproduction is not synonymous with sex; there are many asexual ways to reproduce. But reproducing sexually must improve an individual's reproductive success or else sex would not persist.'**
> **Matt Ridley, *The Red Queen***

The evolutionary process now really began to crack on with building the skyscrapers of life. New variants started to dig more and more trenches and foundations. Among the most significant of these was the major surge forward that took place when eukaryote mutations led to them branching away from the mother cells, and joining themselves together to create the early multicellular life forms of sponges. This was a similar strategy to the way bacteria had agglomerated themselves into cyanobacteria.

As I said earlier, however, Nature hates giving up on old ways of working, and there are still examples around of how organisms can increase their presence, yet without making any changes to their underlying elements. Things like slime moulds and fungi, for instance, might grow in scale, but they still only consist of a collection of similar cells, all of which are largely doing the same thing.

Now evolution began to create far more complicated structures in which cells started to carry out quite *separate and different functions*. Biologists studying the earliest fossils reckon this started around 700 million years ago.

These fossil records suggest that the specialisation trick probably created embryonic nerves and muscles as the first things to emerge. Creatures then continued to refine their functions and actions for the next hundred million years or so. As a result, very basic and yet structurally differentiated organisms like flat worms began to emerge, and genes began to get the hang of the benefits that could come from different cells working together as a team.

Why was this happening?

It was because life was discovering more sophisticated ways of getting things to divide up their labour… so that they could be more *efficient*. If it did this, there would then be energy savings that could be used to carry out other jobs.

The next alterations to appear were the early signs of vertebrae, followed by nerve systems that joined up and created embryonic command centres that behaved like protobrains. Yet these steps still needed catalysing if they were to get to the complicated processes we have today… and life found that the great stimulus for this would ironically come with what appeared to be catastrophic interventions - environmental disasters that would clear out vast numbers of living things. When these happened, the old ways were swept off the table, but this was exactly what allowed new kinds of organisms to bloom in the changed conditions.

Of course, these calamities seem counterintuitive to our current way of seeing things, in which we view environmental change and species loss as appalling events. We do everything we can to prevent them, yet the history of life on earth shows that these are precisely what lights the blue touch papers of evolutionary change.

London's Natural History Museum, for example, estimates that something like ten to twenty billion species could have evolved and then disappeared in the last 545 million years, largely as the result of violent fluctuations to the climate. These colossal numbers rather put into context the anxieties biologists have today about endangered species, but this is understandable because we're concerned with a different time frame.

Nonetheless, how was it that so many came and went - and why did they have to go?

First, the more that species emerged, the more those already in existence would have had to refine their strategies to meet the competition for ecological niches. Many would have simply been squeezed out of existence.

Secondly, the planet (admittedly viewed from a distance of hundreds of millions of years later) was in a state of frequent, revolutionary mayhem. Climate change could be dramatic, with temperatures going up and down in a way we've never had to experience. Sometimes the land would be tropical hot, and sometimes it became so cold that it was covered in thick ice sheets that killed everything beneath them.

Landmasses themselves were always on the move. Continents were colliding and new environments brought with them the competition of other biosystems. Volcanoes erupted, sea levels rose and fell, salinity and acidity went through wild variations, oxygen levels fluctuated, asteroids impacted… and many of these natural disasters led to mass extinction events that periodically shook the genetic dice.

Things were changing in evolutionary terms, too, and new life forms would find alliances that continuously repeated the symbiotic gains of the 1+1=3 model. Plants that grew on land, for example, appeared about 450 million years ago as a result of tiny algae that swallowed a cyanobacteria, an arrangement that would eventually lead to the cyanobacteria getting a refuge, and the host being passed sugar through its bacterial parasite.

Predatory as this no doubt sounds, it is almost certainly how the arrangement between plants and photosynthetic chloroplasts would have first originated. We tend to view land plants as a basic component of our biosphere and food chains, and yet, incredibly, it turns out that they only began to emerge after 90% of the Earth's history.

'Life itself turned our planet blue and green, as tiny photosynthetic

bacteria cleansed the oceans of air and sea and filled them with oxygen.

Powered by this new and potent source of energy, life erupted.

Flowers bloom and beckon, intricate corals hide darting goldfish,

vast monsters lurk in black depths, trees reach for the sky, animals buzz and

lumber and see. And in the midst of it all, we are moved by the untold

mysteries of this creation, we cosmic assemblies of molecules that feel and

But as evolutionary events picked up speed, and ever increasing diversity and variety blossomed with sexual reproduction… what came where?

The first things, as I said, were organisms in which lots of similar eukaryotes got together to form multicellular enterprises. The earliest of these were sponge-like organisms that remained largely unchallenged until the point at which cells with specialised functions began to evolve.

This breakthrough was when complex life really kicked off, and it was followed by the extraordinary burst of evolutionary change that arose with the Cambrian Explosion. It was this that led to many of the major branches of life becoming established.

What triggered it? There are several theories.

Some biologists think it might have been caused by the development of sight. Seeing things speeded up change. Others point to the sudden emergence around this time of what's known as Runaway Glaciation. This led to thick ice covering most of

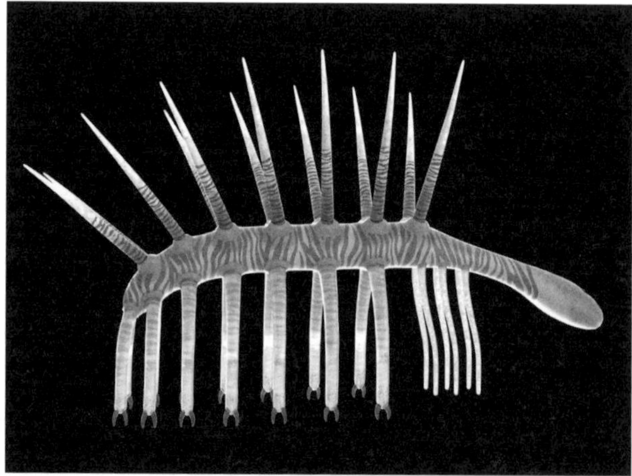

Prehistory can involve a lot of guesswork. *Hallucigenia* lived for 500 million years but paleobiologists spent ages trying to work out which way up it must have been.

the planet and its effect was to create evolutionary bottlenecks. When it eventually melted, scientists believe that speciation came about far more rapidly. And last, there's a school of thought that believes it was the fluctuations in atmospheric oxygen that supercharged multicellular evolution.

Whatever the true factors driving this extraordinary period, animals now began to appear in the fossil record for the first time, even though most of these unique lineages were to later become extinct.

A further thirty million years or so after the Cambrian Explosion started, the emergence of a completely new branch of eukaryotic life called fungi began to take hold. This was a life form that had found ways of not photosynthesising energy for their food, but of living off organic matter externally, and thus making it decompose. This has actually led biologists to regard them, in evolutionary terms, as closer to animals than to plants.

In chronological order there then came a vast number of strange tubular and frond-shaped organisms called biota, and thirty million years after this saw the emergence of the early flatworms with their primitive nervous systems. At roughly the same time, things such as trilobites and the early crustaceans were also appearing. Primitive vertebrates like jawless fish then followed, and after them, marine life forms which seem to have evolved primitive gill systems not once, but many times.

Around 450 million years ago the first of the five great mass extinctions hit, probably in two waves, leading to a colossal advance and then retreat of the ice shelves, making it the only recorded widespread collapse due to global cooling.

Permafrost would have killed off most of the existing organisms and worse was to come when higher temperatures returned. This led the ice to melt and sea levels probably rose by as much as two hundred metres, completely wiping out all the myriad organisms that had so painfully established their habitats on the shoreline.

With one exception, mass extinctions then came about at roughly two hundred million year intervals - all of them with the same effect of extinguishing vast proportions of the species that were alive at the time. But one might ask why these appalling calamities had such a catalytic impact on evolution and on the rate of speciation? And why did life proliferate so much after them?

The underlying answer to both these questions is because each extinction event seems to throw the previous rulebook out of the window. As the American palaeontologist John Alroy puts it: 'Mass extinction fundamentally changes the dynamics. It changes the composition of the biosphere forever.' It's at times like this that natural selection becomes most evident.

Organisms that might have experienced deleterious mutations suddenly found themselves with exactly the right biology for the new environment. What would have been wrong could turn out to be bang on - because the revised organism had exactly the right quirks to fit in with the changed conditions. In this way, the gene won again and again - because sexual reproduction had created multiple levels of diversity, and this had thrown up any number of safety nets to ensure that life was preserved. New conditions simply meant new opportunities.

'It takes just one big natural disaster to wipe (everything) away and remind us that, here on Earth, we're still at the mercy of Nature.'
Neil deGrasse Tyson, *Universe Down to Earth*

And so our world was built. Back around 1.8 billion years ago the three basic 'Domains' of life - archaea, bacteria and eukarya - had been established. Then, although opinions vary somewhat, it was probably by around 450 million years ago that the six Kingdoms were in place: plants, animals, fungi and the three subdivisions of microorganisms.

From then on, the pace of change picked up. Evolutionary decisions piled up on other decisions. Mutations meant life leapt forward. Yes, innovative species would frequently work, but the gene persisted with its tried and trusted methods of keeping the old systems in place. Single-celled microorganisms, as ever, continued to sit alongside novelty. Behavioural strategies became more and more refined as organisms evolved to extract the greatest possible energy from each other, and to package this up in countless different ways. Very little ever disappeared completely.

'Once multicellular organisms were on the scene, the pace picked up. The subsequent fan-out of plants and animals - from ferns and flowers to insects, reptiles, birds and mammals - has populated the world today with millions of different species. In the process, millions of other species have come and gone.'
Daniel Dennett, *Darwin's Dangerous Idea*

It's probably tedious to list out what came where. Nevertheless it's fair to say that wildly changing conditions saw life come out of the oceans, go back into them, adapt to survive enormous changes and mass extinctions, compete by fighting each other, or sometimes winning by creating innovative symbiotic arrangements.

Colossal numbers of species came and went, whole groups of things like the dinosaurs arose and died out, birds evolved any number of times, mammals then arrived and organisms adapted and adapted, becoming ever more complex, yet never once during all this time did the gene rest from doing its job of keeping life swimming against the destructive tide of the 2nd Law.

And then, one day, a ghost ancestor of ours, about whom nothing is known, must have originated a new branch of life before it, too, died out. This line split again, one branch leading down to the chimpanzees and the other to a rather weedy, forest-dwelling biped. And it's from this second branch, a couple of hundred thousand years ago - *after 99.995% of the time that there's been life on earth - there came us, Homo sapiens.*

Put in this context, we've hardly arrived. And yet, and yet… we're the first things that were ever to speak and develop imagination, the first organisms to weigh up decisions and to consider what was best for itself, and to have consciousness and emotions, self-examination and culture.

**'We, like all the animals and plants that have ever
lived, are recent crashers at the party of life on Earth.'**
Neil Shubin, *The Universe Within*

We were also the first to decide on how we should behave, and how to adapt to cope with wide ranges of environments and conditions. And we put all these attributes together in just a blink of an eye, the great majority of them in the last 10,000 years or so. Yet we're now the top wallies, the alpha species, the ones who like to think they control everything.

But how did we do it? What had we arrived at in such a short time that nothing else in 3.8 billion years of change had ever come near to?

And what did all this 3.8 billion add up to anyway? What did it all tell us about ourselves - if anything?

You think it was tough for Sisyphus? Evolution's even worse.

CHAPTER TEN

PHEW. THAT'S QUITE A LOT TO TAKE IN... PERHAPS IT'S TIME FOR A BIT OF A CATCH UP? MAYBE EVEN TO SUGGEST WHAT ALL THIS HISTORY ADDS UP TO?

Can billions of years of evolutionary change really be summarised in the handful of pages that it's taken to get this far - and read in roughly the time it takes to produce half a dozen bacterial mutations?

Maybe. But even so, is it really possible to see a discernible direction of travel in it all? Are there any bedrock certainties to have emerged as one looks at the Earth's journey from inhospitable dust to the sophisticated and largely ordered state we have now?

It seems preposterous when it's put like that, yet many evolutionary theorists say they can, indeed, see an arc of development from when life first appeared to the present day - a time, ironically, when so many also claim that humans are doing their level best to destroy it.

There used to be a joke around that if you had a million monkeys pounding a million typewriters over a million years you'd end up with the works of Shakespeare. Social media has rather disproved this for literature, but are we really to believe that complex life arose from random mutations, and that Nature has pulled off the monkey/Shakespeare outcome with biochemistry?

Or is there more of a discernable shape to life's history?

Perhaps the most unremarkable of observations is to say that from the very moment of life's creation onwards, every single living thing has been focused on nothing other than its self-preservation. This simple truth points us towards seeing an organism's only underlying purpose as the need to live long enough to reproduce.

Once this is done, its next task is to ensure that the offspring also survive… against odds that were, and are, appalling. But the very fact that life keeps going is surely proof that the strategies and decisions that living things arrived at have been successful.

From the first second that Luca - our Last Universal Common Ancestor - wriggled its mythical toes like a molecular version of Frankenstein's monster, the real business of it, and its descendants, has been to contend with the existential threats of an unremittingly hostile world. The sole aim of every life form is that it should get its genes out into the world's gene pool and, vitally, to produce more of them than any of their competition.

This drive to be the 'fittest' may sound straightforward enough, yet the entire history of life's struggle for existence shows just how accurate Homer Simpson's pained retort was that 'trying is just the first step towards failure.'

Even the most successful branches of the taxonomic tree have shown they can be torn off in the wildness of changing environmental conditions. This can sometimes happen so quickly that even the best adapted can disappear in a blink. The Sun might be our principal source of energy, for instance, but volcanic eruptions can blot it out in hours.

The gases that make up our atmosphere might be central to an organism's function, but they too can change too quickly for most organisms to adapt. And, of course, the surface of the planet might sometimes be water, but then it can become dry land, or revert once new life had become settled.

These weren't the only threats. Quite suddenly, for example, another species might have liked the look of whatever it was that an organism had come to depend on.

'We now know that all extant living creatures derive from a single common ancestor called Luca. It's hard to think of a more unifying view of life. All living things are linked to a single-celled creature, the deepest root to the complex-branching tree of life. If we could play the movie backwards we would find that this microscopic primogenesis is at the starting point of biological evolution, the sole actor in what would be a very dramatic story, lasting some 3.5 billion years leading to us.
Alex Vikoulov, *Noogenesis: Computational Biology*

Life has never stood on firm ground. Calamities have always been lurking, and mass extinctions can repeatedly sweep millions of years of slow evolution away in a kind of Sisyphean tragedy.

However hard things have tried, however deep the foundations of life appear to have been dug, the habitats that living things rely on are ultimately rickety. In a world of unpredictable events, of interruptions to energy sources, and the constant menace of things trying to suck the life out of one another, there is only so much that the organism can do to protect itself.

Sexual reproduction, however, was undoubtedly one of the major steps forward to improving security. Evolution was then able to introduce variety and diversity to the biosphere - and to create increased numbers of safety nets, even if individual life expectations might have been no more certain.

'Evolution is Nature's creative way of pushing living organisms to higher degrees of complexity.'
Alvin Conway, *Sapienta*

The reason for this was that the more life forms abounded, the more there were of them to become competitive threats. Not the least of these problems arose when an organism was viewed as a food source, a parasite's host. If these issues were not challenging enough, all life also had to contend with the iron laws of existence: of natural forces like gravity, the critical need to take energy from the Sun, the exchange of atmospheric gases, and behind everything else, the immutable and unchanging Laws of Thermodynamics.

'Extinction is the rule. Survival is the exception.'
Carl Sagan, *Cosmos*

Grab whatever energy you can, says the 1st Law. Everything is falling apart, says the 2nd. And together they insist that nothing can survive forever. Yet a combination of the genius of self-replicating molecules, together with the ruthless strategies of the gene, refuse to accept that these laws cannot be circumvented.

Yes, it's true that virtually everything that's ever lived has gone extinct - yet life itself goes on, in different forms and in different ways, but on it goes. The gene is only focused on ensuring that *something survives*. It 'cares' nothing for the fate of individual vehicles; only for the continuation of life itself. That's its job.

This has become known as the Selfish Gene Theory, yet to term its compulsion as 'selfish' seems ironic, because the gene's *effects* can only be described as profoundly

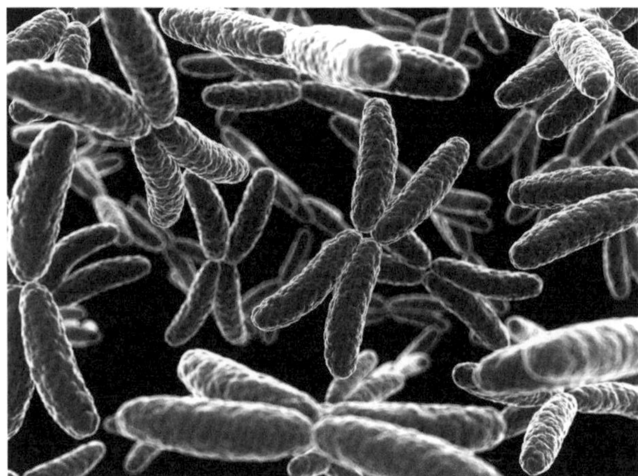

Really, how selfish can you get?

unselfish. Logically, if its processes ensure that something survives, then the evolution of the gene's actions have led to life's success. Establishing the strategy of creating multiple, diverse life forms to spread the risk of being wiped out has worked - and every single thing that's alive is a witness and beneficiary of the gene's single-minded approach. The end result of all this is… more security.

Change suits the gene. Tomorrow is always a better day.

**'Gene-centric sociobiology looks at survival and reproduction
from the point of view of the gene, not the individual.'
Frans de Waal. *Good Natured. The Origins of Right and
Wrong in Humans and Animals***

But while adaptations and complexity, variety and diversity might be advantageous, it never gives up on the old ways either. Thank goodness for that, we might conclude, because there must have been many times in the history of the world when environmental lurches and mass extinctions carried away sexy innovations, and yet it was the boring, primitive organisms that somehow kept life going.

And it was from these basic things that entirely new evolutionary branches could kick off again.

In this sense, while sexual reproduction can be seen as the major breakthrough in the gene's risk reduction strategy, it was the asexual, cell splitting mechanism of mitosis that's actually kept the show on the road. Passing on 100% of one's genes is arguably a limiting and cautious strategy, but it remains the nearest thing to catastrophe insurance that life has ever produced.

Add this all up and one can only agree with the original proposition of this book that anything one can see in life must indeed have made the right survival decisions. From prokaryotes to eukaryotes, to multicellular agglomerations, and from there on to specialised cells, the mechanics of decision-making through reproduction can now be seen as the vital factors in keeping life going.

This is why Darwin was proved to be more right than he could ever have imagined once the action of DNA had become understood. He could never have known it, but we can now see how gene expression, protein synthesis and individual traits work hand in hand with the environment to produce the phenotypes that interact, and so create ecological niches.

But it's also now plain how decision-making has reached out through extensions to the phenotype and, though it's less well understood, through epigenetic action. By doing this, an organism's outward face is always best suited to its surroundings. And over the long march of evolutionary time this approach can now be seen as the major driver for the different behavioural choices that are so evident.

If the cooperation biologists have identified in prokaryotes is anything to go by, survival tactics must have developed very early on in the story of life. Bacteria evolved to live in gigantic colonies, yet they've continued to share their world with an overwhelming number of other species like themselves, and also with colossal varieties of parasitic viruses.

Yet the outcome is as intricate as any human community has ever managed. Yes, they may only be basic organisms, but they display the most remarkably sophisticated strategies to arrive at their balanced existence.

The way they exist is extraordinary. They share genetic material so they can mutate their way out of trouble. They'll sacrifice themselves so that others in their colony can survive. And they're able to come up with ways of neutralising the attacks of threats like parasitic viral bacteriophages.

From the first archaea onwards to ever more complex life forms, these are the tactics that have persisted to maximise the survival chances of living things. Nonetheless, we're still left with the great paradox of life, that in the resulting, seething biosphere in which every single thing is doing its best to win, *nothing ever does so forever.*

How extraordinary this is. What can it mean? How can the underlying forces of environmental roulette, of constant competition, of species' success and failure, and of never-ending evolution, all be working towards the aim of organisms finding what evolutionary biologists call a 'stable state' - a way of living that cannot be bettered by others - and yet nothing ever achieves it?

Does this mean that collapse and entropy result? No, quite evidently it doesn't… the world remains in balance. And so what else are we left to reflect on, must be the conclusion, that it can only be *the continual failure of individuals and species that accounts for the continual success of life as a whole.*

Clearly the behavioural strategies that organisms evolved have been central to this success. Everything may be in competition, the logic of the gene would suggest, in a world where survival depends on being fitter than one's rivals. And yet all the breakthroughs in the development of complexity - from atomic bonding to compounds, to genetic inheritance and through to the most staggering novelties of symbiotic relationships - have almost always relied on things working together to make 1+1=3.

In making this observation, the story of life has shown again and again that the pressure of competition appears to be making demands that something beats another, but this frequently doesn't actually happen.

Why not?

It's because individual sacrifice and collaborative strategies work best for members of the same colony, and it's this group success that benefits the individual members. As politicians like to say, a rising tide lifts all boats.

The way communities organise and work for each other is just one of the examples of how all life forms, from bacteria to rhinos, appear to be playing a role in a highly complex and yet balanced whole. Yet even with the trillions of moving parts there are, all of them are still looking out for themselves.

How does all this work… when there's no central organiser, no controlling force, and no conductor waving his baton at the wild orchestra of competing organisms? Paradoxically there isn't confusion and collapse in all this, but an organising mechanism that leads to *balance and order*. Quite how this happens is what these books are exploring.

But what does order mean anyway? Well, I suppose it provokes an image of organisms living placid and unthreatened lives, all rubbing along contentedly in stable relationships. Instead, we see the opposite to this everywhere around us.

Yes, cooperation must hold things together, because shared fate provides the glue. But if that's the case, and if the gene is so effective and so selfish as to make itself 'immortal', then why doesn't it allow its vehicles to also survive? Why does it let the very things it relies on… die?

And - rather more self-interestedly - why does it let *us* die?

'I wish I'd spent more time looking up trivia on the internet.'

IF THE GENE IS COMPLETELY FOCUSED ON KEEPING LIFE GOING... WHY DOES IT LET THINGS DIE?

Why does the gene appear to stand idly by and let its organisms shuffle off? If its whole job is to keep life going - and it relies on its vehicles to do that - why hasn't it managed to evolve a way of stopping them falling off their perches?

The answer has to be the same one that's been given to pretty well every other question about how the gene works… it's because doing this suits it. Hang on, though, if the chemistry that's called 'the gene' is so breathtakingly brilliant in the way it's developed its strategies - then how has death so clearly evolved to be part of its great plan? Well, for the gene, death is a life strategy. It somehow concluded that getting rid of old organisms once they'd reproduced was a terrific idea… as long as a new bunch of offspring served its purpose better than the ones who had been carrying it around.

To explain this a bit further, maybe the place to start is by asking *how* things die, rather than why. There are two ways: by accident or by design, by outside actions or by internal ones. External causes can occur at any second because of environmental changes; and things get eaten, squashed, infected with diseases or any of the thousands of ways we tut about when facing up to the violence of Nature and the fragile hold we have on life.

The gene has factored all these in, of course, and individual strategies have evolved to mitigate them. Mutational evolution, for example, has resulted in certain species and groups producing more offspring than others as a way of reducing risk and, in general, the gene-based theory of evolution favours younger members of colonies. It does this because the young have a better chance of surviving long enough to reproduce, largely by having life cycles that make them more robust and reactive to danger in their early years.

The second method of death is possibly more interesting however. And it might illustrate why getting rid of its vehicles can suit the gene's purpose.

Essentially, the idea appears to be that our genes 'want' to have periodic clear-outs so it can make newer, shinier, better versions of things, hopefully with more reproductive potential, less old tech and more mutational adaptations that will fit in with changing external conditions. This is how life works: the gene's actions versus the environment, the gene's strategies versus the Laws of Thermodynamics, and the gene maximising the cascade of energy from the Sun through to the creation of order. To do all these things, it needs to keep the roulette wheel of mutations spinning - and that means encouraging reproduction.

Hold on a minute, you're probably thinking... if death is a strategy for life, then why don't single-celled organisms like bacteria die? Well, of course, they do in one sense because individuals come to an end. But in another, they don't because 100% of their genes pass down to the next generation, and short of the occasional minor mutation, the colony stays genetically the same. This, arguably, therefore makes their genes pretty well immortal.

But these simple creatures were, and still are, stuck in a kind of biological dead end. They can never develop on a larger scale; they can't respond to many of the sudden changes in their surroundings. And there's only a limited amount of diversity they can ever produce.

'Life had to invent death to evolve.'
Freeman Dyson, *Origins of Life*

The evolution of eukaryotes was a big step forward in giving the gene more options. They, too, pass on all their genes through mitosis, yet they have the underlying tensions of the symbiotic relationship inside them as a constant threat to their existence. One theory, for example, about the reasons for more advanced organisms dying is that the mitochondrial element of cells has never been wholly satisfied with its marriage to the nucleus, and there are times when it seems to be pressing for a fairly dramatic kind of divorce - by making the things that carry it around die.

When life evolved to multicellularity, the gene could be said to have used the diversity that then arose to experiment with a range of solutions, even toying with the idea of extraordinary longevity. Examples of this show up in the evolution of creatures with very long lives. Among the most remarkable of these might be a species of jellyfish that's capable of reverting to its polyp stage when it becomes old or environmentally stressed, shedding parts of itself and dropping to the ocean floor. Once there, it starts growing a new body. Theoretically this makes it immune to internal causes of death but, even so, while a fresh suit of clothes might be great, it doesn't stop it suffering from external problems like being eaten. Brilliant though this might be, though, it plainly wasn't such a startling success as an evolutionary novelty that it led to other organisms following its lead.

Then there are some bizarre creatures called tardigrades (more merrily known as moss piglets) that can withstand the kind of extreme conditions that would kill anything else. Nothing appears to freak them. Staggering temperatures? Soaring atmospheric pressures? Radiation levels that would kill us all? Drought or lack of food? Pah, they cope with all these and more. They seem almost impossible to kill. However, they've never progressed beyond their tiny size, and however astonishing their biochemistry might be, the decision-making processes that led to them coming on the scene haven't been passed on to other organisms.

There are also amazing species like some of the flatworms who can reproduce themselves from tiny fragments if they're attacked or chopped up. If a minute fraction of their body is still intact, even as small as one part in three hundred, it can regenerate back to the complete organism.

But if weird phenomena like this are so remarkable, then why didn't evolutionary performances like these get handed on to other species? Why can't we grow a new leg if we lose one in an accident, or manage to survive a vast range of environmental threats? Perhaps it was that whatever biological breakthroughs led to these odd examples, they couldn't be replicated on the scale of larger multicellular organisms. Maybe there simply weren't enough evolutionary advantages for their biochemical decisions to kick on into other species? Maybe they were just weird mutational accidents?

More to the point, these kinds of elongated lifecycles simply aren't in the gene's interests. It doesn't want old things hanging around forever, stuck in their evolutionary cul de sacs. The gene wants novelty and diversity to give it more throws of the dice to combat change and extinction. It doesn't want stasis; it wants movement.

And if the advent of internally generated deaths came with the arrival of multicellular life forms, it can only mean that sexual reproduction was the agent of change. Sex leads to death. (What would Philip Larkin have made of that?) Nonetheless, that's the only conclusion one can come to. And it must therefore follow

that once something's reproduced, then its genes have little further need for it. The parent's done its job, and logically the gene is more than happy to see its spent vehicles shoved out of the way so that new generations can refresh the species - and whole new species might also come along.

What does this all mean?

As with the invention of sexual reproduction itself, one can again see the underlying battle between what's good for an individual organism - even though it's doing its best to survive - and what's good for the gene. Getting rid of old stock and having yet more adaptations out in the world is pure genius. As ever, the gene is going to win; the gene is what's keeping life going. The individual is always just a temporary vehicle.

> **'Younger people are, on average, more likely to be alive. So, if your genes**
> **have to choose between investing in the survival and/or reproduction**
> **of young you versus old you, they'll pick young you.'**
> **Suzanne Sadedin, *Biologically Speaking, This Is Why Humans Are Born To Die***

But if genetic death arose with the invention of sex cells that only pass on half a parent genes, then what's happening to the somatic cells, the body cells that keep dividing to make two new ones? If these are supposedly renewing the body's structure, why do things seem to go wrong with age?

Ageing is something that's particularly noticeable in us humans. Instead of being refreshed as we get older, we obviously do the opposite. We deteriorate, our skin loses its elasticity, our muscles harden, the spring in our step disappears and the thousand and one other things that typify the elderly become clear at a glance. No doubt if you were to survey people about what's going on, you'd be told that we're 'wearing out', and that death is the end result of this. But if that's the case, why are our cells bothering to renew themselves?

The answer becomes clearer when one understands why these cells are splitting in the first place. Initially, of course, the obvious reason is that things are born small and have to grow to become adults. They need to get bigger and cell division is the way they do this. However, once they've achieved full size, the process continues because doing so revitalises the body as a defence against parasites, and it's also the body's way of making repairs where they're required. Certain parts of our bodies need greater activity than others to achieve this.

> **'The body concentrates order. It continuously self-repairs.**
> **Every five days you get a new stomach lining. You get a new liver every**
> **two months. Your skin replaces itself every six weeks.**
> **Every year, 98% of the atoms in your body are replaced.**
> **This non-stop chemical replacement, metabolism, is a sure sign of life.'**
> **Lynn Margulis and Dorion Sagan, *What Is Life?***

So far, so good, yet while the process may look like renewal, it's also leading to major problems. This happens because when the body cells are unzipping their DNA to make two identical versions of themselves through mitosis, damage is being done because the repetitive action is continuously shortening their strands. Just like a clothes zip that has one of the little teeth always left on its own at the end of a line, the DNA strands will behave in exactly the same way. They, too, will always have a snippet on one side that will be higher than on the other.

To stop the chromosomes unravelling from this ragged chemical ending, there's a DNA sequence called a telomere that's stuck on the final bit. Biologists often describe this as being like the little plastic caps at the end of shoelaces, and it's the telomere that prevents the chromosome from folding in on itself. This is necessary to prevent it losing genetic information.

What all this means is that when the cell divides, the enzyme that duplicates DNA can't continue all the way up to the tip of the chromosome - and the end bit goes missing. It therefore becomes shorter each time the cell divides. The telomeres get shorter too, and in time the end result is that the cell can no longer keep splitting.

A brilliant American biologist called Leonard Hayflick worked all this out back in the 1960s, and he arrived at the finding that there was a ceiling to the number of times a cell *could* divide. His conclusion (it became known as the Hayflick Limit) was that they could only split between forty and sixty times. This has now established itself as the cornerstone rule for biologists when they say that while longevity is genetically determined (we live longer if our ancestors did), the rate of ageing remains epigenetic (if we bash ourselves about during our lifetimes, then we'll age faster). Mother was right again: take care of yourself is the message.

I doubt if any of this is particularly surprising, because everything so obviously deteriorates with age. It also explains the extraordinary rise in global life expectancies as the average is more dependent on the eradication of diseases and terrible living conditions - and therefore early deaths - than it is on people actually living longer adult lives.

But there are other problems that cells have to face besides the chemical challenges. They have to put up with constant physical ones too. These arise because the cell interior is mainly water, and water molecules are careering around at enormously high speeds, smashing into the protein-making machinery of the mitochondria at billions of times a second.

Scientists call this 'thermal motion' because the collisions are subject to the same laws of physics as energy exchanges between hot and cold objects are, or gas molecules, or any of our metabolic processes. The upshot of this violent bombardment on the cell's engine, though, is that it makes doing its job a lot harder. If it were happening to us, it would be a bit like trying to change a car tyre in the middle of a hurricane.

The genius that is the cell responds to these assaults by turning the thermal chaos into order - and then using its energy. This looks like a good thing, but of course it can only last so long. The 2nd Law won't be denied, and like all living things when they act to decrease entropy locally, there's a corresponding increase in entropy somewhere else to offset the reduction.

In the long run, therefore, the whole process ends up tending to disorder. The smashing and bashing threatens the cell's integrity, and this means that a lot of its proteins' energy is spent in trying to heal itself. This is a never-ending fight that sadly accounts for why things deform by what's known as senescence - something scientists regard as an illustration of the triumph of physics over biology.

'By definition, there must be a finite amount of energy generated during the life cycle of any organism which is then distributed throughout the period between birth and death in response to selective pressures for reproductive success. As a result, the bioenergetics are optimised during the reproductive phase, followed by a progressive loss of energy during the post-reproductive phase of life, leading to a breakdown in cell-cell communication, ageing and ultimately death as a result of the progressive increase in entropy.'
John Torday and Virender Rehan, *Evolutionary Biology: Cell-Cell Communication and Complex Diseases*

What does this all add up to? It probably means that, yet again, we're seeing the hand of the gene at work. With cellular deterioration happening at the same time as inevitable telomere shortening, the ageing process results in the decline of older generations in favour of younger ones. New is better than old. As Ernest Fraenkel, the professor of biological engineering at MIT put it: 'The strategy that Nature seems to use over and over is to let cells and organisms that have accumulated damage die off - and give their progeny a fresh start to go on and conquer the world.'

Certain species can also be utterly ruthless about speeding up the process. Things like salmon, spiders, fruit flies and huge numbers of insects don't hang around cluttering the place up - they reproduce and then immediately die. On the other hand, there are many other species, including us thank goodness, that need to stay alive to rear their young. In these cases, Nature has evolved to let them survive long enough to do this; indeed, sometimes even long enough to help nurture their children's children as well.

But sooner or later, cells begin to fail and the old then become vulnerable. Since that's the case, perhaps we should all follow the advice of the British anthropologist Ashley Montagu who said: 'The idea is to die young… as late as possible'. This clearing out strategy is natural selection in action. We tend not to reproduce in our older years, and individuals who've become diminished by senescence are more open to disease and accidents. Add these two factors up, and random chance is therefore working to act on population sizes.

Where does this end up? The obvious conclusion is that evolution has no incentive to engineer living things for immortality. As Leonard Hayflick himself summed it up: 'Natural selection diminishes after reproductive success because the species will not benefit from members favoured for greater longevity.'

But there are other kinds of assaults that the cell suffers from as well. There are also problems, for instance, with the metabolism of mitochondria reducing its energy supply, and this in turn can damage DNA and so trigger a vicious cycle of detrimental effects. Then there are harmful radiation and copying errors.

'The common denominator that underlies all modern theories of ageing is change in molecular structure and, hence, function. The ultimate cause is an increasing loss of molecular fidelity and an increase in molecular disorder.'
Leonard Hayflick, *Biological Aging Is No Longer an Unsolved Problem*.

All these things lead to cells malfunctioning and tissues deteriorating. The repair mechanisms can never completely reverse the damage. The result? It's hardly surprising that we end up not looking so great. Rather more seriously, the accumulated damage can lead to terminal diseases and system collapses. This all means that we don't die of getting old, but we certainly die of the underlying pathologies that the running down of our bodies invites.

The way that cells divide and repair themselves can only achieve so much. They also die as a response to overwhelming stress or trauma. Tissues that are subject to being hit, for example, or burnt, or possibly damaged by something like a traumatically induced heart attack, are the kind of externally generated injuries that lead to necrosis. This is when cells burst open and die, and the area around them becomes inflamed.

But there's also another, fascinating way in which cells die that harks all the way back to their origins as prokaryotes, and to the strategy they use for dealing with parasites. They commit suicide. Just as their ancestors found, this is a brilliant way of clearing out exhausted cells as well as playing a major role in helping the immune system ward off viral infections.

These suicides occur because cell splitting reaches its limit. When they can't divide any longer, they know the jig's up and communicate with each other, just as they do in bacterial colonies, sending each other signals that it's time to go. The DNA in the nucleus then condenses and fragments, the tiny cytoskeleton collapses, and the mess is cleared up by immune cells that ingest the debris.

This process is happening at something like a million cells a second in human bodies and is known as apoptosis from the Greek for 'falling down' (rather like autumn leaves) or more generally as programmed cell death (PCD). But what's making cells do this? It's because there's the most intricate genomic tango going on in all multicellular organisms at every moment of every day in which, on the one hand, cells are dividing, growing and renewing the body, but on the other, when they've reached their limit, they're being balanced out by the PCD process.

Mitosis and apoptosis are therefore working hand in hand - but it's a delicate dance and it depends on both processes being finely tuned. Sadly, it can often go wonky. Too much cell splitting, for instance, can lead to growths like cancers, while too much suicidal cell death can result in diseases like Huntington's and Parkinson's.

'The number of cells in our bodies is defined by an equilibrium of opposing forces: mitosis adds cells, while Programmed Cell Death removes them. Just as too much cell division can lead to a pathological increase in cell numbers, so can too little cell death.'
Robert Horvitz, *2002 Nobel Prizewinner for Medicine*

If you take a step back from all this and try to detect whether a pattern runs through the themes and decisions of evolution from the earliest of single-celled creatures to the present - is death playing its part? It would appear so. That's because we, like all multicellular creatures, are homes to gigantic numbers of specialised life forms that are continuously communicating with each other, working out what's best for themselves and for the whole. In this sense, our bodies are hugely complex, yet they're also balanced and cooperative communities in which the individual aims of the participants have come together to serve their community… every bit as much as bees or ants might do in their own colonies.

And sitting over it all? The gene, as ever. Only the product of chemicals, of course, but with all the appearance of holding the conductor's baton, keeping the beat of the orchestra of life going on a day-to-day basis, but with its eyes firmly focused on the next concert. That one will always be better than this.

Yet if the gene's actions are so devoted to the future, how can it know if the mutations it's so plainly trying to provoke will be good for its vehicles' life chances? (I know, it sounds yet again as if one's giving it a personality - but it's hard to avoid the feeling.) How does the gene know whether mutations won't make matters worse, and lead to life becoming *more* precarious rather than less?

How is it working to ward off the entropic threat to existence?

Belching chimneys might have been good news for industry -
but perhaps they weren't for the peppered moth.

CHAPTER TWELVE

SO SEX LEADS TO DEATH. AND DEATH HELPS CLEAR OUT OLD GENERATIONS TO LET MUTATIONS INTRODUCE DIVERSITY. THIS SOUNDS LIKE A CLEVER PLAN, BUT HOW CAN THE GENE BE SURE THAT MUTATIONS ARE GOING TO MAKE THINGS BETTER, AND NOT WORSE?

How can the gene's actions produce the right outcomes, the right 'decisions' for survival?

Good question... because if the gene's way of working runs the risk of making things worse by introducing mutations that could undermine a vehicle's chances - how can that possibly be a strategic thing to do?

The answer is obvious, if rather brutal. It's because it doesn't matter. And that's because outcomes are as random in mutations as predictions are in the tennis fraud. Looked at in this way, why should the gene 'care'?

The way the sexual reproduction system works is for it to encourage the flow of genes - and yet also to allow the occasional error to occur. The gene 'wants' these to happen to provoke change - because any change is good for its survival chances, in the same way the tennis fraud works for the benefit of the fraudster, not the gullible punters.

But just to persist with one's understandable sense of bafflement… if a species is a vehicle for the gene, then surely having a way of reproducing that could plunge it, and the genes residing in it, into existential danger would seem to be a crazy idea? Well, obviously there must be a method in the madness or the sheer weight of billions of years of evolution wouldn't have allowed all these procedures and processes to continue. They would have failed; life would have come to an end, and it clearly hasn't.

So, why not? And how does it all work?

First of all, to repeat what was said somewhere earlier, there are two possible outcomes from mutations… whatever changes they lead to can either increase an organism's fitness, or reduce it. (There are also those that have a neutral effect, which might increase genetic variation, but which leave no long-term observable consequences.)

Beneficial mutations, we know, lead to vital advantages for survival that improve the proliferation of the species. Astonishingly, though, scientists believe that bad ones - what they call deleterious mutations - occur far more frequently than the other two kinds. And these could well bring about, as the medical ethicist Leonard Fleck said: '… premature death, or serious health problems that drastically compromise the capacity of affected individuals to carry out normal or near normal life plans.' That all sounds fairly doom-laden, but if these mutations look like they're speeding up the work of the 2nd Law in that they're making life fall apart, then how come we're still here?

> **'Random mutations much more easily debilitate genes than**
> **improve them, and that this is true even of the helpful mutations.'**
> **Michael Behe, *Darwin's Black Box***

Well, if one goes back to the staggering statistic that 99.9% of all the species that have ever lived are believed to have become extinct, I suppose one could argue that these adverse mutations must have been one of the major reasons for their departure.

But life goes on, and it's our turn to be around now, and we're still surrounded by enormous genetic diversity… so how is it that we've turned out all right and others have failed in the past? Or, to be more exact, what does this show us about how individuals and species fit into the vast community of living things that remain - and have evolved to be, somehow, in balance?

> **'Evolutionary plasticity can be purchased only at the ruthlessly dear price**
> **of continuously sacrificing some individuals to death from unfavourable mutations.**
> **Bemoaning this imperfection of Nature has, however, no place in**
> **the scientific treatment of the subject.'**
> **Theodosius Dobzhansky, *Genetics and the Origin of Species***

Maybe it's worth remembering how mutations work in the first place. Scientists tell us that they're all due to DNA coding errors, but while that's true, they actually come about in a number of different ways.

Some occur when a nucleotide on a stretch of DNA happens to be replaced in a chemical slip-up by another one, in a process known as point mutation. Then there could be additions or losses when a chromosome breaks and a segment of DNA is deleted or replaced with something else. These are probably the main two causes, but there are many rarer types too.

However they come about, though, the results are always the same: a slightly different bunch of proteins get produced than normal. And it's this revised chemistry that has an effect on what the offspring then inherits.

This doesn't happen every time, because the body's monitoring systems pick up most of the mistakes as they happen and eliminate them. However, some of them get through and these then interact with the environment, or with other mutations, or with the surrounding population.

The changes then lead to 'adaptations' - and these adaptations are how organisms evolve. For anyone who likes things to say the same ('why can't they ever leave things alone, eh?') this never-ending uncertainty in life would appear to be scary. Looked at another way, however, if they didn't happen then everything would carry on unaltered, and species would inevitably get wiped out when their surroundings changed in a way that didn't suit them.

It's because of mutations that not every member of a species will be caught flat-footed when calamities like this come along… because some of them will have changed in such a way that they now have whatever is needed to survive in the new conditions.

'The secrets of evolution are death and time - the deaths of enormous numbers of life forms that were imperfectly adapted to the environment; and time for a long succession of small mutations.'
Carl Sagan, *Cosmos*

There are three ways in which this could happen:

First, there might be a physiological alteration that turns out to be dead right for a changing environment. An organism, for example, might have mutated a higher or lower temperature tolerance and this could be just what's needed to cope with sudden climate change.

Secondly, an organism could change physically, and their offspring might then find they'd inherited new ways of fighting off the threats they'd been facing from other species. This is particularly useful in a world where so many things are threatened by changes that take place in members of their own species, or are dominated by parasitic life forms.

And thirdly, they might develop a trait that brings with it an evolutionary advantage. Giraffes make a good example of this because they developed their long necks over an enormous period of time, but the mutations that led to this happening resulted in exactly the right adaptation to let them have a food source that others couldn't reach.

'Evolution is creative. That's how we got giraffes.'
Kurt Vonnegut, *A Man Without a Country*

Mutations, of course, are what make natural selection work. But they can also make it go wrong because if the rate at which they occur is too slow then a population can't evolve fast enough to cope with the changes around them. On the other hand, if they accumulate too fast, then natural selection can't eliminate them, and they can lead to what biologists call an 'error catastrophe', which can end rather badly… well, extinction anyway.

Existential decline is particularly true for creatures like bacteria and amoebas that use asexual methods of reproducing. Here, if mutations result in them becoming less fit, then a chain of events can follow which would almost certainly lead to something the American geneticist Hermann Muller called a 'ratchet', because it only works in one direction and therefore can't be reversed.

This happens because the constant cell splitting process means that all the same genes in these organisms are getting passed down to the next generation in their entirety, and consequently their offspring are less able to cope when something goes wrong.

The only good thing is that once an extinction does take place, the bad mutation dies out along with the species. One goes, they all go. This is rather reminiscent of Sir Walter Raleigh's last words before his head was chopped off. Apparently, he had a bad head cold and said, as he felt the axe's blade: 'Tis a sharp remedy, but a sure one for all ills.'

The downward momentum of the ratchet is less of a problem in sexually reproductive species than it is in asexual. The difference arises because the genetic exchange between chromosomes can generally separate between good and bad mutations. If things are unfortunate enough to get too many nasty changes, they might die out. But others can be luckier and end up with hardly any long-term effects.

Is the process really that mechanical?

Possibly not. And that's because natural selection doesn't just work at the genetic level. Effects also depend on what happens next - on how the newly mutated phenotype then fits into its environment. Outcomes are then shaped by the way the 'new' individual and its group behaves from that point onwards. A more accurate conclusion, therefore, would be that what affects fitness - and survival - may not just be down to mutations, but on how these changes are then expressed through behaviour.

What kind of behaviour?

Well, if we go back, for example, to the question of what makes animals warn each other about predators sneaking up on them, then a mutation that leads to an individual member of the colony changing its behaviour so that it doesn't help his pals by crying out (what biologists rather coyly call a 'cheater') then is this good or bad? It's true that it must be good for the 'adapted' individual because it gets to survive by keeping quiet - it doesn't get eaten and others do - and it could therefore be said to be theoretically 'fitter'.

> **'The demonstration of effects, good or bad, proves nothing.**
> **To prove adaptation one must demonstrate a functional design.'**
> **George Williams, *Adaptation and Natural Selection***

However, if its genes then spread at the expense of others who might have been more prepared to sacrifice themselves for the good of the colony, then these 'cheating' genes can become too dominant in the species. The process then ultimately works *against* the species' interests because its defence systems become weakened. The great biologist JBS Haldane called this phenomenon 'evolutionary suicide'.

Oddly enough it turns out that this kind of genetic cascade isn't as rare as one might imagine. And the end result of it is seen by behavioural scientists as yet another example of the great conundrum of life… the choice that's been raised already in this book between whether it's better to be 'selfish' and win by beating others (like cheaters not crying out) or to be 'unselfish' and win by helping your group win (by altruistically calling out a warning) and by preserving the non-cheating genes in the gene pool. Much more on this later.

So what happens in us humans? Do we have to cope with harmful mutations too?

We certainly do, and biologists generally agree that we incur them at a surprisingly high rate. Each of us can apparently expect to inherit around two deleterious changes from our parents, and these can lead to the kind of diseases that have a strong genetic

'Boy, what a depressing day.
We studied heredity.'

element, such as diabetes, cystic fibrosis and schizophrenia. (More Larkin: 'They fuck you up, your mum and dad'.)

While this is true, one of the ways that Nature has evolved to steer us and other organisms away from continuous disasters is by being less selective in how it hands these sorts of diseases down. This means they often only come along once the victim's reproductive years are over - in other words, when we're past our child producing age, and are therefore too old to pass them on.

But here's the surprise (although it probably shouldn't be as the long history of evolution has thrown up so many examples) what looks like it should be a bad mutation can actually turn out to be good, and what would look as if it was good can often be bad.

As an example of this, if one parent is carrying a certain mutation, it might confer resistance to a disease. But if both parents are carrying it, then it can lead to big trouble. This is one of the reasons why people in small communities with a limited gene pool have to take care about who they reproduce with. And it's also the reason why, in wider communities, there are cultural mores against marrying a close relation.

Sickle cell anaemia, for instance, comes from both parents having a particular mutation. But if only one of them is carrying it, the result can be evolutionarily advantageous because the offspring might then inherit a resistance to malaria.

This 'what's bad can be good, and good can be bad' randomness can even show up in a remarkably short span of time. Evolution as a result of mutations doesn't always have to take the millions of years it's always believed to. One of the most famous examples of this was what became known as 'industrial melanism', during which the extraordinary evolution of the tiny, peppered moth was being studied while its changes were actually going on.

The background to this was that the moth's habitat was on the bark of birch trees, and because this surface is usually pale, the moths' light colouring made them almost invisible for birds to see. However, when a mutation came along which led some of them to develop darker wings, it naturally meant that they were now easier for birds to spot - and therefore more liable to be eaten.

'New mutations don't create new species; they create offspring that are impaired.'
Lynn Margulis, *Origins of Sex: Three Billion Years of Genetic Recombinations*

But this mutation also came at a time when the environment itself was changing. Because of the emissions from the new-fangled factories of the Industrial Revolution, chimneys were spewing out soot and this was darkening the trees' barks. What would have been a disadvantage for the moths when they were light-coloured now became exactly what was needed for them to stay camouflaged.

Of course, the numbers of the poor things declined precipitously during the time the generations were moving from one wing colour to another, but in the end the pale moth became as dark as the satanic mills that had so threatened its existence in the first place.

The story doesn't end there either, because after 150 years or so of heavy industry, legislation was introduced to clean up the factory output. The atmosphere became purer, and tree barks began to turn pale again… and so did the peppered moth. Would these colour mutations therefore be described as 'good' or 'bad'? Or just random? What's not in doubt is that it was natural selection in action.

Then again, some mutations can appear to be of little consequence but can actually be part of a process that ends up with a species splitting into two. This apparent weirdness arises when something's faced by two different stimuli, usually introduced by changes to the environment.

Land masses, for example, frequently drifted apart in the development of the Earth's surface, and if conditions varied from one place to another, then mutations to the same species made it adapt in completely different ways to their new environments.

Another stimulus might be changes to what an organism feeds on. The humble maggot fly is a case that's been much studied, and like the peppered moth, it shows up how quickly an apparently trivial change to an organism can take it in an entirely new direction. What happened was that when apple trees were introduced into America, the hawthorn fruit fly began to lay its eggs on the new imports rather than on hawthorns. After less than a couple of centuries the maggot flies had become two distinct species, with completely different populations, and all because of a minuscule change in the brain that led one branch to prefer the smell of apples, whilst the other kept faith with hawthorns.

This kind of speciation goes right back to the original contention of the book … that different living things are the result of behavioural decisions. As the biologist Sharon Olsson of the University of Notre Dame summed it up: 'Changes in behaviour can lead to the evolution of new species, particularly when these behaviours influence habitat choice. Yet the neural bases of such changes are relatively unknown.'

Mutations that lead to splits are therefore difficult to classify as either beneficial or deleterious because while branching might be said to weaken the species' original line, diversity leads to the gene's security. What seems to be clear, though, is that mutations which have the potential to drive a population to extinction could equally end up with it having a completely different outcome, and to be later judged by history as having been hugely successful.

This contention has recently been illustrated when geneticists found they could replicate the natural process by manipulating engineered DNA into disease-giving organisms. In doing this they've been able to neutralise their effects. There's now much hope, for example, that this is how they might get on top of one of the world's greatest killers, the malarial mosquito, and so make being bitten irritating, but not fatal.

I guess the summary to it all is… it's complicated.

The huge range of effects that mutations can have on fitness - some advantageous, some deleterious - comes about because they're reacting with changing external factors. Because of this it's almost impossible to predict what results evolutionary forces will produce in populations. There's also the question of whether the genetic variations that produce traits turn out to be common changes with small effects - or rare changes with large effects.

But the one thing that can be concluded with certainty is that the survival of the gene remains paramount. Whether this comes at the expense of the individual organism that's carrying it, or whether it sees whole groups of these organisms become extinct, seems to be immaterial. The gene is in the driving seat, whether it's described as selfish, or its effects as unselfish, because its strategy for keeping life going depends on the creation of complex structures and better adapted organisms.

It doesn't 'mind' how it gets there. And it certainly shows no sign of being bothered by which species come, and which go as it's achieving its aim.

What's strange about the gene's 'master plan', however, is that none of the millions of vehicles it's ever produced can ever be said to have won. You'd think the immensely long history of evolution would have ended up with a process that made organisms less vulnerable to environmental and genetic threats, and therefore more likely to survive. Yet it seems to do the opposite. Because its mutational strategy has random outcomes, it theoretically risks weakening things if changes occur when there aren't any environmental alterations to match it.

'The function of mutations is to maintain the
stock of genetic variance at a high level.'
Sir Ronald Fisher, *The Genetical Theory of Natural Selection*

The end result of having an arbitrary system such as this is that some types of organisms and species can last for tens of millions of years, while others disappear very quickly. Whether they're long or short-lived, however, the only certainty is that *nothing* lasts forever. And that's because every single living thing suffers from the same two problems in the end.

The first of these is that advanced life forms are only able to change through vertical gene transfer - from parent to offspring - and this is such a slow and uncertain process that it needs long periods of evolutionary time before a mutation turns out to be either beneficial or damaging.

Only two types of creature seem to escape this problem: single-celled organisms, such as bacteria, that can exchange DNA horizontally. And the other one is us. Why us? Because we humans are arguably the only multicellular organism that can make non-vertical adaptations.

What? Do we get genetic material other than from our parents?

Of course not, but what we do share with the earliest of microbial life forms is our ability to *change quickly*, to assess danger, to look ahead and be worried at the threats, to alter our behaviour, to change habitats and, generally, to find ways of surviving existential problems. In many ways, *H. sapiens* could claim to be the best thing that Nature's ever created for winning under a wide range of different conditions. Neil deGrasse Tyson mused on these unique abilities in *Letters From an Astrophysicist* when he wrote: 'Dinosaurs are extinct today because they lacked opposable thumbs and the brainpower to build a space programme.'

The second reason nothing ever succeeds for long, let alone forever, is because every single organism in life has weaknesses. And these weaknesses are constantly being exploited by other things which are trying to grab their ordered energy, eat them, take over aspects of their environmental niches, and in general provide a deadly challenge to their survival. At root, this continuous warfare may explain how the kingdoms of life are held in balance, because any kind of success in an organism is an invitation for others to exploit it.

But these facts are also contradicted by the equally constant force of cooperation and the endless search for the gains that come from 1+1=3 strategies. If things aren't competing, they're trying to find mutually beneficial ways of existing, where they can act together for their joint benefit.

So can there really be a coherent explanation for the vast exercise that is 'life' other than the gene-based theory of evolution?

Personally, I don't see how there can be... it all seems to make such complete sense. And yet the two geniuses that first deduced how all this worked - and had the vision to imagine life forms arranged as a 'tree of life', all descending from a single common ancestor - *had no knowledge of the gene, nor any understanding of genetics.*

These two astonishing people were Charles Darwin and Alfred Russel Wallace, and the most extraordinary thing about them was that they were flying completely blind and managed to reach their conclusions simply on observation. And yet they came up with the theory that so many people continue to believe is the right answer.

How could they possibly have guessed at what was going on? The answer makes a great story, saturated with ambition and ruthless tactics, false starts and lucky coincidences. A bit like life, really.

Before we get on to Darwin and Wallace, though, what came before they turned everything upside down? Did *everyone* think God was responsible for the order of life, and that it was His will that had placed the different plants and creatures in Creation?

Or were there other theories as well?

The map that changed the world. 'Fossils have... wonderful order and regularity with which Nature has disposed of these singular productions and assigned to each class its peculiar stratum.' William Smith

HOW DID PEOPLE THINK EVOLUTION WORKED BEFORE DARWIN AND WALLACE CAME ALONG? IF GOD WASN'T THE ONLY ONE MAKING DECISIONS, WHAT ELSE DID THEY IMAGINE WAS HAPPENING?

It's tricky to be too precise about when the Scientific Revolution began to dominate European thinking. But in general historians tend to date it to around the late Renaissance, probably some time about the middle of the sixteenth century.

That would make sense because it was about then that increasingly sophisticated telescopes and measuring instruments began to be used, and these led to courageous early 'enquirers' coming up with a series of outrageous claims that were later, of course, found to be completely correct. These were the men who set about rejecting two thousand years of Greek-originated certainties, and the rock-solid religious beliefs that had dominated philosophical thought up to that point.

The upheaval they caused was taking place at roughly the same time as the invention of mass printing was unleashing mass knowledge - and mass questioning. This was the long period that's become known as the Age of Enlightenment.

Why enlightenment? It was because it brought to an end people having to believe in everything they'd been told. Now men like Copernicus and Galileo were challenging the accepted order with the aim of 'enlightening' others, by putting forward extraordinary new theories about how the Universe worked. But there were many more who were less than thrilled at this ambition. In particular, the religious authorities weren't too keen on having their doctrines trampled on.

> **'I do not feel obliged to believe that the same God who has endowed us with sense, reason and intellect has intended us to forgo their use.'**
>
> **Galileo Galilei**

A hundred or so more years after the revolution had started, Isaac Newton burst onto the world stage. Among the other brilliant investigations he worked on, his studies of optics, and the laws of motion and gravitational forces were all huge breakthroughs.

But he also brought an entirely new philosophical dimension to scientific discovery. This was because of his unwavering belief that everything should be questioned, that superstition should be rejected, and that it was what we *didn't* know that was more intriguing than just accepting the assumptions of the past.

In just a short period, knowledge was no longer only in the hands of the powerful. Quite the opposite - all the old certainties were now being thrown in the air. Yet while Newton was being recognised in his lifetime as a great scientific genius, he himself saw only the excitement of what was yet to be unearthed. He described himself as like a boy '… playing on the seashore and diverting myself in now and then finding a smoother pebble or a prettier shell than the ordinary, whilst the great ocean of truth lay all undiscovered before me.'

Suddenly, it was all right to question things. Rather, it was a time of great opportunity for educated men to put forward entirely new ways of viewing scientific 'facts', and even for leisured amateurs such as clergymen and aristocrats to spend their time re-examining old beliefs. Some of them were even using research-based methods to explore the empirical evidence for extraordinary new theories.

One of the most obvious consequences of this explosion of ideas was the epic arm wrestle that broke out between the religious convictions on the God-given order of life forms (with us humans at the top, of course) and the new kinds of scientific inquiry that were spreading throughout Europe. Neither side seemed to be listening to the other, yet both were trying in their different ways to answer the most basic of questions: Who were we? Where had we come from? And why did we behave in the ways that we did?

> **'The greatest scientific discovery was the discovery of ignorance. Once humans realised how little they knew about the world, they suddenly had a very good reason to seek new knowledge, which opened up the scientific road to progress.'**
> **Yuval Noah Harari, *Homo Deus: A History of Tomorrow***

In 1656, for example, at roughly the time that the invention of the microscope was leading to the discovery of the cell, and to an understanding of the structure of complex organisms, the Bishop of Armagh, James Ussher (a scholar of such standing that he managed to be admired by both Charles I and his arch-enemy, Oliver Cromwell) was dealing with more important matters. Poring over ancient Hebrew texts, he managed to work backwards from when people believed Noah's Flood had taken place (2349 BC, apparently) to date the precise moment at which God had created the Universe.

It was, he said, at six o'clock on the evening of 22 October, 4004 BC as measured on the Julian calendar.

**'The inventions of microscopy and telescopy shattered
the boundaries of ordinary human perception and
fuelled the Scientific Revolution.'
Richard Borden, *Ecology and Experience***

A Cambridge academic named John Lightfoot immediately took issue with this, and claimed that the saintly prelate had got his sums wrong. A more accurate computation of the moment God had fired his starting pistol, he pronounced, showed it wasn't until nine o'clock the following morning.

Nonetheless, the still widespread assumption that 'everyone believed in God's plan until Charles Darwin came along' would actually appear to be wide of the mark. The sheer diversity of organisms on the planet, and the increasingly studied verities of life and death, made questioning people argue that the way the world worked was a matter in which science would one day transcend both religion and philosophy.

By the late eighteenth century, for example, a couple of generations before Darwin, many scholars were in agreement with the Scottish geologist James Hutton who was saying that the implication of rock formations meant that the age of the Earth was nigh on immeasurable.

With what seems incredible prescience he claimed: '… in conceiving an indefinite variety among individuals… those which depart most from the best adapted constitution, will be the most liable to perish while, on the other hand, those organised bodies which most approach to the best constitution for the present circumstances, will be best adapted to continue, in preserving themselves and multiplying the individuals of their race.'

Hutton's pioneering views were then followed by one of those extraordinary self-taught geniuses who began to crop up as the Industrial Revolution took root at a time when talent and intelligence were being valued more highly than birth, or a classical education.

The genius was William Smith, son of an Oxfordshire blacksmith, a dreamy child, fascinated with stones and fossils. He'd left home in 1791 for the boom city of Bath, and had begun working as a surveyor for the canal-building entrepreneurs who were building the transport infrastructure that would fuel the growth of the manufacturing industries.

James Hutton in 1798. Has his description of natural selection ever been bettered?

By the time he was twenty-three, his extensive digging had led to a new nickname, Strata Smith, and he was soon publishing his *Principles of Faunal Succession*. This was a book that used the fossils he'd found embedded in rocks as the basis of a theory that claimed sea creatures had been laid down in sediments, and that his excavations showed that the oldest were at the bottom.

A map of the strata of the entire British Isles followed some years later, together with his inescapable conclusion that there'd been profound changes to the Earth's surface - 'evolution' he called it - that showed that life was far, far older than any creationist might have believed from reading the Bible's narrative. In his great book, *The Map That Changed the World*, Simon Winchester describes Smith's masterpiece as having: '… an importance, symbolic and real… that underpins all knowledge, all understanding.'

Many geologists saw in this strata map the evidence that the Earth had been convulsed by repeated 'catastrophes' over a long period of time. These had thrown up mountains and land masses they said, and no doubt had driven some species to extinction while others arose.

Catastrophism was the name of the new theory, and it quickly became the accepted belief of influential scientists such as the French natural historian, the Comte de Buffon, and his compatriot, the physicist Joseph Fourier. Both of them, remarkably, speculated that the planet had begun as a molten ball and had then experienced dramatic and violent changes while it cooled.

How was this crazy evolution stuff going to be squared away by religious leaders? What did they think of it all - and how did it fit in with their beliefs?

One of the answers came from the wildly eccentric Professor of Geology at Oxford, a palaeontologist and high churchman (and ancestor of mine!) called William Buckland. In spite of being an eminent scientist he came up with a world-class piece of spin to explain the established church's position. Yes, he said, God had indeed created the world in six days but… because the universe was still unformed, there hadn't yet been the same definition of a day that we have now. In fact, he went on, these 'days' were more like periods of millions of years.

'The days of the Mosaic creation are not to be strictly construed as implying the same length of time which is at present occupied by a single revolution of our globe, but PERIODS of a much longer extent.'
William Buckland, *Vindiciae Geologicae*

This explanation might have settled the nerves of the Synod of the Church of England, but it certainly didn't wash with an ex-student of Buckland's called Charles Lyell. He wasn't going to swallow the ecclesiastical wriggle, and he certainly wasn't going to have anything to do with the idea that the world had been made by unimaginable catastrophes.

Instead, he postulated, it had been transformed in an imperceptibly slow way with sediments forming rocks, and the planet undergoing rhythmic cycles of destruction and restoration. These would have made the Earth suitable for the plants, animals and humanity that one could see now. The process, he said, was still going on, and his theory - what became known by the snappy name of 'uniformitarianism' - was rammed home by the forcefulness of his personality.

Lyell became something of a superstar, writing popular geology books posing as travel guides for a growing audience of people hungry for insights into the origins of the human race. He wrote and rewrote his *Principles of Geology* in a series of volumes that laid out his doctrine that 'the present is the key to the past.'

By now, around the 1830s, the idea that there had been some kind of evolution of life on earth was no longer in much doubt. Instead, the new breed of scientists that was emerging spent their time speculating on what the exact mechanism for it had to be. Jean-Baptiste Lamarck's views were all the rage for a bit, and traditional thinking was rocked by his theory that life forms had begun simple, and had then progressively become more complex. This approach hinged on his conviction that organisms could transform themselves into higher states, and that over long enough periods of time they would end up looking quite different to their original forms.

> **'The greatest scientists in history are great precisely because they broke with consensus. There is no such thing as consensus science. If it's consensus, it isn't science. If it's science, it isn't consensus.'**
> **Michael Crichton, *Prey***

But then along came Charles Darwin and Alfred Russel Wallace and nothing was ever the same again. Together these two saw through the Earth's swirling mass of interlocking organisms to the idea of cumulative *natural selection*. This was a completely novel explanation for how all living things had arisen, a sustained piece of brilliance that Richard Dawkins was to later describe as: '… the only theory capable of explaining the existence of organised complexity.'

But who were these two? And what did they actually say?

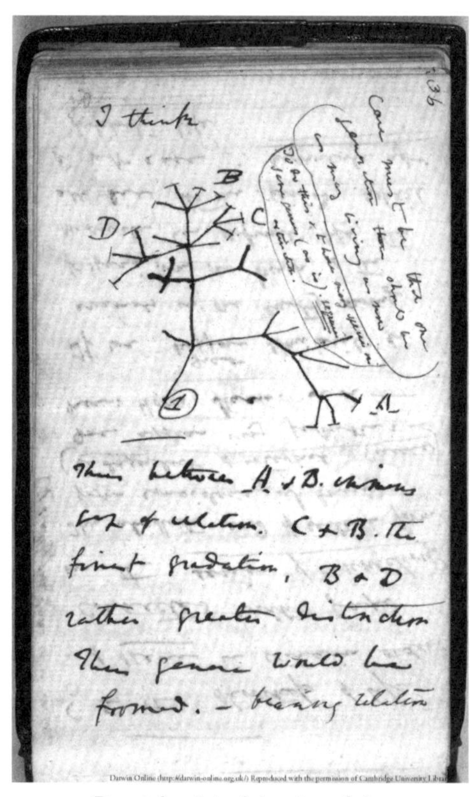

Darwin's original drawing of the branching that ended up with the cocker spaniel, Virginia creeper, five million different species of fungi... and us.

CHAPTER FOURTEEN

FEW WOULD DISAGREE THAT CHARLES DARWIN WAS A VISIONARY GENIUS, BUT WHO WAS THE OTHER PERSON - ALFRED RUSSEL WALLACE? THE TWO OF THEM ARE SUPPOSED TO HAVE SOMEHOW WORKED TOGETHER, BUT WHO CAME UP WITH THE RIGHT ANSWER? AND WHAT WAS IT?

There must have been something going on in the constellation of Aquarius on 12 February 1809 when Charles Darwin and Abraham Lincoln were both born on the same day. Like Lincoln, Darwin's early years were unpromising, and neither would become generally recognised until they were in their forties. Both lost their mothers early, both experienced the tragedy of a child's death - and each of them knew the unstoppable power of a well-described truth.

Unlike Lincoln, though, Darwin was born into a family of worldly success and powerful intellects, an intimidating start in which nothing less than genius would do. Both his grandfathers were world-famous: Erasmus Darwin as a distinguished physician and natural philosopher and, on his mother's side, Josiah Wedgwood, a rich inventor and one of the leading entrepreneurs of the Industrial Revolution - as well as being the founder of the family pottery company.

But poor Charles looked like a complete dud. His own father was a society doctor made wealthy from a series of successful investments, and once the boy was through school, he was sent off to study medicine in Edinburgh. He didn't last long, not taking much interest in anything and greatly preferring to shoot and fish. In particular, he loathed the brutality of early operations, and the last straw came when he saw a child having its leg amputated.

With no doubt a heavy sigh, his father entered him for Cambridge to be trained for the Anglican clergy. Again he fell short, eventually managing a pass degree, but becoming less and less interested in theology, and increasingly fascinated by natural philosophy and geology.

Then fate took a hand when one of his university botany tutors recommended him as a self-funded, gentleman naturalist to join a surveying ship, *HMS Beagle*, that was about to embark on a long voyage to chart the South American coastline. He nearly didn't get the berth when he met the captain, a young man named Robert FitzRoy (who would later go on to become famous himself as the originator of daily weather forecasts). FitzRoy was a believer in the new craze for physiognomy, and he had an instant aversion to Darwin's nose, convinced that its shape indicated laziness.

The *Beagle* - 'little more than a cricket pitch' long in Darwin's words - sailed in 1831 for a voyage of two years that turned into five, 500 days of them at sea and 1,200 on land. It was during this time that the mildly interested amateur turned into one of the deepest-thinking naturalists of his age.

The voyage took them to Uruguay, then down to Argentina and the long coast of Patagonia, and through the Strait of Magellan. It was here that Darwin saw the naked people of Tierra del Fuego, somehow surviving in the sub-zero temperatures '… inconceivably wild… I could not have believed how wide the difference was between savage and civilised man'. Could they really, he wondered, be related to him? How could it possibly have come about that these prehistoric barbarians were, as he was: '…descended from Noah and his wife?'

Darwin studied them closely, even sending two men and a girl back to England, but eventually the little ship left the ice floes. Setting a course North, the *Beagle* then beat up the Chilean seaboard to arrive some months later at the Galapagos Islands, 600 miles west of Ecuador in the Pacific Ocean.

It was here that Darwin began to shake that noble head of his, troubled and uncomprehending at what he saw. As he travelled around the archipelago of twenty-one islands and the numerous rocks and islets that made it up, he knew that the fauna there had hardly ever been seen by another human, and yet its birds and animal life looked as if a shrewd farmer had been pursuing a dedicated programme of selective breeding.

How had these things adapted themselves so exactly to the demands of their environments in the way they had? No hand of man had been involved in producing the beneficial traits they showed, even though a breeder would have taken many generations to arrive at them. But here Nature seemed to have done the work - admittedly not as quickly, but certainly as effectively.

Darwin looked for clues in the geography of the place, but the islands were clearly separated by sea channels that were too wide for animals to hop from one to another. And yet he could see that certain types of birds, particularly finches (although they were later shown to be more closely related to mockingbirds) had somehow managed to adapt their bills in completely novel ways so that they could pick up the different seeds that grew on the unconnected islands.

Animal life, too, showed astonishing adaptations. The giant tortoises, for example, had also managed to change themselves to deal with the differing environmental conditions.

'I never dreamed that islands… most of them within sight
of each other, formed of precisely the same rocks, placed under
a quite similar climate, would have been differently tenanted.'
Charles Darwin, *On The Origin of Species*

What could it all mean? And then the penny dropped.

In his wonderful novel *This Thing of Darkness*, much of which is set during the *Beagle's* voyage, Harry Thompson imagines the conversation that took place between Darwin and the God-fearing FitzRoy:

'Those species were not created on the sixth day. They have - they have -

'Transmuted?' FitzRoy uttered the word calmly but grimly.

'Yes, damn it, they have transmuted into existence, in relatively recent geological times.'

FitzRoy, a Muscular Christian, rejects this, and Thompson has him say later in the book:

'What you speak of is adaptation. Variation within a species. Species themselves are immutable.'

'I tell you they were different species.'

Why was Darwin thinking like this? Was it because, even though he was no ornithologist, he'd become convinced that what he was seeing were birds with a recent common ancestor - that had become quite separate species because they'd adapted to fit their environments? If this was true, he could only conclude, they were far from being examples of Lamarckian complexity. And even though they might be able to fly to other islands - they wouldn't be able to breed with the other birds there. This was because they were now new species... they had branched away from the original line.

How this realisation must have racked him. How he'd have immediately known the explosion of anger his theory would arouse if he went public with it. If birds could change like this, then what else could?

He continued to agonise: if there was the branching he could see, then where was the background for it? How far back did it go? Back to what? Could there only be one thing, one trunk to the tree, from which every subsequent branch had emerged? And what did that imply about where we humans had come from?

As with so many people when they first learn about the theory - it was understanding how the mechanism had overcome the problems of the intermediate phases that most concerned him. Harry Thompson, for example, goes on to imagine FitzRoy putting this most crushing of objections to Darwin: where were these stages in the fossil record?

'If wings grew from forelegs, where are the half-winged animals, and how could they have half-flown? If lungs grew from gills, where are the half-lunged fish and how could they have half-breathed?'

Darwin was himself unsettled by this gap in the theory, but not for the first time he dealt with it by having a fit of the vapours (a ducking technique he would use repeatedly when his beliefs became public and the balloon went up). He'd always suffered from weak health, but it somehow seemed to be at its worst when unpleasant questions were being asked. Then, as later, he insisted that his ideas should be taken as a whole, and not picked apart by questions of detail. Future generations of scientists, he said, would come up with the complete answer.

In 1836 the *Beagle* eventually arrived back in Britain, and Darwin then busied himself with building his reputation as a naturalist, publishing a widely read account of the voyage called *Journal of Researches*, and then becoming a specialist in, of all things, barnacles. But even as he slogged away on his eight-year, four volume study of these odd arthropods, he continued to ponder and develop his thoughts about evolution - transmutation he called it - although he knew better than to tell anyone but a few close friends about his conclusions.

That was because his problems were many. And they were all pretty bleak.

First, he could imagine only too well the backlash that ideas like this would provoke from the country's Christian backbone. Whatever else it did, his theory would undermine the belief that God had created and sustained the natural and human hierarchies. Anything that denied this fact would threaten the social order - and even provide ammunition for the dreaded Chartists and revolutionaries. Such thoughts, his friends told him, could undermine the whole moral fabric of society, and bring 'deadly mischief in its train'.

Secondly, he knew that there were great gaps in the evidence that he'd need if he was to back up the theory. FitzRoy's objections would have worried him like a broken tooth - *where were the stages?* He was quite sure they'd be found, or certainly explained with further research, but he had no proper training in biological science. And anyway, he simply didn't have the time to conduct field studies or to correspond with others about their findings.

But thirdly, he'd have been concerned about a big hole in his reasoning, a hole which he couldn't fill. It was this. Why did some animals act in an altruistic way? They obviously did, and yet they did so without the key component one sees in humans of a nobility of intention towards others. But nonetheless these animals acted as if they were similarly selfless. Why, if this wasn't the case, would some of them put their lives in danger for the sake of their communities, and even sacrifice their own lives for the good of others?

Animals like birds and rabbits cried out when a predator was near, even though they'd be calling attention to their own position and plunging themselves into danger. Why would they care about others if doing so led to their own deaths? Surely if every living thing was created with the sole intention of surviving so that it could reproduce - then they should be keeping quiet and letting something else get eaten. And yet they didn't.

And the problem went further still. What about so many of the insects?

Some of the members within a colony of certain kinds of insects - in fact, frequently the majority of them - were born sterile, and unable to reproduce. And yet they played a full part in the life of the colony. Why, if evolution was all about survival and the reproduction of the species, were some of them doomed to never pass their lines on?

Yet these bees and ants and termites, and all the other insects that were made this way, seemed to be willing to labour all their lives for the good of others in their colony, even to the point of committing suicide by stinging intruders, or of working themselves to death.

Surely natural selection demanded that their only interest should be in reproducing, in making their bloodlines survive? Surely this kicked into touch the theory that natural selection programmed the way animals and insects behaved?

How Darwin must have stroked that great beard of his, staring out of the window again and again and forgetting his barnacles for a minute to chew over the problems. But he carried on working, and books and honours followed; he was elected to prestigious scientific bodies, he had friends in high places, and for many years he placed his family and advancement ahead of his secret beliefs.

Then at some point he read a book that had been a bestseller forty or so years before, but which had since lapsed in popularity. This was the *Essay on the Principles of Population* by a Church of England vicar named Thomas Malthus, and its central message was the gloomy prediction that while the number of humans on the planet would progress logarithmically (selfish people would keep insisting on breeding), the food supply would only progress arithmetically (farmers wouldn't be able to keep up). In other words, we were inevitably doomed.

The Malthusian vision saw the cheery end of the story as… death and destruction. Violent breakdowns to society would become endemic, he forecast, and hideous culls would be necessary to chop back the rutting hoards, insensible to their brutish fate. Not very Christian, one wouldn't have thought, but arguments like this were pretty standard fare at a time when the educated classes were saying that the flood of working people pouring into the manufacturing industries was expanding the new cities so quickly that they were bound to come to a terrible end.

Darwin set humans to one side, but he could see the same great issues of life and death were being acted out in every other organism. If the food supply was limited, how would this make things respond?

Then the light went on in his head. It was because only the strongest and healthiest would survive! Organisms would die off in exactly the same way that Malthus was predicting for mankind; but some of them changed, some of them managed to survive because they became other, better-adapted things… they became varieties. And even new species.

But the ghastly realisation that had so shaken him in the Galapagos remained. If animals and plants could respond to these pressures by transmutation, then what did it mean for where man had come from? Lamarck had dared to suggest thirty years earlier that we were somehow descended from apes, and look where that had got him.

Another public mauling also gave him pause. In 1844, a Scottish publisher and amateur geologist called Robert Chambers had anonymously published a book called *Vestiges of the Natural History of Creation* that put forward an extremely speculative and frequently silly evolutionary hypothesis.

The reason that Chambers had decided on keeping his name off the book became clear as soon as people began reading its central argument. In it, he put forward the theory that species underwent progressive transmutations in much the same way that Lamarck had advocated. Yet, with a certain amount of wriggling, he did his best to distance himself from the Frenchman's evolutionary mechanisms.

Chambers had another reason for keeping his head down. While he wanted the sales revenue the book was producing, he certainly didn't want to get his publishing company involved in a scandal. He needn't have worried. *Vestiges* was a sensation, and nobody discovered until years later who its author was. Everyone took it up, even the royal family; Prince Albert was particularly keen on popular science and he liked to read it aloud to the Queen. She, apparently, loved it.

Underlying the book's success was the realisation that evolution had come out of the public bar and its uneducated moralising, and into the drawing rooms of respectable people. Darwin may have thought that the speculation behind the secretive author's arguments were largely rubbish, but he quietly watched from the sidelines, patiently waiting to see whether its publication would open up an opportunity for him.

But then opinion turned. A Cambridge don, the Reverend Adam Sedgwick, the Professor of Geology at the university, labelled it a 'foul book' that suggested 'religion is a lie, morality is moonshine, and… man and woman are only better beasts than the animals.'

Darwin had seen enough. Back into his shell he retreated, determined that from now on his research would continue in secret. Among his fellow scientists, Charles Lyell would share his ideas, but very few others besides him. The *Vestiges* row eventually died down, but Darwin continued to sit on his thoughts for years, terrified of the outrage the natural selection theory would provoke, and yet burning with ambition to be recognised for what he felt he'd discovered.

And then, one day, a letter arrived from the ends of the Earth, an island called Ternate in eastern Indonesia, from a man he vaguely remembered corresponding with called Alfred Russel Wallace. It was addressed to Lyell - now Sir Charles Lyell, the unquestioned Great Man of natural history - but Wallace wrote to say that he didn't have his address, and how grateful he'd be if Darwin could pass it on.

Darwin opened the letter. How his heart must have dropped as he saw the title of the enclosed monograph. He raced on, and as he turned the twenty-four pages in his hand he must have known that, from that moment, his entire discovery of the mechanism for evolution would be claimed by this man… and that his own ideas had been *forestalled*. Unless that was, he did something he'd been avoiding for two decades, something that would change his life forever. He would have to go public.

But who was this Alfred Russel Wallace anyway? That was the worst of it. He was just an ex-schoolmaster, a Welshman, up from nothing. He was simply a man whose father had gone bust, and who was now reduced to earning a living as a specimen hunter in the Far East, sending back plants and insects to his rich collector clients. He wasn't a gentleman naturalist at all; he was a tradesman, a 'flycatcher', a man who most certainly wasn't on the same posh circuit as the likes of Darwin and Lyell. What was to be done?

Darwin was in a panic. He had to find Lyell… and quickly.

But how on earth had Wallace seen through to the truth? Recalling the events much later to a journalist, Wallace said he'd been collecting on the islands of Bali and Lombok, only twenty miles or so apart and yet, like Darwin in the Galapagos, he was struck and baffled by the realisation that he was seeing completely different adaptations among the plants and animals there. More than that, they were completely different *species*, yet they were clearly related.

'(Mutations) give accidents as well as adaptation a place in evolution

and at one stroke explains the facts which puzzled earlier selectionists,

notably the much greater degree of divergence shown by island than

mainland forms, by forms in isolated lakes than in continuous river systems.'

Julian Huxley, *Evolution: The Modern Synthesis*

Like Darwin, he'd also been very influenced by reading Malthus a few years previously. Now he'd fallen ill and was lying in his hammock, ravaged by a bout of malaria, turning over Malthus's depressing conclusions in his mind… when the clouds parted and the whole beautiful picture of creation came to him in an instant. And with it a realisation of the entire process of evolution.

As Tom Wolfe describes the moment so brilliantly in his book *The Kingdom of Speech*: '… he had another kind of fever, an exhilarating fever… a fervid desire to record his revelation and show the world - now! For two days and two nights… during every halfway tranquil moment between the chills, the rattling ribs, the fevers, and the sweats… he writes and he writes, writes, writes a twenty plus page manuscript entitled *On the Tendency of Varieties to Depart Indefinitely from the Original Type*. He has done it! His will be the first description ever published of the evolution of the species through natural selection. He sent it off to England on the next boat.'

Now Darwin was reading his letter with mounting despair. Here it all was, he saw, and even he had to be struck by the pithy certainty of the writing and the clarity of the mechanism. 'The answer', Wallace wrote, 'is clearly that on the whole the best fitted live… then suddenly it flashed upon me that this self-acting process would necessarily improve the race, because in every generation the inferior would inevitably be killed off and the superior remain - that is, the fittest would survive.'

Darwin eventually tracked down Lyell and told him the worst. As Harry Thompson imagined their meeting, he has Darwin saying in anguish: 'I never saw a more striking coincidence. I have been collecting facts for twenty-five years and Wallace reached the same conclusions as myself after thinking about the matter for just three days!'

'Nothing in biology makes sense except in the light of evolution.'
Theodosius Dobzhansky, *Genetics and the Origin of Species*

What was to be done? Lyell took charge. There was, he said, a delayed meeting of the Linnean Society coming up. Why not expose your thoughts there - and Wallace's paper - at the same time? That way, his and Darwin's discoveries would have equal status.

There was obviously no time to get Wallace's agreement to this - a great shame but he was seven thousand miles away, and anyway how could he object to having his insights exposed? Wouldn't he be pleased in fact? Then, Lyell continued, at some point they'd send a letter to Wallace telling him what had happened. In the meantime, why didn't Darwin knuckle down and finally write the book on natural selection that he'd been planning for twenty years?

The Society's meeting was held on a hot day in July, 1858. Neither Lyell nor Darwin was there, and the papers were delivered and received with drowsy indifference. No one ever mentioned them again. But honour was satisfied, and Lyell wrote to Wallace later that year and reported on the 'equal credit' that the papers had received.

Wallace must have been pretty surprised. He'd only sent his article off to ask for opinions and now here he was, being written to by the Great Man himself, telling him that his ideas had gone public. But he took it well, and when he returned to England four years later, he generously lived out the rest of his life playing second fiddle to Darwin's virtuoso lead. He even later published a book called *Darwinism*, and over the years his loyalty was well rewarded by a respectful scientific establishment.

'What about me indeed!'

By the time he died in 1913, Wallace was clothed in a mass of academic honours, a Fellowship of the Royal Society, and the award of the Order of Merit. But there was something rather more meaningful as well, something that made his name immortal… a wiggly line was now drawn on maps of the world that covered the two thousand miles or so that lay between Bali in the south and the northernmost extent of the Philippines. It was called the Wallace Line, and to one side of it naturalists now formally recognised the flora and fauna as belonging to Asia, and on the other, to Australasia.

But what had Darwin been doing before Wallace returned?

He'd taken himself away and got on with it. *On the Origin of Species* appeared the following year and, surprisingly, while sales were muted (Chambers took advantage of the interest to republish *Vestiges* and it outsold *Origin* by five to one) it provoked considerable discussion in the academic community. But with this came exactly the review that Darwin had most dreaded: 'If a monkey has become a man', he read with horror, 'what may not a man become?'

Darwin went to ground and left it to his friends to defend him. Two of them became famous for it: Thomas Huxley for his pugnacious speeches and hostile explanations that earned him the nickname, 'Darwin's Bulldog'; and the social commentator Herbert Spencer (who was, speaking of fitness, the only one of eight siblings to survive to adulthood).

It was Spencer who was to give the world perhaps the most misunderstood summation in history when he described the Darwinian principle as 'survival of the fittest'. This was to become the damaging oversimplification that's always used as a half-baked argument by so many of the racists, eugenicists and political supremacists we continue to be saddled with. And any number of sadistic gym masters as well.

In Germany, the publication of a translation of *Origin* was received with enthusiasm. Nietzsche seized on it… 'God is dead' he said it meant. And there were many others who were only too happy to interpret it as a rallying call for a process of national renewal.

What did other scientists think of it?

Well, naturalists had clearly been assuming for years that the development of complex organisms must also have complex explanations to account for them. But Darwin and Wallace's theory had shown that instead of this, it was an astonishingly simple process. Natural selection occurred *naturally*, they said, and, in many ways, it was so obvious that there was little to be discovered. 'How extremely stupid of me not to have thought of that!' was Thomas Huxley's response when he first read about it. And part of the reason that many biologists supported the thinking was because it so closely resembled the way that animal breeders and plant propagators would improve their stock.

'The publication of the Darwin and Wallace papers in 1858, and still more
that of the '*Origin*' in 1859, had the effect… of the flash of light
which to a man who has lost himself in a dark night, suddenly reveals a road.'
Thomas Huxley, *Letter to Asa Gray*

Nonetheless, if it was that simple, how did natural selection actually function?

Neither Darwin nor Wallace knew.

The presence of the gene was as yet unknown, let alone its mechanisms and the way that mutations came about. When he was pressed on how changes occurred, Darwin initially said he thought that successful characteristics must be passed down rather like colours being mixed together to create new ones. Mr Blue and Miss Yellow would produce a family of little shades of Green, he assumed, otherwise every generation would end up as uniform as the one before.

'Darwin himself, notoriously, included Lamarckian inheritance as a booster process (in addition to Natural Selection) in his own version of evolution. He could entertain this idea because he had such a foggy sense of the mechanics of heredity.'
Daniel Dennett, *Darwin's Dangerous Idea*

But the question nagged at him and he later was to become bogged down with a theory he named pangenesis, in which he thought body cells gave off minute particles that travelled around the bloodstream and ended up in the reproductive organs.

This, he said, produced quasi-Lamarckian effects that not only accounted for how environments would cause variations in these particles, but also how traits from remote ancestors could suddenly reappear. Pangenesis had few takers. He needn't have worried, though, because in yet another of those bizarre instances of how scientific breakthroughs seem to come in bundles, an obscure monk in Moravia was setting about cracking the problem at precisely the same time.

His name was Gregor Mendel, and he was the Austrian-born abbot of a monastery in what's now part of the Czech Republic. Like Darwin, he was a highly educated man whose great passion in life, besides God, was pottering about in the abbey's kitchen garden. Working entirely alone, he'd become intrigued by how different vegetables seemed to inherit characteristics from the previous generation.

To try and understand what lay behind it, he began to experiment with cross-breeding peas to see whether it was possible to predict which traits they'd end up with: how their phenotypes would turn out, in other words.

During a seven-year period leading up to 1863, at exactly the time that Darwin was shaking up society's understanding of inheritance, he hybridised tens of thousands of peas, carefully noting things down like their size and shape, height and colour and discovering over time that there was a strict mathematical ratio to the outcomes.

From this he developed the rules of heredity, now referred to as the Laws of Mendelian Inheritance, in which he deduced that the reproductive material (genes) must come in pairs, and that they're inherited as distinct units from each parent. It was these, he concluded, that produced the future physical manifestations.

Once he had this overall idea, he tracked the segregation of parental units and the appearances they produced in the offspring. In this way he saw through to the mechanism of dominant and recessive traits. He also recognised that different characteristics occur separately from one another, and how this meant that the inheritance of one trait need not necessarily be dependent on the inheritance of another.

'Those traits that pass into hybrid association entirely or almost entirely unchanged, thus themselves representing the traits of the hybrid, are termed dominating and those that become latent in the association, recessive.'
Gregor Mendel, *Experiments in Plant Hybridisation*

Then, for some reason Mendel completely gave up on his research. One story has it that he was told to drop it by a superior; another that he simply got bored. Either way, he published his findings in 1866 to the kind of reception that made Darwin and Wallace's first exposure of natural selection look like a Hollywood opening. No one took the slightest notice and his papers were burnt when he died as part of, of all things, a row about how much tax was due on his estate. It was a further three decades before his work was rediscovered and he was hailed as the 'father of genetics'.

But in spite of Darwin's haziness about the mechanism, what did he and Wallace think were the *effects* of natural selection? What were the 'rules'? There were three they both concluded.

First, that evolution could expand an organism's advantage over the competition in the struggle for existence… but no further.

Secondly, that it couldn't produce any changes that were bad for the organism.

And, thirdly, that it couldn't generate any organ that was useless. How wholly understandable are these explanations - and just how far away is the real meaning of natural selection from the interpretations of 'superiority' so beloved of the pub bore.

So there it is. The whole extraordinary tale of what lies behind every single thing on earth. Of how we've progressed from 'three of four cells floating in a pool of warm water' as Darwin described it and ended up, in the words of his own summary, with: 'One general law, leading to the advancement of all organic things, namely: multiply, vary, let the strongest live and the weakest die.'

Perhaps the last part should give all those politicians and amateur geneticists pause… 'let' he says. Not 'force'.

The prevalence of beneficial traits, he insisted, will increase at the expense of traits that do not confer survivability. Mutations may be random, but the process of natural selection is anything but. It culls all mistakes except those that help. It accumulates advantageous alterations, eventually building vehicles more efficient and complex than what was there before. How beautiful it all is.

But who pulled everything together? Who glued Darwinian principles to the hard maths of Mendel in what has become known as 'the modern synthesis?' This was carried out by a man who's been sometimes described as 'the greatest of Darwin's successors', a genius of a statistician called Sir Ronald Fisher.

In 1930 Fisher published *The Genetical Theory of Natural Selection*, a book that defined the science of population genetics and revitalised the concept of sexual selection. This seminal work included a whole host of extraordinary insights that included: the inverse relationship between the scale of a mutation and the likelihood of it impacting on an organism's fitness, the critical role of parental care, the need for signalling in selecting a reproductive mate, the reasons populations tend to end up with equal males and females, and a whole host of other things that we now take for granted. It's hardly surprising that the book's been called the 'natural successor to *On the Origin of Species.*'

It was also Fisher who spotted that natural selection was leading to exactly the same outcomes that the 2nd Law of Thermodynamics does in life. Death uses the mechanism of inheritance to lead to more complex, better fitted life as a survival strategy, he wrote, every bit as much as the 2nd Law ensures that the certainty of entropy makes everything exploit order wherever it can. In this sense, he concluded, natural selection: '… should hold the supreme position among the biological sciences.'

'Elegant in its simplicity, so far-reaching in its implications, today
we regard Darwin's theory of evolution by natural selection as one
of the fundamental rules underpinning the world as we know it.'
Steve Brusatte, *The Rise and Fall of Dinosaurs*

But it's just possible you're still musing on one of the great arguments against Darwin's Big Idea; the one put so ruthlessly by Captain FitzRoy: Where are the stages? Ah now, it turns out that the multitude of researchers that came after him have, indeed, done Darwin proud because, bit by bit, they've found the evidence.

In a scientific field that's been crawled over time and again to find just one aberration in the fossil record, one example of something in the wrong order, none have ever come to light. But what, so many people ask, about astonishingly complicated functions rather than morphology? What, for example, about sight? Doesn't the extraordinary mechanism of the human eye simply cry out as proof of creative design?

'If it could be demonstrated that any complex organ existed, which could not
possibly have been formed by numerous successive, slight modifications, then
my theory would absolutely break down. But I can find no such case.'
Charles Darwin, *On the Origin of Species*

Yet it seems that all the evolutionary stages are accounted for, and all of them make sense. Primitive eyes can be seen throughout the animal kingdom, and even plants will turn towards the Sun. Some creatures have light sensitive sections on their skin at the bottom of indentations in their cell walls. Mucus in the wall itself can then harden to form a rudimentary lens.

Give it a few million years and enough positive selection and you've got yourself the unreal abilities of a raptor. Compared to these extraordinary creatures with their binocular vision, night enhancement and staggering powers of triangulation, it's us humans who could be said to have 'half sight'. After all, researchers have found that certain hawks can spot the movement of a small rodent at a distance of over a mile, while the latest statistics record that 61% of us poor humans need some kind of vision aid like spectacles.

**'A totally blind process can by definition lead to
anything; it can even lead to vision itself.'
Jacques Monod, *Chance and Necessity***

Then again, snails could be said to have a halfway house on the road to a fully formed eye, but even their basic equipment does the job well enough to keep the little things safe and for them to flourish.

Yet, in spite of all the trawling by biologists and evolutionary theorists, looking for flaws in the theory, this 'half stage' objection remains the most commonly quoted when general discussions about natural selection crop up. But, as Richard Dawkins rather crossly put it: 'There is no refutation of Darwinian evolution in existence. If a refutation ever were to come about, it would come from a scientist, not an idiot.'

**'One of my little boys Horace, said to me, 'there are a terrible number of adders here;
but if everyone killed as many as they could, they would sting less' - I answered
'of course they would be fewer' Horace 'Of course, but I did not mean that; what
I meant was, that the more timid adders, which run away and do not sting
would be saved, and after a time none of the adders would sting' - Natural selection!!'
Charles Darwin, *In a letter to Asa Gray***

Is that it then? Is this how 'decisions' get made and how life ended up with everything, the cocker spaniel, the Virginia creeper, five million different species of fungi... and us?

No, it is not, it's just part of the story. Sure, natural selection makes new things... but then what? How do they work? Are they right for what's needed to prosper in their surroundings and competition? How do they then behave so they can 'win'?

Perhaps the last words should go to someone who is going to play a big part in the next stage of the story, the evolutionary theorist Lynn Margulis. As she put it: 'All scientists agree that evolution has occurred - that all life comes from a common ancestry, that there has been extinction, and that new taxa, new biological groups, have arisen. The question is, is natural selection enough to explain evolution? Is it the driver of evolution?'

A good question.

                                        The Secrets of Life - Book One

Eugenics. The wrong way.

CHAPTER FIFTEEN

COULD LYNN MARGULIS HAVE BEEN RIGHT IN SAYING THAT NATURAL SELECTION ALONE WASN'T ENOUGH TO EXPLAIN EVOLUTION? BUT WHO WAS SHE AND WHAT DID SHE MEAN? AND IF SHE AND OTHER PEOPLE WITH SIMILAR VIEWS WERE CORRECT, WHAT ARE NOW REGARDED AS SOME OF THE OTHER MAJOR DRIVERS OF EVOLUTIONARY CHANGE?

When Darwin's great theory first appeared there were, unsurprisingly, many in the Victorian public who were pretty uncomfortable about the 'descended from the apes' bit of the story. That wasn't the least of it either, as large sections of society weren't entirely happy with the idea that God was no longer responsible for saying what went where in life.

But at a time when most prevailing social beliefs were being shaped by the success of the British Empire, the way that the global order was shaking itself down into tiers and classes, and winners and losers, seemed to have its roots in a kind of Darwinian reasoning.

After all, commentators began saying, wasn't Britain and its people, together with their ways of dispensing laws and ethics, showing the world that their version of civilisation was producing the fittest people? Couldn't they be said to be improving the 'backward' in their own image with education and training, even with those muscular ball games of theirs? And anyway, wasn't there a necessary public debate to be had about how to restrict the 'downward pull of the underclass and their hectic, Malthusian breeding habits?'

'The perpetual tendency of the race of man to increase beyond the means of subsistence is one of the general laws of animated nature, which we can have no reason to expect to change.'
Thomas Malthus, *An Essay on The Principle of Population*

Darwin's mild and humane character made him largely duck these kinds of absurd interpretations and, in his own way, he tried to resist what was becoming a climate of grim pessimism about the drag effect of 'lesser beings' and 'lower orders'. At its ugliest, he must have been concerned to see how this new sort of social thinking was leading people towards interpreting natural selection in human terms. Then - as now - one would hear interpretations of his theory in which fitness was linked to 'social success', strength to 'superiority', and progress with 'civilisation'.

One of the most worrying of the human interpretation brigade was Darwin's own cousin, an exceptionally brilliant polymath called Francis Galton. Born in 1822, Galton was one of those child prodigies who were translating Sophocles at Cambridge before they'd lost their milk teeth. And although he was principally a mathematician, it was in the new field of statistical research that his ground-breaking work had first been conducted.

He'd become fascinated by what kinds of backgrounds were likely to produce great geniuses (like himself!) and he began to question whether Darwin's theories meant that there wasn't a place for what was later termed 'genetic determinism' in which controlled breeding programmes could encourage 'fitter' humans.

Galton thought that there might be a role for introducing some kind of ranking mechanism that awarded high achieving families with merit points. Once they'd pocketed a good score, it would allow superior people like themselves to breed with other superior people, and before long the world would end up with a whole bunch of the Darwin/ Wedgwood/ Galton-style pedigrees that he himself was lucky enough to be a part of.

By measuring certain human traits to establish supremacy, went his logic, it might be possible to match up the desirable qualities and cut out the unwelcome - a process he called 'eugenics' - meaning 'good stock, or kin'. After all, he said as he was coining the phrase 'nature versus nurture', surely it was plain that polishing the product of natural selection with good manners and education would never produce the degrees of improvement that one could achieve by sexually combining the 'inborn qualities of a race'? Wasn't this exactly what Cousin Charles had explained about animal breeding in one of the chapters in the *Origin* entitled 'Variation under Domestication'? Why couldn't human ability be measured and made to become equally heritable?

'Had neither Daewin nor Wallace existed, someone else would have come up with a similar theory; many practical people, whether pigeon fanciers, or dog breeders, already understood the practical principles quite well.'
Rory Sutherland, *This idea Is Brilliant*

Well, we all know where that led. If you could breed better humans, claimed Galton's disciples, then it was a hop, skip and a jump to getting rid of the duff ones. Why not, they said, manipulate the 'inferior classes' into subjugation, reduction or even extinction? From small beginnings, and doubtless good intentions, the road to hell rose up… and over the next sixty or seventy years the eugenics movement became an increasingly accepted aspect of social planning. And increasingly vicious.

Throughout the 1920s and 1930s it was, surprisingly, the supposedly humane Scandinavian countries that led the world in enacting sterilisation laws. A bill to do the same thing in the UK was put before Parliament in 1931 - although thankfully it failed to pass. But other countries were less squeamish, and by 1938 an astonishing thirty-three American states had introduced compulsory sterilisation laws that covered certain categories of mental and physical disability.

The Nazis went even further, of course, and when their atrocities were finally exposed, eugenics was consigned to the dustbin of history and every piece of worldwide legislation was repealed. But why should the swing have been so far in the other direction, some people continued to ask? If a savage animal like the Arctic fox could be turned into a family pet in only thirty-five generations, why couldn't we improve the human race with similar breeding approaches?

The answer is more obvious to us now than it would have been when Darwin's maxim of 'let' rather than 'force' in his explanation of natural selection was being overlooked. Even fifty years ago, scientists had no real understanding of the gene-based theory of evolution, nor an appreciation of how the gene did its job. Certainly no one was thinking about it as if it had some kind of strategic motivation. Yet without the random influence of genetic recombination, we now know, we would never have the diversity that leads to speciation.

This is particularly true of the human race. Eugenicists and top-down 'men of system' will always imagine that they can manipulate society by influencing the breeding process. But the true glory of *H. sapiens* is that there's never a way of predicting what extraordinary people life will suddenly introduce, even in the most troubled of circumstances. No one can plan for it, and even individuals born with the most unpromising of backgrounds and parentage can turn out to be precisely what could be right for society's needs. As the wonderful line on Sylvia Plath's headstone from the Ming folk tale, *Monkey* puts it: 'Even in the midst of fierce flames, the Golden Lotus may be planted.'

Personally, I've always been moved by the legendary (but, sadly, probably fictional) story of the two great physicians discussing the merits of prescribed abortion. To shape their discussion, they're using various examples to find where the lines might lie between the rights of the individual, medical dangers, societal protection and general morality.

'Let me put another case to you', says the first. 'The father is syphilitic and the mother's consumptive. Their first child was born deaf. The second was deaf and blind. The third died after a few days, and the fourth is tubercular, probably fatally so. The mother is pregnant again. What would you recommend?'

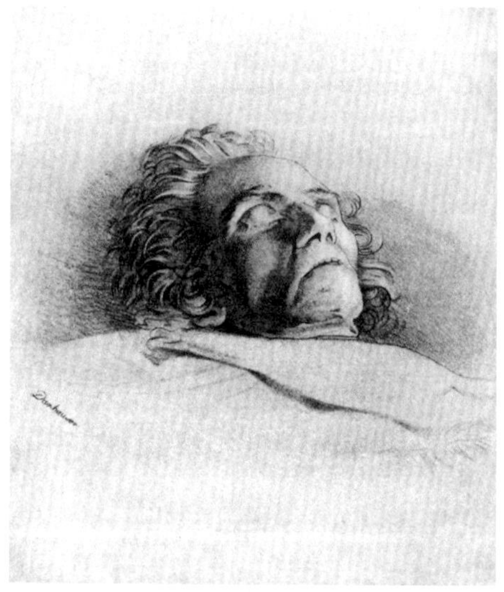

'I shall hear in heaven.'

'She should have a termination as soon as possible', says the other, hotly. 'You cannot bring another child like this into the world.'

'Yes, I agree with your logic', replies the first. 'Your conclusion is admirable. The only trouble is… you've just killed Beethoven.'

But although the reasoning that led to eugenics might now make us shudder, it can still be dispiriting to recognise how deeply its underlying beliefs have lodged in us. Even after biologists have given us our modern insights into the role of the gene, it's not that rare to hear people insisting that organisms behave as if nothing matters other than a hideous and never-ending fight to the death.

These views make people look at our interconnected world, in which species and individuals coexist and press in on each other, ruthlessly taking one another's energy by eating their neighbours, and all they can see is the Hobbesian vision of *'bellum omnium contra omnes'* - a war of all against all.

Frequently, they'll then shake their heads and repeat Tennyson's line that Nature is 'red in tooth and claw', and that life is nothing but an eternal struggle. It's also one, they then say, that we humans continue to act out in our dealings with each other. 'Kill or be killed' they mutter sagely - that must be the axiom of the successful. Surely, it has to be the guiding principle if one's to stand a chance in the rat race?

Yet we now know that recent scientific findings insist that this is a superficial observation of the way life works. Yes, organisms may see each other as food sources and they certainly display no sentimentality when it comes to following their instincts about survival. The 1st Law directs everything to grab each other's ordered energy, and non-human life cycles very clearly depend on this. 'Nature is one big restaurant' as Woody Allen put it. And yes, too, we must accept that every single living thing is programmed for self-preservation so that it can then reproduce - and that to achieve this aim, organisms must constantly win against their competition.

But what Darwin, Wallace, Fisher or even some of their successors could never have guessed, is that the strategies to achieve this all stem from something they were unaware of - an understanding of the mechanism of self-replicating molecules and the subsequent role of the gene. It is the exposure of the gene-based theory that now allows us to see evolution as the gigantic interaction of organisms acting as the survival mechanism for life itself… not its vehicles.

This is the mechanism that ensures that *something* survives. Whatever happens to environmental conditions on earth, it is the gene rather than individual life forms that shows how to win in life. What lies behind the clarity of this inference, is that it's the *interaction* of the different strategies that species adopt that means that life itself will win through.

The inescapable conclusion that evolutionary biologists have now given us is that it is the continuous and inevitable failure of living things - both individuals and species - that is the key to understanding the continuing success of our existence on earth. Vehicles may be temporary, says the gene, but that means life will be permanent.

One of the most important of the visionaries who was to see through the vast mix of different organisms, living and extinct, and showed that there were discernible patterns of behaviour within it all, was an extraordinary scientific rebel called Lynn Margulis.

Margulis was an evolutionary theorist, married to the great astrophysicist, Carl Sagan, (you can imagine the idle chatter round *that* breakfast table) who made herself unpopular in the 1960s and 1970s by claiming there was more than just the Darwinian explanation of competition and genetic mutations that were leading to new species. 'Natural selection', she would repeatedly say, 'eliminates and maybe maintains, but it doesn't create.'

What was also critical, according to her, was the potential for two, or even more, quite separate lineages to merge together to bring about a wholly new organism. As she put it: 'If you really want to study evolution, you've got to go outside sometime, because you'll see symbioses everywhere.'

She claimed this process led to what she called endosymbiosis. According to her theories, one life form had merged with another at different points in the Earth's history, and in doing so had created entirely new lines. In the shorthand this book has been using, she said that 1+1 had made 3. In saying this, she distinguished between the biological and chemical actions of these mergers, and what's more widely known as ectosymbiosis. This is a different mechanism that takes place *outside* of organisms and not within them, and which is the process by which different things cooperate in life to find mutual benefits.

The core of her hypothesis for endosymbiosis was that life had sometimes evolved through things getting together - whether by accident or design - and the greatest proofs of this, she claimed, were the ones she used in her 1970 book *On the Origin of Eukaryotic Cells*. In this she showed what I tried to describe earlier: that the cells that accounted for the starting point of all complex life forms derived from two separate, single celled, bacteria-like creatures that had symbiotically merged to form the eukaryote cell of our common ancestry.

'With cells and genetic material of different species merging and genes continually duplicating and repurposing, life's history flows more like a braided and meandering river than a straight channel.'
Neil Shubin, *Some Assembly Required*

The idea was met with considerable resistance at the time and it wasn't until some years later that she was vindicated when DNA was found in mitochondria. Once researchers knew what they were looking for, other examples of endosymbiosis were then exposed, such as the chloroplasts that provide photosynthesis in plant life, or how nitrogen-fixing bacteria lived in the roots of pulses.

What does this all mean? At base it's nothing but another example of how the 'war of all against all' view of life is profoundly flawed. Lynn Margulis's explanations showed the reverse - of how the ability of things to form endosymbiotic relationships was a major driving force in evolution. This was because it explained how genetic variation could also arise from the *transfer of nuclear information* during this kind of collaborative action.

As the evidence built, however, it became clear that a far bigger principle had been at work throughout the entirety of evolution. This was because symbioses, whether within their biochemistry or between different organisms, gave a new insight into understanding how the entire superstew of living things coexist. And, just as importantly, how this process leads to their success or failure.

Not only was evolutionary pressure making things occupy every conceivable ecological niche possible, Margulis and other biologists were now saying, but there was also a process going on that was deciding how they should then *behave* towards each other.

'The view of evolution as a chronic bloody competition among individuals and species, a popular distortion of Darwin's notion of 'survival of the fittest,' dissolves before a new view of continual cooperation, strong interaction, and mutual dependence among life forms. Life did not take over the globe by combat, but by networking. Life forms multiplied and complexified by co-opting others, not just by killing them.'
Lynn Margulis, *Microcosmos: Four Billion Years of Evolution from Our Microbial Ancestors*

How does all this work? It happens because there are a large number of components meshing together in the shape-changing machine of life that will collectively decide what does well or badly, and what factors increase or decrease an organism's fitness.

But behind all this, it is the action of the gene that can be seen as the trigger for the process. At its heart is the paradox of its function, because the way the gene's incredible replication ability works in one direction is being constantly counteracted by its inbuilt error-making production line pulling in another. This is what makes the gene's results so stable, and yet also so periodically inventive. It's a two-way action that produces both consistency in the species, and yet the ever-present possibility of mutational variations to the genotype.

It's at this point that the environment then comes into play. This is because the strategies that genotypes harness to survive within an environment refine a species' phenotype and its behaviour. This behaviour will decide how something interacts with the things around it, how it can protect itself against them, and how it can benefit from their presence.

Where does all this end up? It inevitably leads, first, to different species having different kinds of physical approaches that help them do well in different kinds of environmental conditions. And secondly, it leads to behavioural strategies that are going to maximise a life form's chances of coexisting with other organisms. This is largely how natural selection results in the creation of ecological niches.

'Natural selection involves no plan, no goal and no direction - just genes increasing and decreasing in frequency depending on whether individuals with those genes have, relative to other individuals, greater or lesser reproductive success.'
Rudolph Nesse, *Why We Get Sick*

What kind of behavioural strategies? Well, being predatory, for example, something that's seen when organisms simply live off others, grabbing their energy by eating them, or stealing their habitats. This is a way of living that suggests that everything is trying to win by beating everything else, rather like a huge crowd of people that have fallen in the sea and are frantically trying to stay alive by desperately snatching at each other. The end result? Some might survive but most will drown.

Or are organisms trying to find another way of surviving? By cooperating with each other? In doing this, perhaps they're attempting to create the sort of 1+1=3 solutions that the long history of life has shown can lead to breakthroughs? Instead of drowning each other in a frenzy of selfishness, suggests this approach, living things would be working together to build rafts. Yes, energy is spent helping others, *but in the end everyone benefits because the entire community wins.*

Now, if you were the gene (and to remind you, your job is to find a way of keeping life going in a world in which the 2nd Law of Thermodynamics is making everything fall apart) you'd want to introduce an endless and hugely diverse number of organisms, behaving in a wide range of strategies. Only by doing this can you build all the millions of safety nets you reckon are needed for life to survive the random lurches that come along when environmental conditions change.

Have you succeeded? Yes, you very largely have… the world is not only full of things designed to create every conceivable niche possible, but you're also using a range of behavioural strategies so that organisms use other life forms to help their survival.

**'Of course, genes can't pull the levers of behaviour directly.
But they affect the wiring and workings of the brain, and the brain
is the seat of drives, temperaments and patterns of thought.'**
Steven Pinker, *The Blank Slate*

But surely, you're probably saying, this process has got to be complete by now? There can't be that many niches, or even strategies, that are left unexplored? You'd be surprised. No, of course there's unlikely to be an undiscovered valley in the Andes where sabre-toothed antelopes roam free, and flying tortoises are sucking nectar from colossal peonies. Larger organisms take a very long time to evolve, and the chances of finding a few that biologists don't know about are slim. But there are any number of smaller creatures, many of them insects, that are discovered each year, and more still are constantly being generated by evolutionary pressure.

As an example, you'd think that a tidy English garden would be the last place to find anything new. Yet a retired zoologist named Jennifer Owen spent thirty years seeing how many different species she could find in her small, well-kept garden in a suburb of Leicester. Extraordinarily, she found a total of 2,673 species of flora and fauna in under a quarter of an acre, that included 80 different types of spider, 375 kinds of moth, 442 species of beetle - and 529 species of parasitic wasp of which fifteen were previously not thought to exist in the UK… and four were entirely undescribed species.

But where are these new lines coming from, and why? They're arriving as a result of decisions - actions that are being taken by organisms as the consequence of evolutionary effects. Some of these are coming about because things might be trying to generate niches, some are because decisions are being taken that result in 'fitter' organisms occurring when challenged by deviant mutations, and some are emerging because different life forms are reacting to changes in the environment. And then there are some that are finding a better way of doing things, a more productive form of behaviour in other words.

But what are these different behavioural strategies? What are the different ways of dealing with each other - of creating and benefitting from symbioses?

**The emerald cockroach wasp. Not very nice...
but incredibly creative.**

CHAPTER SIXTEEN

DO ORGANISMS REALLY MAKE 'DECISIONS' ABOUT HOW THEY'RE GOING TO BEHAVE? AND, IF SO, WHAT ARE THE BENEFITS OF THE DIFFERENT STRATEGIES THEY'VE ARRIVED AT?

The profound schism between the selfishness of a zero sum 'fighting each other to avoid drowning' approach, and the cooperative, non-zero 'communal raft building' instinct has already cropped up a couple of times in this book. And, with this come the bigger questions about why living things should choose a behavioural strategy at all.

To begin with, it's always been plain that life was built by organisms taking energy from something else. This was how they coped with the 1st Law. But life had also evolved by incentiving vehicles to share tasks, divide labour, and by doing this, to create surplus energy. The benefits of having different kinds of symbioses might therefore have been obvious, but what were the different ways of achieving them? If living things have always tried to find associations that got the most out of their coexistence, then where did these strategies end up?

Well, at its most stripped down, one can pretty quickly arrive at a decision spectrum that would look something like this:

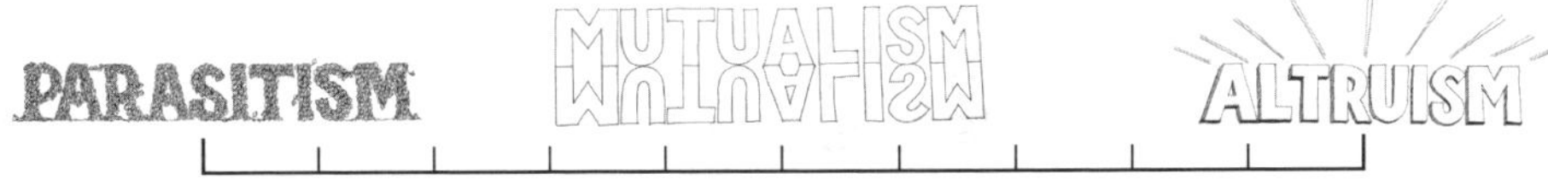

The Behavioural Spectrum of life.

Why doesn't everything behave in the same way, though? Why do organisms choose to adopt so many different positions, slicing and dicing their approaches on what might be called the Behavioural Spectrum of life? If they're all trying to arrive at an optimal survival strategy, then what made them invent so many different tactics for overcoming the problems posed by the Laws of Thermodynamics?

In looking at the Spectrum, it's plain that strategies range from the energy grabbers at one end who are parasitic or predatory, while down the opposing pole are species that are prepared to sacrifice themselves in some way to help others, particularly those from within the same colony.

And it's a Spectrum that is evident everywhere one looks. As an example, even at the microbial level, life is a series of checks and balances, thrusts and parries, as the parasitic actions of viruses and the defensive strategies of bacteria - including giving up their lives - dance together in an endless process of ensuring that nothing ever succeeds to the exclusion of others. In this, as in everything else, having organisms win or lose are secondary to the gene's intentions.

And in the middle of the Spectrum? Mutualism?

That represents the position where symbiotic organisms could be said to be in some kind of equally rewarding relationship. Both of them would be benefitting from the involvement of the other, either entirely relying on them for their existence, or partially if they're able to survive without them - but are greatly diminished if they don't have their help.

Many of us would probably have thought of this as what 'symbiotic' actually means, but biologists use the term far more widely. Their perception is that if an organism gets any kind of benefit from combining with another, then it's behaving symbiotically - even if one of the organisms might be acquiring what appears to be a *disproportionate* share of the gains compared to the other.

Set against this, however, is the belief that although asymmetric benefits can still suit both parties, there's frequently a latent tension, and even the risk of revenge, as the underdog tries to get a bigger slice of the outcomes.

Indeed, many microbiologists believe that this even takes place at a cellular level. As I think I said before, there are theories that certain illnesses could well have their origin in the ancient squabbles between the nucleus and the mitochondria as they coexist in eukaryotic cells.

Isn't this all very familiar to our own world? Doesn't it reflect exactly how humans behave towards each other in our own lives? Many of our problems seem to stem from wanting to gain from relationships - and yet we so often have the nagging anxiety that we're being taken advantage of. Immanuel Kant saw through to the profound tension we have in dealing with others when he said that we 'cannot bear them, but we cannot bear to leave'.

Do we humans have a similar Behavioural Spectrum? Clearly we do. We tend to use the word 'parasitic' as an insult, but we openly acknowledge that we also have snatchers and takers in our societies every bit as much as the nicer types. We have our own terms for them, of course, such as 'sociopathic', or the slightly more salty 'utter bastard' to describe one pole, and then descriptions like altruistic, self-sacrificing or saintly at the other.

But more to the point, where we depart from other organisms is that *we humans have evolved the ability to slide easily up and down the Spectrum*. Unlike other living things we don't stay in an ecological niche, just one position, but instead we adapt, bluff, dissemble and generally hop around, changing where we are in a second. We can be one thing one moment, and something entirely different the next.

It's a uniquely human ability. It's what makes us so brilliant at surviving and yet it's also what makes us so frustratingly difficult to understand.

Other organisms in the natural world can't do this. They've largely evolved to 'decide' on their niche, and then they stick with it. If they do make a change, it takes a hugely lengthy time for mutations to bring it about - rather than the microseconds with which we flit around.

'Contemporary biologists in general do not believe that behaviour evolved for a greater good. They assume that if bats, bees, dolphins, and other animals help one another, there must be benefits for each and every participant or their kin, otherwise the trait would not have spread.'

Frans de Waal. *Good Natured. The Origins of Right and Wrong in Humans and Animals*

We're also tricky when it comes to our behaviour because we overlay emotions and morality on top of our decisions. We endlessly argue with each other, and ourselves, about what the 'right thing to do' is.

None of the world's other living things are bothered by these questions. They don't adopt life strategies on the basis of thoughts or feelings. Instead, they evolve their niches as ways of surviving in the superstew of life forms… all of which are equally out for themselves. Perhaps this is one of the reasons why so many people say they prefer animals to humans - because they're so much easier to predict?

So what are some examples of these positions? And what do they tell us about how the millions of organisms on earth have managed to remain in balance… and why nothing ever wins forever?

Perhaps the most engrossing place to start is at the parasitic end of the Spectrum. As in our own lives, of course, it's an extremely seductive idea to simply let others do all the work, have them arrive at energy and order, and then to simply snaffle up what they've done. In evolutionary terms one can therefore see the attraction of being at the zero sum, selfish end because it's the simplest way of beating the competition. Even the term parasite comes from the Latin expression for 'eating at the table of another.'

But surely there are gigantic risks involved in the strategy?

After all, if something is actively reducing its food source, but without doing anything to ensure its continued supply, then it would suggest a high degree of uncertainty about whether the host organisms are going to run out. Kill too many of them, in short, and you'll kill yourselves. And yet the idea must work because there are *more* parasitic species than any other grouping

The reason for this is that even within the term 'parasitic' biologists have drawn up a further scale that's defined by varying levels of 'virulence', depending on how much things dominate and take from other organisms. The most extreme version of this are the parasitoids - who always kill their host - while down the cosier end of the scale are many others who'll keep their hosts alive, and sometimes even reward them with benefits.

What's the difference between a parasitoid and a predator, you might ask? After all, a lion doesn't exactly keep a lamb in great health when it gets hold of it. Not much, is the answer, as both kill for their food, but the difference is that predators feed off multiple prey while these kinds of parasites have evolved to only target a single organism.

On the 'yuk to cuddly' scale, parasitoids are generally so horrid that even Darwin said his faith in God was eroded by looking at them. There are even - in one of the most astonishing examples of how life forms will find even the tiniest of life's niches - parasitoids that feed on other parasitoids.

‘I cannot persuade myself that a beneficent and omnipotent God would have designedly created the Ichneumonidæ [parasitic wasps] with the

The Secrets of Life - Book One

One of the most noted examples of how extreme this approach can be (and also of the almost infinite adaptability of Nature) is arguably the emerald cockroach wasp. This little beauty has so refined its methods that it can make the most talented of brain surgeons look like a blundering oaf. What happens is that when the wasp has selected a victim, it initially injects a tiny area of the cockroach's nerve clusters, and this has the effect of paralysing its front legs.

The wasp now has to move fast. It only has about three minutes before the Mickey Finn wears off. But this is enough time for it to nip up onto the cockroach's back and to find the exact spot on its head where it can give it an injection of toxins, targeting precisely the ganglia that control the doped thing's escape reflexes. This second shot makes it relax, and then to start grooming itself: a process that releases all sorts of good chemicals that the wasp's offspring are going to use as nutrients.

The wasp then chews off a portion of the roach's antennae to control the amount of venom it's going to receive, before it leads the now-addled insect into its burrow, rather like a child with a docile bull at an agricultural show. The analogy isn't that far from the truth as the cockroach is about six times the size of its tormentor.

Once it's stuck the poor thing in the burrow's entrance, the wasp then piles stones up to close it. It's at this point, I'm sorry to say, that it lays an egg in its new best friend's abdomen. In time, larvae will hatch, ready programmed with instincts to feed on the cockroach's organs in exactly the right order to provide fresh meat for themselves - while still keeping the host alive, at least for a time.

Nice, huh? A science-fiction nightmare?

Maybe, but among our appalled sensibilities, there also has to be an equal measure of admiration for the precision of the operation that makes all this possible. Just how long must the evolutionary process have been experimenting to have arrived at such an extraordinary outcome?

And how many errors must there have been along the way? 'Natural selection is a mechanism for generating an exceedingly high degree of improbability', Sir Ronald Fisher wrote in his synthesis, and who could disagree with him when you read examples like this.

But what, you're no doubt wondering, could a parasitoid's host possibly get out of this grisly relationship? How can being eaten alive conceivably be described as symbiotic? Well, it couldn't, of course, for the *individual* cockroach, but it certainly could for those members of its species who avoid the awful fate.

That's because the threat of the wasp's attacks keeps competitors out of the cockroach's niche, and in that sense the individual is behaving altruistically for its colony because by 'sacrificing' itself, it's acting to the great benefit of others. If the action of the gene can make Nature pull off stunts of this level of complexity, you can only stand back and admire its creativity.

Parasites that have the power to control their host's behaviour may be terrifying to the imagination, but they're also critical to the balance of life. They keep the population of competitors down, they check pests, they control other parasites, and they provide a constant challenge to make sure that nothing wins for long.

And as with everything else, they're also carrying out the gene's intentions. They're doing this by hurrying up death, getting out new generations, testing an organism's fitness, and by then by returning the whole shebang of nutrients to the food chain as they recycle their host's energy.

So hats off to them I suppose, even the very names of things at this end of the Spectrum make one shudder at the ruthlessness with which they carry out their tasks. The emerald cockroach wasp may be a natural born killer but it sounds quite stylish compared to others like the zombie ant fungus, the spined assassin bug, the kamikaze horsehair worm, the green-banded broodsac, or - one to make us men go quiet - the castrator barnacle.

'Parasitism evolves and moves through any system... The less variation there is in a system, the more readily parasites will evolve to infest it.'
Daniel Suarez, *Daemon*

Moving a little up the Spectrum and one sees parasitic cunning passing beyond the brutality of parasitoids. Now things really start to manipulate their host's behaviour. There are some, for example, that have two separate hosts, each of which performs a different function in its life cycle. One of the best known of these is a single-celled eukaryotic organism whose ultimate ambition is to end up in a cat's stomach, because this is where it reproduces.

But how to get there? Ha, by first planting itself in the brain of a rat or a mouse - and then playing around with its neurological wiring so the poor thing becomes programmed to now adore the smell of cat urine. This makes it come out of hiding and try to snuggle up with its furry enemy. Fairly predictably, the cat eats it… and the parasite gets its wish.

In the same way, the viral parasite that causes rabies makes its victims go wild, biting and scratching people to open up wounds so the terrible condition can be passed on.

Even the early stages of the flu virus, amazingly, makes infected people want to socialise rather than stay at home. In doing this the virus is somehow manipulating its host's brain to want to mingle with others, and therefore to pass on the illness to a whole new bunch of potential victims.

Progressing still further up the Spectrum leads to parasites that don't kill their hosts, but instead succeed by keeping them alive.

As they do this, the parasites are reducing the fitness of their host while increasing their own. In this way they're exploiting the 1st Law by taking in ordered energy, but they are also allowing their symbiotic partners to continue to live and therefore generate further energy that they'll consume later. Biologists have termed this position as 'optimal virulence' although, within it, there's a further, extensive scale that runs from the violent aggression of waterborne diseases like cholera and dengue fever, right up to the way many minor irritants act parasitically, but represent only a mild threat to the host's life.

As with viruses, pathogens and bacteria, the relationship between parasites and their hosts is rarely ever truly 'good' or totally 'bad'. As far as the gene is concerned, each party is reliant on the other in an endless struggle for ecological success. In doing this the process is reducing the risk of anything 'winning', and yet it's providing the creative tension that can produce mutations, new biochemistry and novel species.

That gene, eh? It sure is clever.

The position on the Spectrum of *not* killing, or even severely undermining the host, would seem to be far more understandable than flat-out parasitoidism. That's because the parasite now has a continual source of nutrients available to it without having to risk its host being killed or even diminished - or having to move on to find another one when it dies. That is, unless it wants to.

And oddly enough, that's exactly how some of them exist: reproducing in one - what's called the primary host - before moving on to have various stages of development in a second. Biologists call these 'trophically transmitted' parasites and the journey from one to the other usually happens when the second of them eats the first - and the parasite goes long for the ride. Just as in the rat and cat horror show, it frequently even plays a role in making this happen.

As another example, there's a particularly nasty flatworm that lives in a snail's body and then travels up through its head and into the eyestalk. Once there its biochemistry changes so that it starts flashing like a ship's hazard light. This attracts birds, who peck it off, and away goes the worm to a cosy new home, where it reproduces and waits to be excreted, then eaten by another snail, at which point the cycle starts all over again.

There's even a subset of these double dealers called 'vector transmitted' parasites who sometimes rely on a third party to carry them from one host to another.

But why did parasites arise? And how did they get to be so clever? Well, I mentioned earlier how ancient their origins are, and how errors in the early self-replicating molecules saw bits break off and form the ancestors of present-day viruses. Ever since then, parasites have been the constant companion of every single organism: the ying to the natural world's yang.

They sometimes even share in the host's evolutionary history, branching off their main genetic lines at the same time as they do, in a process known as co-speciation. And if there's an organism without parasites, then science is yet to find it. When palaeontologists examined the skulls of the mighty *Tyrannosaurus Rex*, for instance, they discovered how they must have been plagued by nasty little fellas living in their heads, boring holes to eat their brains. No wonder they were always in such a bad mood.

But doesn't letting something else do all the work and then living off its efforts have to be a clever way to exist?

Only up to a point it appears, and parasites frequently have to watch their step in evolutionary terms. That's because the elaborate dance that's taking place between them and their hosts depends on a very finely balanced arrangement.

Too great a virulence might be a seductive way of increasing fitness, for example, but the price of doing this could be faster host elimination, and therefore the loss of the parasite's energy source. And the problems of transmission, of course, can mean that parasites have to spare the host long enough so they can find a new home.

Too slight a virulence, on the other hand, can lead to the danger of victims finding a mutation that confers resistance to the parasitic invasion. The equilibrium point is elusive, and the endless attempts to find it are yet another reason for mutations.

One common feature of parasites, however, is that they tend to reproduce faster than their hosts. This means that, over time, the interaction of one on the other usually has a major effect on the pace of evolutionary change. And as life became more complex with the emergence of multicellular organisms, so new positions began to be exploited further up the Spectrum towards what biologists have termed 'commensalism'.

This was the outcome that would take place when successful parasites not only didn't kill their hosts, but the relationship between the two progressed to the point where one now did the other *no harm*, but nor was it helped by the process. This arrangement is very often found in those cases where there are two or even more hosts.

As with organisms evolving their niches to find a degree of security, parasites have endlessly refined their actions throughout evolutionary history in breathtakingly creative ways. Nothing is too sacred. If parasites can live off something, they'll develop a strategy to fit the job. They manage to extract life out of pretty well anything, coming up with a bewildering array of tactics that might use mimicry, aggression, theft, cheating or even modifying their host's behaviour. They can even make them lose some of their traits.

'But if they're so successful, why haven't parasites taken over the world?
The answer is simple: they have. We just haven't noticed. That's because
successful parasites don't kill us; they become part of us, making us perform
all the work to keep them alive and help them reproduce."
Daniel Suarez, *Daemon*

If animals, insects and microbes are examples of the parasitic black arts, then so too are plants and fungi. Some of the most successful strategies see things modifying their host plant's roots, penetrating into their conductive systems and sucking out nutrients and water.

The honey fungus, for example, has to be the uncrowned champion of this, rampaging through such a wide range of plants that a vast and ancient example in Oregon is now recognised as the largest life form on earth. It's grown so huge that it now measures roughly two miles square as it takes energy from neighbouring trees and large shrubs, feeding on the dead wood and consuming the remains saprophytically before moving on. You thought the blue whale was the largest organism? Pah, small beer. This honey fungus monster is thousands of times bigger.

But if evolutionary pressures have made parasites creative, their skills are often matched by the ingenuity of the host's defences. Among these in animal life are physical barriers that block them from entering, such as dry skin or the secretion of toxic chemicals. Some potential hosts even thicken their coatings, or attempt to bat parasites away with body parts such as eyelashes or tails. Others might hose down vulnerable areas with killer enzymes.

There are also any number of cellular and intracellular alarm systems to stop them. These include antibodies, receptors and other tactics of the immune system. The battle isn't entirely one-sided by any means, and the pushing and shoving of invasion and defence is yet another example of the ways in which behaviour acts on fitness - and therefore on the underlying direction of natural selection.

What came after commensalism on the Spectrum? Did the gene rest on its oars once apparently harmful spongers appeared to be neutralised by coexistence?

Hardly. Instead, it led parasites to have such important ecological roles that organisms eventually came up with the invention of sexual reproduction, a mechanism that could speed up novelty in hosts that gave rise to the so-called Red Queen hypothesis. Without this need, creating new life was unlikely to have ever progressed beyond the safe waters of asexual methods.

Yet with the invention of reproduction that involved two sets of genetic material, diversity shot forward and mutations flourished. And natural selection created yet more strategies for life. Genius.

> **'The most wonderful mystery of life may well be the means by which**
> **it created so much diversity from so little physical matter. The biosphere,**
> **all organisms combined, make up about one part in ten billion of**
> **the earth's mass... Yet life has divided into millions of species, the fundamental**
> **units, each playing a unique role in relation to the whole.'**
> **EO Wilson, *The Diversity of Life***

So, what did the gene do next to maximise the role of parasites? If the strategies so far had moved from 'always killing the host' to 'living with it without causing any harm', the great fandango of coexistence now seemed to realise that there could be even more gains if the parasite offered the host some *benefits*.

In doing this life yet again appeared to be searching for the 1+1=3 mechanism that had supercharged the development of so many of its vehicles. In other words, the gene was incentivised to stimulate relationships that could be of mutual benefit... in short, to be *mutualistic*.

But hold on. If the key compulsion in life is to use all one's energies to survive, then why on earth should some organisms actually help others?

What could possibly be in it for them?

A small cleaner fish servicing another species on a coral reef.
An example of Nature refusing to be red in tooth and claw.

CHAPTER SEVENTEEN

IN A WORLD OF APPARENT COMPETITION - IN WHICH SURVIVAL AND REPRODUCTION ARE THE ONLY AIMS - CAN NON-HUMAN LIFE FORMS BEHAVE LIKE US AND ACTUALLY HELP EACH OTHER? AND, IF THEY CAN, THEN WHAT'S MAKING THEM DO IT?

If all the millions of different organisms on earth are so mixed up, living in such close proximity, bashing into each other, competing to invent niches to be secure in, fighting for energy, programmed by their genes to survive and reproduce… then why would anything ever behave in a way that benefited something else?

And yet everywhere biologists look, it's clear that evolution has thrown up an almost bewildering range of behavioural strategies that are carefully, even brilliantly, designed to form symbiotically rewarding relationships.

Why's that? It's because, like everything else that affects an organism, evolutionary forces are constantly trying to find the best ways of increasing genetic fitness. And symbiotic unions turn out to be very profitable mechanisms for achieving this.

This occurs in different ways. Sometimes the strategy is to get an increase in one's own fitness by reducing the fitness of something else. The ghastly parasitoids, for example, do this by wiping out their individual hosts, even if other members of the species might benefit from their sacrifice.

Further up the Behavioural Spectrum are forms of predation that shade into less asymmetric relationships. What's called amensalism, for example, might see the host harmed but not killed; while commensalism leaves the parasite with some benefits, yet the host isn't reduced in any way.

But this picture of life makes it look as if it's only constant *competition* between the species that leads to gains. Thomas Huxley typified this argument when he'd hammer relentlessly on about how a Malthusian competition for limited resources led inevitably to the shorthand of a 'struggle for existence' in life - a fatalistic landscape that went largely unchallenged for forty or so years.

But then, in 1902, an extraordinary counter-argument was published in a book entitled *Mutual Aid: A Factor in Evolution*, that forced biologists to take another look at the evidence. It wasn't conflict that led to long-term gains, the book's argument proposed, but *cooperation*. And the idea that things would ever willingly collaborate was such a shockingly different way of seeing how the world worked that the scientific establishment was stung into taking notice.

Mutual Aid's author was a Russian aristocrat called Prince Pyotr Kropotkin, a heavily-bearded, political hothead who went around behaving as if he'd stepped from the pages of Joseph Conrad's novel, *The Secret Agent*.

As a young man, Kropotkin had swung completely away from his privileged background, and instead had become an influential anarchist and revolutionary. Arrested and imprisoned in a Czarist jail, he'd been sprung before his trial and had escaped Russia to travel extensively, looking for models of social justice. As he did so he became increasingly convinced that there were strong parallels between the behaviour of organisms in the natural world, and the kind of political philosophies that most interested him.

There must have been something he particularly liked during the years he spent exiled in Brighton, because by the time he wrote *Mutual Aid*, he was convinced that instead of Darwinian competition being the sole driver of change, it was an evolutionary emphasis on collaboration that led to the success of species. And that, he said, included *Homo sapiens*.

> **'Under any circumstances sociability is the**
> **greatest advantage in the struggle for life.'**
> **Pyotr Kropotkin, *Mutual Aid: A Factor in Evolution***

To support his views, he explored the biology of symbiotic relationships and examined the ways that the different parties used them to develop their colonies and communities. And the more he looked, the more he began to highlight the important strategic differences that organisms employed as they'd evolved, not only with their genetically linked relations, but also with other species.

However, Kropotkin went further than simply saying that cooperation had a place in evolution. It played a more important role than this, he said, and his conviction grew that it actually represented the cornerstone of successful survival strategies.

Any close observation of the best equipped and fittest species, he concluded, showed that they were the *most cooperative* and that where '… the practice of mutual aid has attained the greatest development (then the species) are invariably the most numerous, the most prosperous and the most open to further progress.'

The way living things search for the benefits of cooperation, Kropotkin claimed, was based on profound genetic drives. Ever the political activist, he then developed his ideas to propose that these drives were similarly present in humans, so much so that our cultural evolution had elevated collaborative instincts to form the bedrock of our morality.

The evidence that pointed to species' success in biology, the book argued, also gave us the framework to see how our own attitudes, thoughts and feelings were central to *H. sapiens'* successful development. These wishes weren't restricted to cultures or civilisations, but were commonly held across all the various races and peoples on earth.

Prince Kropotkin. Sometimes it takes a maverick outsider to see what the professionals might miss.

Far from human society being a separate and superior construct to the 'tooth and claw' of Nature, he maintained, it was essentially the same product of evolutionary momentum. In other words, however much we may have thought we were some kind of separate, superior race, Kropotkin argued that we employ exactly the same social practices as any organism that enters into an arrangement with another from which both derive benefits.

Further, he said, it was even more obvious when it occurred within a species, where different members would form collaborative colonies of insects, plants, protozoa or bacteria. In short, we could learn from examining and understanding how these worked and, above all, appreciate how cooperation, and not conflict, had led to them becoming successful.

The book was a game changer for biologists, and its influence spread as the twentieth century unfolded. Scientific opinion began to increasingly switch its focus away from seeing natural selection as the merciless grinding process that the Victorians had portrayed it as, and more towards an understanding of how the major stages in evolution had been catalysed by symbiotic events.

The advances that would come later in bacteriology, molecular biology and the growing appreciation of the actions of the gene were all to point biologists in the same direction.

The gains that lay at the heart of the critical transitions in evolution were all now seen to have been due to the action of symbiotic mergers that had transmitted genetic information from one generation to the next. While Lynn Margulis and others would also come to the same conclusion, many feel that Kropotkin provided the original insight.

What kinds of evolutionary transitions would they have been referring to? Well, cooperation had been the motor force behind elements joining up to form compounds. Similarly when compounds were to create self-replicating molecules called genes. It was also what led genes to arrange themselves in such a way as to work together as chromosomes.

In the same manner, the seach for cooperation was what lay behind single-celled, asexual bacteria when they had merged to unleash the entirely new organism of the eukaryotic cell. The invention of sex cells had originated from the same force. And, ultimately, it had also produced the collaborative exercise that meant that cells would specialise and come together to make their unique offspring... of which we're each one.

All these and more - all the steps on the long journey to get to the wildly complicated structures of multicellular organisms - *were all due to the same motivation to share the benefits that came from synergistic arrangements.* Everything could now be seen to have been looking to make 1+1 equal 3. Compared to this profound drive, the evolution of behavioural strategies would seem to be a breeze.

'Cooperation is the architect of creativity throughout evolution,
from cells to multicellular creatures, to anthills to villages
and on to cities. Without cooperation there can be neither
construction nor complexity in evolution.'
Martin Nowak, *SuperCooperators*

All the way along the 3.8 billion years it had taken to get this far, scientists could now see the great truths that lay behind the way that different things had collaborated to create something new.

And yet, behind all this, it was still possible to see that the entire mechanism was based on a paradox. This was for the simple reason that *while the end result might be cooperation… what lay behind the motivation for it was nevertheless genetic self-interest.*

Although acts of cooperation might look like heart-warming examples of spontaneous collaboration and organisational effort, the genetic origins for them were anything but that. Rather, they were generated by the same ruthless survival instincts that made conflict and parasitism possible. The truth was simply that cooperation sometimes worked better as a strategy for producing more fitness improvements than competition did. And the winner in all this activity was, as always, life itself.

It is within this definition of cooperative activity that one can now see how understandable the central stage is on the Behavioural Spectrum - mutualism. This occurs when a symbiosis stems from both parties making mutual gains, and from which *each of them becomes fitter as a result.*

This takes place when two quite different things, even different species, both with their own unique living requirements, each outsource their development needs and futures to the other. They do this to make further evolutionary progress. Why's that? It's because they each needed something from the outside world that they didn't have the resources to create for themselves.

And the result is a net gain for both things.

Here are the gene's self-interested motives displayed at their most subtle. Neither party is working with the other on the basis of generosity or conscious sharing. There is no sympathetic 'reaching out' in the natural world, and no definitions like 'good' or 'bad' that recognise thoughts or emotions. These are human descriptions. In Nature, symbiotic unions are due simply to the endless search for ways to prosper by generating the kind of defensible niches that will give organisms a safe place to reproduce.

What kinds of things emerge as a result? Well, wildly successful things. Take the lichens as a good example. Although botanists see some of their species as examples of commensalism, most regard the lichen's relationship between fungi and photosynthetic algae or cyanobacteria as mutualistic. Whatever one calls it, they're certainly cooperative.

The mutual gains arise in this way: the fungus grows round the algal cells, and while these cells might differ in a vast range of colours, sizes and forms, they're all similar in that none of them have roots that can absorb water or nutrients in the way that plants do. The symbiotic trade-off sees one partner providing the sugar energy that comes from photosynthesis, while the other is retaining water through its surface, which then provides mineral nutrients for the joint venture.

Lichens have hugely benefited from this arrangement. In fact, they've turned out to be such evolutionary winners that they're among the most tried, tested and successful of any organism on earth. So adaptable have they become that they'll grow on pretty well anything, and can modify themselves to succeed in a huge variety of environmental conditions. They've expanded so greatly that they now include some 20,000 known species, and this mutualism marriage turned out to be such an amazingly effective approach that lichens now cover something like six per cent of the globe's surface.

The world's flora is awash in similarly mutualistic associations. Roughly half are believed to contain a fungus on the roots of a vascular host plant, which give them critical roles in the ecology and soil biology of a huge range of habitats. In pollination, too, plants trade food in the form of nectar for the work insects do in carrying reproductive pollen between the sexes.

In the microbial and animal worlds, successful organisms teem with mutualistic arrangements. Sometimes there are even crossovers between the different domains. An example of them getting together is shown in the way that bovine species rely on having bacteria in their intestines to digest food, while the bacteria benefit from the continuous supply of nutrients. Another might be the night flowering species of the desert which are visited by moths. The plants benefit by being pollinated, but the moth also wins by laying its larvae behind to be fed by the plant's seeds and fruits.

Then there are the many instances of what biologists call 'service-service' relationships. The oxpecker of sub-Saharan Africa, for example, is a bird that lives on the backs of zebras and rhinos, happily pecking away at the parasites and bugs on their hides. This might suggest an easy and plentiful supply of food, but they also give something back by cleaning up annoying pests. They go further than that, though, because they also act as a defence mechanism, flying high in the air as their hosts move over open ground, and screaming out a warning if they see predators around.

In the same symbiotic manner, that strange creature, the clownfish is allowed to live in safety among the poisonous tentacles of the sea anemone. But it returns the favour by protecting the plant from being eaten by other fish.

Last, of course, we ourselves wouldn't be here if it wasn't for a form of mutualism. We depend on oxygen and expel carbon dioxide. In turn other organisms suck this up, and respond by making more of the oxygen that's so critical to our futures.

Understanding how these sorts of outsourcing tricks can drive progress provokes a couple of immediate questions. First, how do the different players in such a complicated symbiotic game find each other? And secondly, and possibly more to the point, how did one know whether such an arrangement might do them some good?

The answer to both points is actually much the same. It's a process that echoes all the way down the billions of years of the existence of life on our planet, and the countless species that have been created by natural selection - until it arrives at ourselves. It's as central to the way we live now as it ever was for our forebears… because it all relies on the principle that if you want to get something that will help you, then *you'd better have something to offer in return.*

It depends, therefore, on having coevolution arrive at organisms that employ exactly the same specialisation and exchange mechanisms that we use in our economic and social lives. In this sense, the natural world is acting in the same way as our own, in that if you have an asset that something, or somebody, might want, and if they have something that you need in return, then you've got a deal. This was, and is, how 1+1 found it could make 3.

'In the long history of humankind, (and animalkind too), those who learned to collaborate and improvise most effectively have prevailed.'
Charles Darwin, *On the Origin of Species*

Our very existence, and the way our bodies are constructed, are among the most obvious examples of this. Within us humans are more than 230 different types of specialised cells, all doing different, vital jobs of mutual benefit to each other. Yet they all came together over untold millions of years in a vast series of symbiotic unions that would end up making us the complicated and evolutionarily advanced beings that we are.

Put simply, it suited cells to help each other by transitioning from the model where everything carried out the same jobs used in simple organisms like sponges and slime moulds. While these basic life forms can work together as a common entity, and even have what looks like some kind of guiding brain, they're always going to have limited functions due to of their lack of cell specialisation.

But is it really so surprising that cooperation is to be seen acting in the natural world in precisely the same way that it does in our human communities - and using exactly the same mechanisms? After all, we're all connected because we're all the offspring of Luca, the original cell, and every organism is therefore made of the same biochemical toolkit. That's why we can fit together like a colossal Lego set.

It's for this key reason that Nature isn't constantly faced with trying to make different operating systems work together. However, other problems might arise because not everything has the same kinds of desirable qualities that lead them to achieve balance in their mutualistic relationships. *The upshot of this is that one party is almost invariably going to be contributing more than the other in their symbiotic arrangements.*

Does this matter? Can there really be resentment if both partners are gaining from getting whatever it is that they need, and therefore each of them is becoming fitter? Even when it looks to us as if one side is benefiting more than the other, surely the balance of gains matters far less than whether both parties are getting what they want?

'Every symbiosis, is in its degree, underlain with hostility, and only by proper regulation and elaborate adjustment can the state of mutual benefit be maintained.'
HG Wells, *Ancient Experiments in Cooperation*

Biologists tell us that what's more critical than any assessment of the 'share out' is that the relationship ends up with living things settling down into a niche that's impossible for anything else to invade. And what this means for the organism is… nirvana. A place to snuggle down and live quietly, safe from threat.

But that awful statistic raises its head again… the extinction of 99.9% of species shows this is ultimately a fantasy, an unachievable ambition. Even so, it's what drives things. It's the odyssey of every single organism to seek a way of being secure in its niche for as long as possible… even if it's not to be forever. Why's that? It's because everything is programmed to survive and do anything it can to increase its chances of reproducing - and a solid, defensible base has to help this process. And the gene is behind it all, of course, making its vehicles have the best chance possible of carrying out its overriding 'selfish' aim of keeping life going.

As biologists repeatedly point out, however, even though the upshot of mutualism should suit both partners, the merger of specialisations in any arrangement never appears to be entirely acceptable. There are always tensions and defections. Even with ourselves, how often are we ever entirely happy with our relationships? When do we stop weighing up whether others are taking too much from us - however much we may like or need them? And isn't it a boring feature of life that we're always moaning about arrangements in which we think the other party is getting too much and us not enough? Even though being in the relationship is making our life easier?

'Like all the best relationships, symbiotic ones take work. Every major transition in the history of life - from single celled to multi-cell, from individuals to symbiotic collectives - has to solve the same problem: how can the selfish interests of individuals be overcome to form cooperative groups?'
Ed Yong, *I Contain Multitudes*

Marriages, for instance, have to be endlessly worked on to overcome the problem. Then again, you might resent your boss and think you're underpaid, but nonetheless you stay working at the job to get the money. And while you may like playing in a team, just how much do we hate the glory grabbers… and so on and so on.

Perhaps most of all, what we particularly begrudge are people who take the benefits but don't contribute - cheating and lying while they're at it. Do organisms in Nature do the same thing? Do symbiotic strategies on the Spectrum throw up the same problems? You bet… masses of them. Just like us (hardly that odd really since we spent over 99.99% of our time as non-sentient creatures) there are sharp practices and shysters in the great biological market where organisms are trading their specialisations, every bit as much as there are in our human world.

Charles Darwin acknowledged as much when he wrote in the *Origin*: 'I do not believe that any animal in the world performs an action for the exclusive good of another distinct species, yet each species tries to take advantage of the instincts of others…'

But if things are taking more than they should, then how does this happen? The answers appear in a spread of different tactics. Some simply decide to take but not give. Some plainly lost the ability to contribute over evolutionary time, but still continue to benefit. And others just overstep the mark and take more than their agreed 'share'.

Some of the examples of chicanery that biologists have identified make the conmen in *Dirty Rotten Scoundrels* look like amateurish patsies. There are certain insects, for example, that take nectar from flowers without pollinating them. But do the plants deserve our sympathy? Only up to a point, as many of them display remarkable ways of fighting back. Some clever species, for instance, even deceive pollinating males by producing flowers that look and smell like females. The poor suckers then provide the pollinating services by mistakenly trying to mate with the lookalikes.

Incredibly, there's even cheating at the microbial level. There are bacteria, for example, that fix nitrogen inside the roots of certain plant species. The deal is that the plants get nitrogen and the microbes are given organic acids. However, some of the tiny things are dodgy types who take what they need but contribute precious little in the way of giving back nitrogen. How do the plants respond? They apply sanctions: the acid supply dries up, and suddenly the bacteria have to relearn how to behave fairly.

Then there are all those 'cleaners', like the birds that pick food out of a crocodile's teeth, or the fish that nibble the parasites off the skin of client species. Sometimes they're also duplicitous. Naughty fish, for instance, might try to take too much by feeding on their clients' tissues instead of just picking off parasites. What happens? The cheaters are quickly identified and the client fish chase them away, and then ban them, rather like an unpleasant drunk being told to take a hike from a pub.

There are also ways in which some creatures benefit within a species. Take the selfish members of a wild dog pack, for instance. These will hang back from the effort and dangers of hunting, but are quick to turn up when it's time to tuck into the spoils. The problem, of course, is that one would think that these instances of unwelcome behaviour are logically favoured by natural selection, because by getting something for nothing, it theoretically gives a genetic advantage to the cheat.

We face similar issues in our societies - and the natural world solves its problems in exactly the same way that we do. Just as we get to know which people can't be trusted, we hand out punishments by exposing them - and then *avoiding* them. When this happens they end up with a bad reputation, and this means they get excluded from societal benefits. In short, if people steer clear of them, then ultimately they're the losers. Book Three of this series goes into the mechanisms we use to do this.

Nature has similarly evolved different types of disclosure and punishment tactics.

As with our own societies, these can be unpleasantly brutal. By getting exposed and shut out, the forces of natural selection will affect dishonest types because they're damaging the long-term prospects of their genes. How is that? It's because their biological stock is reduced in mate signalling terms, and they become less attractive to potential partners. After all, who'd want to mix their genes with a known loser?

And so, in time, a paradoxical result emerges in which the cheating strategy becomes a drag on fitness. Dishonest tactics might lead to a win in the short-term, but there's a price to be paid as one looks out into the future, because this is when the opposite outcome kicks in. The result? Trustworthy individuals progressively take over a species' gene pool… *and the strategy of cooperation becomes increasingly dominant.*

'The implications of our new understanding of cooperation are profound. Previously there were two basic principles of evolution - mutation and selection - where the former generates genetic diversity and the latter picks individuals that are best suited to a given environment. For us to understand the creative aspects of evolution we can now see that cooperation is the third principle. For selection you need mutation and, in the same way, for cooperation you need both selection and mutation. From cooperation can emerge the constructive side of evolution, from genes to organisms to language and complex social behaviours. Cooperation is the master architect of evolution.'
Martin Nowak, *SuperCooperators*.

All good, you're no doubt saying. That seems to make sense.

But what's this final place on the Spectrum? Altruism? One can understand how some things might want to take advantage of another by grabbing more than they're giving. This makes sense because there's an incentive in trying to increase one's fitness at the expense of others.

But why on earth would anything make a sacrifice of giving rather than taking? Doesn't this run counter to winning in the great struggle of life? Surely any behaviour that reduces one's own fitness, and increases another's, has to go against every single law of existence?

Surely that's obvious… isn't it?

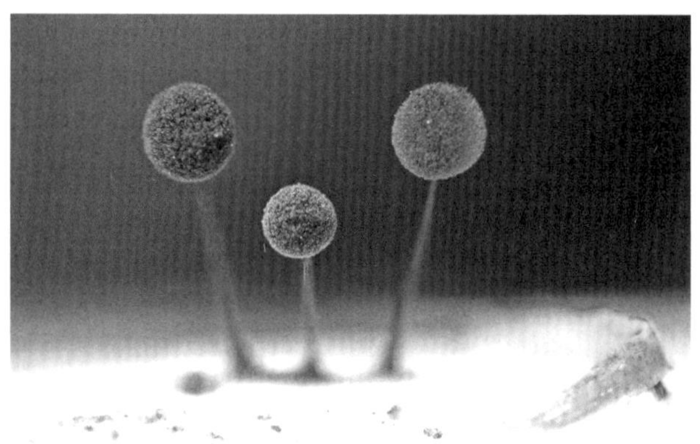

Slime mould spores doing their Sidney Carton imitation:
'We see the lives for which we lay down our lives, peaceful,
useful, prosperous and happy… it is a far, far better thing
that we do, than we have ever done; it is a far, far better
rest that we go to, than we have ever known.'

ALTRUISM? DON'T BE RIDICULOUS - WE ALL KNOW THAT'S A UNIQUELY HUMAN QUALITY. LIVING THINGS ARE PROGRAMMED BY THEIR GENES TO SURVIVE AND REPRODUCE, SO WHY WOULD ANYTHING ACT IN A WAY THAT WASN'T IN ITS SELF-INTERESTS? WHY WOULD IT EVER SACRIFICE ITSELF FOR OTHERS?

In the late summer of 2018, the world's press descended on one of those rare good news stories they occasionally find to cheer up the usual gloom. What made this one such a 'human interest' certainty was that it managed to combine the public's admiration for selfless courage with the 'wow' factor of a bizarre coincidence - and then to have it all wrapped up in a satisfyingly heart-warming ending.

It was about an elderly man called Xu Weifang who'd been sitting at home in Zutang, eastern China when he heard a child shrieking for help. He rushed outside to see a seven-year-old boy thrashing around in the river that ran past his house. Without a second's thought for his own safety - and in spite of being eighty years old and crippled with arthritis - he threw himself in the water and managed to pull the now unconscious child to safety.

That evening he dropped by the local hospital to see how the little fellow was doing. His parents were at the bedside and as they covered Xu with their grateful tears, the old man realised with a shock that he'd met the father before. Thirty years before, in fact, when he'd rescued him from drowning in exactly the same way that he'd saved his son - and from exactly the same river.

Xu was interviewed about it later and with admirable humility said he was pleased to have helped, but admitted that he might not be able to do so again in another thirty years.

Sadly, selfless actions like this don't always have the kind of outcome they deserve.

Not a month before Xu's bravery, and 10,000 kilometres away across the Pacific in California, a heroic young man named Victor Mozqueda hadn't stopped to think of his own safety when he'd jumped into the fast-flowing Kaweah River in the Sequoia National Park to save a small child called Vincent - even though he couldn't swim.

Although he was knocked down several times, a witness later said that Mozqueda 'never let go of him, even when they went down under the currents. The last effort he did was to throw Vincent out… so his father could grab him.' Although a number of fishermen later tried to save Mozqueda, they couldn't find him in the swirling waters, and he was eventually swept away to his death.

Interviewed later, his family confirmed that Victor had never learned to swim but that this wouldn't have mattered to him. He was the type of man, they said, who always tried to help others whenever he could. In a heart-breaking coda to the story, they ended by saying they'd have to open a crowd-funding campaign to pay for his funeral.

What can we do but swell with collective pride at such extraordinary acts? How much higher, we inevitably feel, do these examples of brave and selfless people place us humans above the rest of the world's organisms. St John wrote about our capacity for self-sacrifice when he said that 'greater love hath no man' when brave souls such as Victor laid down their lives for others.

How superior we must be, is the only conclusion, when we compare ourselves to the scrabbling conflicts of the natural world, and to the awful ruthlessness of lower life forms. And how different we are from every other organism, driven by their hardwired compulsions to maximise reproductive success… and never mind anything else.

We might grudgingly accept that the 'Behavioural Spectrum' laid out in the last few chapters shows how similar we are to the rest of Nature in our selfish and even in our sharing strategies. But surely altruistic actions are solely the preserve of our higher consciousness and our unique self-awareness?

It has to be because of these critical differences that we allow ourselves the comforting thought that when push comes to shove, we'd all put ourselves second when life demanded it. Whether it's donating a kidney or jumping on a railway line to save a deranged depressive, caring for an elderly relative or throwing ourselves on a live grenade to protect the platoon, surely actions that cost us so greatly are unique to humanity? Aren't they nothing less than examples of our ability to be truly, morally good?

Hmm, maybe not. Perhaps we're being a little too quick to pat old *Homo sapiens* on the back?

Darwin, himself, cast a cool, scientist's eye on such counter-intuitive behaviour and realised that it was probably grafted onto a paradox. The problem, as he wrote in *The Descent of Man*, his follow-up book to *Origin*, was that: 'He who was ready to sacrifice his life... would often leave no offspring to inherit his noble nature.'

Where would we be, was the implication, if everyone went around being so wonderful, chucking our lives away and taking our altruistic DNA out of the gene pool. Wouldn't that be the quickest way to let the selfish types win?

Of course he must have been right. Cooperation in general poses deep problems for the traditional view of natural selection, but self-sacrifice is particularly baffling because it leads to the certain loss of exactly those unselfish genes.

Yet as Darwin could see only too well - and almost certainly wished he couldn't - altruistic acts were everywhere in Nature, endlessly cocking a snook at his theories.

'One reason people deny that altruism exists is that, looking inward, they doubt the purity of their own motives. We know that even when we appear to act unselfishly, other reasons for our behaviour often rear their heads: the prospect of a future favor, the boost to reputation, or simply the good feeling that comes from appearing to act unselfishly.'
Professor Judith Lichtenberg, Georgetown University

Katherine Hepburn as Rose Sayer in *The African Queen* giving Humphrey Bogart her view of life: 'Nature, Mr Allnut, is what we are put in this world to rise above.'

Why, for instance, are some insects sterile, yet they'd spend their whole lives working for the good of their colony? Wouldn't honey bees that protect their hive sacrifice themselves when they stung an intruder, even though this would kill them? Don't some bats willingly regurgitate their food to help another that's going hungry?

And wouldn't animals that instinctively cry out a warning to others serve a vital function - yet doing so attracts the predator's attention onto themselves?

These kinds of acts are fascinating because they all seem to go against the rules. They do nothing to help things resist the never-ending pressure of the 2nd Law, and they certainly don't ease the struggle for existence. Quite the opposite it would seem. By putting the lives of others ahead of their own, organisms that are making a sacrifice must be paying a terrible genetic price for their altruistic behaviour. Surely this is a deep mystery in the context of behavioural decisions?

'Altruism is not limited to our species. Indeed its presence in other species, and the theoretical challenge this represents, is what gave rise to sociobiology - the contemporary study of animal (including human) behaviour from an evolutionary perspective.'
Frans de Waal. *Good Natured. The Origins of Right and Wrong in Humans and Animals*

Darwin must have seen that we humans are also displaying the same kind of incomprehensible behaviour. Everywhere one looks in human society, there are examples of us admiring the very opposite of looking out for our survival and our potential to reproduce.

What's going on? How can all this be happening when success in life is an evolutionary process that should only reward hard-headed competition? Yet humans view selfishness at the root cause of all vice, all crime, and all sin. Even evil is an exaggerated, appalling form of selfishness.

'The one great difference between man and all other animals is that, for them, evolution must always be a blind force, of which they are quite unconscious; whereas man has, in some measure at least, the possibility of consciously controlling evolution according to his wishes.'
JBS Haldane and Julian Huxley, *Animal Biology*

It's hardly surprising, therefore, that being unselfish is so highly prized. But if this is the case, why are we so suspicious of people's motives when we see them putting the needs of others before their own? Can it be because we secretly understand ourselves only too well, and know how alluring it can be to act altruistically… but only because we want some kind of *reward* out of it?

This is one of the reasons why so many people wonder if there's such a thing as true altruism. Certainly, the numerous theories of psychological egoism would put this in doubt, a line of thinking that leads some to the sad conclusion that acts of self-sacrifice can never be entirely devoid of the hope, even the expectation that there'll be some kind of recognition or return from putting someone ahead of ourselves.

Francis Hutcheson, one of the giants of moral philosophy in the Scottish Enlightenment of the eighteenth century (and the man who foresaw Utilitarianism with his famous phrase: 'the greatest happiness for the greatest number') was particularly keen on examining the motives behind good deeds. What he called 'moral sense' played a key part in his ethical system, and he encouraged people to constantly weigh up the 'advantages or disadvantages of actions'. That's how we would learn about ourselves, he said.

His point was, I think, that we were rarely in a position to calmly calculate all the factors at play before we have to make a decision. Generally, they're intuitive choices, taken in the blink of an eye, and because they happen so fast we don't have the time for empirical judgement-making. In other words, acting on instinct showed us what we were really like, and deciding whether something was right or wrong shouldn't involve a calculation of our own self-interest.

What did he think this showed us? We were certainly capable of benevolence, he said, but: 'While we are only intending the good of others, we undesignedly promote our greatest private good'.

Take the instance, he proposed, of why a man should throw himself in a river to save someone who was drowning. Was the hero doing this out of pure concern for the person in danger - or was he doing it out of vanity?

Even if nobody saw the act, was it ever entirely decoupled from our need for self-congratulation, self-love or some kind of personal gratification? But if that's the case, was there ever such a thing as 'pure' altruism?

Ouch.

'What we value so much, the altruistic 'good' side of human nature,

can also have a dark side. Altruism can be the back door to hell.'

Barbara Oakley, *Pathological Altruism*

If people set themselves up as altruists, went the inevitable logic, then they'd better be the real thing, or they deserved to have society hold its nose at them. Nobody's safe from this kind of thinking - and how careful it makes us. How we despise the immodest, how suspicious we are of the boastful, and how we hate the morally fraudulent. Even our greatest icons can be laid bare to the polemicist's gaze.'

As an example, consider the saintly Mother Teresa - literally so since her canonisation in 2016 - who was given a mauling by Christopher Hitchens in his book *The Missionary Position*. His accusation was brutal: at base, he said, she was less committed to loving the poor than she was to 'loving poverty'. And in doing this, she was motivated not by pure altruism, but by wanting the world's approbation for her fundamentalist, Roman Catholic beliefs.

Hitchens even spent time picking over her acceptance speech for the Nobel Peace Prize and its condemnation of contraception, a view he chose to interpret as displaying a lack of sympathy for women's empowerment. Last, by accepting the hospitality and donations of 'crooks, millionaires and criminals', she was allowing these sorts of people vicarious access to altruistic acts, without the personal effort and cost they should rightly take.

Ouch, and ouch again.

Even if we can see the arguments in Hitchens' brilliant writing, it's almost impossible not to wonder whether anybody is ever really altruistic when measured by these cynical criteria. If Mother Teresa can be portrayed as an Aunt Sally, then is it actually possible to satisfy the public's scrutiny over the question of whether a person is ever *truly* unselfish.

What makes this so? Nobody would question poor Victor Mozqueda's motives, but is that simply because he had the advantage of only being in the public eye for such a brief instance that nobody had time to find fault with him? Or that, sadly, his sacrifice led to his death, and so elevated him above criticism?

> **'These seemingly odd behaviours, where… people sacrifice themselves for their social groups… despite their own best interests is extremely common historically. They must come very naturally to us *Homo sapiens*. Are they in our genes? Although we now know that genes do not determine specific behaviours, they do cause us to have certain tendencies. We can override these tendencies, especially since we have evolved the ability to anticipate negative consequences to our behaviour and change it accordingly. Still… we all must have some sort of strong genetic tendency to explain it.'**
>
> **David Allen, *Psychology Today***

Religious teaching, of course, has always seen charitable actions as the way to God. But without the promise of eternal paradise, the whole concept of altruism has always been so illogical that there wasn't even a word to describe what it meant until the middle of the 19th century - let alone to see it formalised into a philosophical or ethical doctrine.

That was when a strange misfit with a long history of mental illness called Auguste Comte founded a philosophical movement known as 'positivism'. The central belief of its followers was that individuals should recognise a moral obligation to renounce selfishness and to serve others. He coined the word for this as 'altruism' after the Latin root, *alteri*, or 'other people'.

Comte was no doubt reacting to the savagery that had been unleashed by the French Revolution, and he urged his acolytes to acknowledge that only by constantly living for the sake of others could one embrace a 'religion of humanity'. By doing this, he said, we might eventually hope to escape our egocentric motives of expecting approval, or even pleasure, from selfless actions.

But is this kind of 'pure' altruism - of giving at a cost to oneself and without the expectation of gain - a realistic ambition?

Perhaps so. In the last few years, neuroscientists have made huge progress in understanding our 'social brain' and the structure and circuitry that indicates our intentions. Using sophisticated kit like functional MRIs, they've been discovering specific regions tucked away within the cortex that are hardwired for giving. By seeing whether they can make them light up, they've recorded significant variations in neural activity in response to stimuli that suggest altruism in action.

What's interesting is that research subjects who'd said they were altruistic by nature did, indeed, show higher activity in testing, particularly when they were told that the rewards being offered could go to charity.

The reverse results were also true, and these led researchers to be able to predict how people were going to score on an altruistic self-assessment scale. This measurement turned out to be so accurate that if someone thought they were more self-sacrificing than they actually were, then the research scientists could clearly see their shortcomings.

As the neuroscientist Donald Pfaff says in *The Altruistic Brain*: '… the brain is wired to propel us towards empathetic behaviour and feelings leading towards altruistic behaviours… (and that) this knowledge of our brain's wiring can, in turn, add to our capacity for benevolence'. Reactions to this wiring shows up particularly as one of the side effects of volunteering. Strong neurobiological connections induced by this kind of selfless behaviour are consistently seen to lead to better general health and a sense of well-being. It's hardly surprising that so many religions promote altruism as a cornerstone duty for their followers.

> **'Random acts of kindness have been shown to help those with depression. Counter-intuitively, new research shows that the benefit goes to the person doing the kind act. It's one of the reasons why I've recommended volunteering to those who have come to me with depression.'**
> **Max Pemberton, *Consultant psychiatrist, quoted in the Daily Mail***

But if this is what's driving us humans… then what is leading non-sentient organisms to make their own sacrifices? If they don't have the kinds of complex self-examination (and self-criticism) that we humans do, what's making them have similarly altruistic behavioural strategies? Is there really any evidence for it?

There's a mass of it. And in many ways it's much easier to be objective about the ways in which other life forms act, for the precise reason that they're not caught up in any suspicions about their psychological motives. One could almost argue that their sacrifices are a *purer* form of altruism than we ever manage. If their fitness is the only thing that should matter to them, then organisms in the natural world are going against the struggle for existence when they act in ways that cost them - and where others very obviously benefit.

> **'A simple interpretation of biological evolution says that nature selects for selfishness. Always. Selfish genes increase survival, so are the ones that get passed on. If altruistic genes happen to poke their heads up, they are quickly whacked… But here is the thing: all highly social mammals sacrifice their own needs for others, as do birds. In the first instance, the beneficiaries are offspring, but they can also be mates, kin and friends.'**
> **Patricia Churchland, *New Scientist***

Like what?

Well, there are any number of examples of organisms coming to strange arrangements where one is altruistic to another in the expectation that fitness benefits would be returned in time. Cleaner fish on coral reefs, for instance, provide services to larger species by removing parasites from their flesh - yet they're rewarded by having a secure source of food. Similarly, there are species of bacteria that supply important nutrients to other organisms, and they're recompensed with a secure place to live at a fitness cost to their new host.

But if these are examples of altruism occurring between species, then there are far more interesting illustrations in the way it exists *within* species. In fact, so ingrained has this become, that it defines their life cycles.

Bacteria may be the most basic of life forms but they're utterly selfless when it comes to protecting their colony if it's under attack. Among other defence mechanisms, they use mass suicide as a way of stopping invading viruses. If humans behaved like that, they'd become the stuff of legend.

Eukaryotic organisms are the same. They may have evolved after bacteria and have far more complicated biochemistry, but they also use similar techniques. Protozoas like amoebas, for example, have completely unselfish strategies to ensure the continuing health, not just of themselves, but of their community as well.

If environmental conditions become very stressed - a period of drought, for instance - amoebas stop acting as individuals, and all get together instead to form a structure called a slime mould. This doesn't sound too pretty, but it now behaves in the most beautifully unselfish manner. What happens is that they form themselves into a kind of stalk, and the ones at the top wait for an animal - or sometimes just the wind - to carry them away to another location in the hope that they'll find better environmental conditions where they can make a fresh start.

At this point the stalk, which has huge numbers of individual amoebas packed together in it, then dries out and dies. But how does the process of deciding which of them is going to live get handled? Is there some kind of voting system or lottery followed by a boss amoeba giving an embarrassed cough and saying: 'Oh, Pete… the rest of us have put our heads together and… ah, I'm afraid you've been chosen to be one of the brave chaps that isn't going to make it?'

In many ways the slime mould - with which, by the way, we share 70% of our DNA, so it's not completely alien to us - is displaying a form of altruism that's at least as self-sacrificing as anything we've ever come up with.

Yet is there a National Stalk Day to commemorate the fallen? Of course not. But seeing this kind of strategy does seem to prompt the question that if pond life can behave in such an admirable manner, is there a deeper reason for their behaviour that we don't share? Or should we be applying a different definition from them to us?

Examples of altruistic acts in non-humans abound. From single-celled organisms to social insects, and on up to higher life forms with their alarm calls and sacrificial strategies, evolution has programmed living things to help one another - even when they're paying an enormous price for doing so. And such behaviour isn't rare; in fact, it's widely seen throughout the animal kingdom, and particularly so in species with complex social structures.

What complicates the issue of altruism for us humans is that we have higher levels of consciousness, and we've evolved elaborate cultures over time that apply thoughts and feelings to our decisions. Other organisms may perform the most astonishing actions that benefit their groups, but the experts tell us they're just that - acts, strategies, tactics - and that they don't have the same emotional content that governs our behaviour (and makes us so ambivalent about our motives).

In biochemical terms, we humans are as much a population of socially interacting cells as any other living thing is. Biologists have long seen that when these tiny elements get together to function as superorganisms, they have a 'group mind' that's driving their behaviour and influencing their decisions.

The types of self-sacrifice one sees could be said to be helping the group survive in exactly the same way that the immortal gene is directing every other evolutionary action. They are all aimed at ensuring that *something* survives, even if every individual is eventually going to face death.

The central principle of altruism, as David Sloan Wilson says in his magisterial book *Does Altruism Exist?* is that in a world in which life is a team game: '... group level functional organisation evolves primarily by natural selection *between* groups'. What does this mean? Well, it goes right back to the anecdote of the bear chasing the men, and its conclusion that what matters isn't that death is avoidable, but only that it should happen to someone else.

As Wilson says to explain altruism's attractiveness as a strategy: 'The foundational principle is that natural selection is based on *relative* fitness.' Not *absolute* fitness. If there's something a species can do for its benefit, then it will do it.

This still leaves us with the question of how the mechanism works. Why would evolution have come up with a strategy that results in things paying such a colossal genetic cost for helping others? *Make the right decisions so you can survive to reproduce* was the definition of success at the beginning of this book… so why would some things deliberately choose to do the opposite?

What could make them decide *not* to pass their genes on?

'The only thing that really matters at a conference is that John Maynard Smith must be in residence and there must be a spacious, convivial bar... he will charm and amuse... and is wise, sympathetic and witty.' Richard Dawkins

WHY WOULD AN ORGANISM DELIBERATELY CHOOSE TO BE ALTRUISTIC - PUT ITS LIFE IN DANGER OR REDUCE ITS FITNESS FOR OTHERS? IF EVOLUTIONARY SUCCESS IS ALL ABOUT BEING ABLE TO REPRODUCE, WHY DOES THE 'SELFISH GENE' LET IT DECIDE NOT TO?

One autumn evening in 1955 an oddly unmatched pair of tweedy types walked up Gower Street, away from the university complex, and joined the scrum of people having an after-work drink in the Old Orange Tree pub on the corner with the Euston Road. One was burly and beetle-browed, with a strong physical presence and a military moustache. The other was slighter and scruffy but with a charming manner, his hair swept back and smiling eyes blinking behind large round glasses.

The older of the two was world-famous and the other one soon would be. Both were Old Etonians, both were notably radical in their political views - Bloomsbury communists, committed to Marxist philosophy - and both loved nothing more than a knockabout scientific argument.

The larger man was JBS Haldane, one of the giants of British science, a mathematician, biochemist and evolutionary biologist who had, among other things, combined the Darwinian principle of natural selection with the logic of Mendelian inheritance. By doing this he'd pioneered the concept of population genetics in the 1920s.

After a career as a don at both Oxford and Cambridge, he now held the chair of Professor of Genetics at University College, London. The drinking pal was one of his graduate students, John Maynard Smith, a brilliant maverick who'd studied mathematics and engineering at Cambridge and done war work as an aircraft designer. He'd now abandoned his career in aviation (planes were 'noisy and old-fashioned', he said) and had embarked on a second degree in which he was particularly researching fruit fly genetics.

The legend of the evening goes that after a pint or two the conversation turned for some reason to the old chestnut of whether one would jump into a river to rescue a drowning man.

'Well', asked Maynard Smith, 'would you risk your life… if it was your brother?'

According to Smith's later recollection of the conversation, the famously irascible Haldane 'calculated on the back of an envelope for some minutes before announcing that he would only go in if he could save two brothers, but not one. Or eight cousins, but not seven.'

How they laughed - and then moved on to other things and other pints. But in one of the few recorded occasions when *in vino veritas* didn't include someone having to later apologise for a regretted remark, Maynard Smith found himself turning over his professor's remarks in his head the following day.

Gradually, he became fixated about what lay behind them. The more he thought about it, the more it seemed to him that Haldane had summed up a powerful scientific idea - one that would shine a light on the nature of social behaviour, the gene's role in evolution, the reason certain life forms didn't procreate, ritualised aggression, gender balance… and human progress.

Not a bad list.

What had almost certainly driven Haldane's feverish calculations was the work done in the early 1920s by an American geneticist called Sewall Wright on the 'coefficient of relationship' between two individuals, which was, essentially, a measure of inbreeding.

But where Haldane's boozy leap had taken him was to the realisation that if there was a risk of disaster in an altruistic act - a real chance that you might die and therefore lose your opportunity to reproduce - then you'd want to know your genes would be carried on by the close family members you'd saved. The closer they're related to you the better. If it was a sibling then you would need to save two to make your sacrifice worthwhile. If it was a cousin then you'd need eight.

The reason Haldane had arrived at these numbers was that the whole beauty - and yet the danger - of sexual reproduction was that it made living things lose half their genes every time they created a new offspring.

And what his great brain had worked out was the effect of Mendelian inheritance laws. These meant that if there was a likelihood of death by failing to be a heroic rescuer, then the best chance of your genes being carried on was by saving close relations of *your generation*. Why your generation? Because they shared more of your genes than your own children would ever do.

The conclusion the two men were to come to as they pursued the idea later was that the phenomenon of 'pure altruism' that one sees everywhere in Nature - of things laying down their lives for their colony and not getting the chance to reproduce - was actually neither 'pure' nor 'altruistic'

Instead of this, they felt that they might have come up with the solution to Darwin's terrible headache. This had arisen because if natural selection was all about getting more genes out than the competition - being 'fitter' - then the reasoning behind why Nature chose to make certain organisms sterile had always been an embarrassing hole in his argument.

Now they could see why this happened. It was because evolution had somehow come up with the brilliant idea of getting family or colony members to carry out reproduction on somebody else's behalf. Here, at last, Haldane and Maynard Smith could see why so many of the world's most successful insect species were using this superficially counter-productive strategy. What had always appeared to be a *cost* to the group's chances - by having lots of sterile members - could actually end up as a *gain*.

Deep within these kinds of altruistic organisms, they could now see that the twin compulsions that drive all living things to survive and then, secondly, to reproduce, had plainly separated out over evolutionary time.

Now each of the individuals had specialised its skills and was sharing in the benefits. Some were specialising in ensuring the well-being and survival of the colony, and some were specialising in ensuring its reproductive capacity. 1+1=3 was at work again. It was arguably the ultimate example of cooperation in action.

'Haldane had latched on to a profound insight about the evolution of cooperation. He had seen that genetically related organisms may, in certain circumstances, have an evolutionary incentive to help one another. He had also seen that incentives come in degrees, and that the size of the incentive depends on the closeness of the helper's genetic relationship to the potential beneficiary.'
Jonathan Birch, *The Philosophy of Social Evolution*

At first sight the altruistic actors might look as if they were deliberately decreasing their fitness by being unable to breed, but they were hardly wasting their lives if they were increasing the fitness of a near relative. As the American neuroscientist Jonah Lehrer was to later summarise the phenomenon in a *New Yorker* essay entitled *'Kin and Kind'*: 'Instead of having sex, we're saving kin.'

Suddenly one of Nature's most powerful, genetically dominant strategies had been exposed. And, with it, came an understanding of what led to all those altruistic acts that can appear so baffling - from the behaviour of suicidal bacteria and eukaryotes, to the cohesion of human families and societies. *What was now plain was that altruistic acts were the glue that held collections of related individuals together.*

What kind of colonies and species were most likely to use the method?

Social insects were the most evident. Take a beehive as an example. Within it, the tasks of the colony are specialised: the queen is the only member able to lay fertilised eggs, but she's capable of producing up to two thousand of these in a single day. She's able to do this because she mated early in her life, and then stored the sperm in her body to be used over the following two or even three years.

Then there are the worker bees who are by far the largest group within the hive. They're always female and the great majority will be sterile. But even those who can produce unfertilised eggs, will only give birth to drones. Workers carry out pretty well all the tasks of the colony, foraging for nectar and pollen, feeding the larvae, looking after the queen, caring for the drones and defending the hive with their lives.

For their part, the drones are all male. They only have a single task, and that's for one of them to fertilise the queen. While this life of idleness might look like first prize in the lottery of the hive's existence, drones are always at risk of being chucked out by workers if the colony becomes stressed through such things as drought or a lack of food. Nonetheless, the core point is that since the lucky one who mates with the queen will be carrying the genes of one of the worker bees, *the genes stay within the community.*

Bees are an example of what are known as 'eusocial' (truly social) insects which means that they, together with others like the ants and termites, have one great distinction from the great majority of other societies, and certainly from our own. And that is that they have far more females than males, while others like ours settle down to be roughly 50:50. The answer to why this imbalance has evolved is now obvious as the females aren't concerned with mating, they're letting their kin do that.

The rather sad conclusion to this kind of collective approach is that even after its hard-working, selfless service to the colony, the death of a sterile worker has no more impact on the continuing health of the hive than the loss of a chloroplast bacterium does on the genes of a lichen, or a dead leaf does when it falls from a tree. Actually, the impact is the opposite, as the birth of a worker bee or the unfolding of a new leaf brings with it renewed energy for the collective entity.

Now the suggestion that Haldane's insight had sprung completely unformed is probably wide of the mark. Both he and Ronald Fisher had already guessed that organisms could increase their fitness by harnessing their close relatives, but neither had recognised where this might take them. Nor had they attempted to formalise the process mathematically.

However, it was at this point that a man Richard Dawkins was later to call 'the most distinguished Darwinian since Darwin' was to join the story. Enter William 'Bill' Hamilton, another immense intellect who'd studied at the LSE after Cambridge, and had then also become a graduate scientist at UCL.

In a letter to the *New Scientist* many years later, Hamilton related how he'd become involved. He had heard the tale of Haldane's 'back of an envelope' insight, he wrote, and thought it would be interesting to pursue the mathematical proof of the underlying altruism. The ambition was to cost him, he put it: '… reams of paper and two years of thought.'

'Tortured by self-doubt and loneliness' as Dawkins was to describe him, Hamilton became a bizarre sight, sitting on the benches at Waterloo Station deep into the night, alternately observing people's behaviour for inspiration, and cudgelling his brains to find a mathematical explanation for the displays of altruism in the natural world. Eventually it dawned on him that Darwin might have been wrong. The great man's comment that if something sacrificed itself then its altruistic genes would leave the gene pool… might not tell the whole story.

Instead, Hamilton became more and more convinced that the opposite could be true. This was because if an organism was prepared to give up its life for others, then there must be a strong likelihood that by saving its close relatives, there might be *more* copies of its genes coming through into the gene pool than if the altruistic death hadn't come about.

Once he'd finished bashing away at the problem, what Hamilton's mathematical approach exposed was that if an individual died, but in doing so somehow saved, for example, ten close relatives, it was highly likely that the altruistic genes that made this sacrifice happen wouldn't just be preserved… but they would *multiply*.

The research stage took him still longer to complete, and it wasn't until 1964 that he published his findings in two papers entitled *The Genetical Evolution of Social Behaviour*. Like so many scientific breakthroughs, there wasn't much interest in them at first, but as time passed his ideas led to a complete shift in the understanding of evolutionary biology. What had he seen? It was nothing less than the revelation that if organisms were doing things altruistically - for the good of their kin - then if you looked behind this activity, it was evident that they were actually doing it *for the good of their own genes*.

If you've been following the gist of this book, the role of the gene may not come as a total surprise. But at the time of Hamilton's papers the realisation was a completely new way of looking at evolution. The gene wasn't just the mechanism for heredity, he was saying, but it was the eternal constant that had led to the entire shebang of strategies and decisions, genotypes, phenotypes, extended phenotypes and every other driver of fitness. In short, his insight established the principle of what was to become known as the 'gene-based theory of evolution'.

At the base of this interpretation was the understanding that instead of the selfish gene insisting on the bleak compulsion that things should act only to preserve their own lives, and therefore chances of reproducing, *this new way of seeing evolution was arguing that cooperation, symbioses and altruism all logically stemmed from genetic self-interest.*

In saying this, the theory was holding that the last thing the gene was doing was being selfish. Rather, the opposite effect was taking place because it was motivating its vehicles to be profoundly unselfish. Yes, behaving in this way might simply be another strategy in the race for superior fitness, but it was very obviously suiting those communities in which it was being used.

And us? Does the theory have a meaning for mankind?

Of course it does, because in exactly the same way that organisms can increase their fitness by being self-sacrificial, we are similarly incentivised to care for one another. Doing so plainly helps establish our reputations as cooperators, and this is bound to increase the symbiotic gains we can make by dealing with others like ourselves. And to collectively become part of a cohesive, winning community.

'But on the two occasions when I have pulled possibly drowning people out of the water (at an infinitesimal risk to myself) I had no time to make such calculations. Paleolithic men did not make them. It is clear that genes making for conduct of this kind would only have a chance of spreading in rather small populations where most of the children were fairly near relatives of the man who risked his life.'

Jonathan Birch, *Quoting JBS Haldane in The Philosophy of Social Evolution*

Hamilton went on to call the altruistic strategy 'inclusive fitness' because it was clear that the success of a colony was due to a specialisation and exchange mechanism that would include a number of different, but related individuals who weren't themselves responsible for the breeding process.

However, other biologists began to use the term originally employed by John Maynard Smith of 'kin selection' which describes a gene's eye view of what it's doing. In choosing this wording he particularly wanted to distinguish Hamilton's description of colony success through altruism from the generally accepted belief that organisms were sacrificing themselves for 'the good of their group'. This approach was labelled 'group selection', and while it seemed to explain the advantage to the community, it never confronted the incentives that were needed to make an individual organism chuck away its genetic drive to reproduce.

This was the issue that Hamilton had set out to wrestle to the ground. What was in it for the altruist? His aim had been to model mathematically the requirements that made the sacrificial strategy worth it. And, after long years of effort, he did - and, in doing so, he managed to show that not only did close kin carry on the genetic line for the altruist, but that this was also then carried on by those *offspring* that were raised by these relatives, but scaled by the degree of their relatedness.

Where did this end up?

Well, his great achievement wasn't only to see how the mechanism worked, but to reduce the relationship to a simple notation that was to become known throughout evolutionary biology as Hamilton's Rule. What it said was that altruism worked as a powerful reproductive strategy - as long as what you got out of it was more than what you put in. Seems simple enough.

But how did one arrive at whether the risk was worth it? His answer was the elegant principle of rB>C, a classic risk and reward notation in which the reproductive benefit of increased fitness was represented by 'B', and the degree of relatedness was 'r'. The measurement of this degree was crucial because one's own generation of siblings was more important, genetically, than one's offspring.

And the combination of these two factors had to be more, he said, than the reproductive cost, which he notated as 'C' - in short, what it had taken to make this benefit happen. Perhaps Jonah Lehrer's summary is easier to follow: 'Genes for altruism could evolve if the benefit (B) of an action exceeded the cost (C) to the individual, once relatedness (r) was taken into account.'

Over time, the sheer brilliance of Hamilton's Rule gained momentum - and evolutionary biologists did a lot of forehead slapping as the implications mounted. But the fact that he'd reduced a natural process to a mathematical relationship meant that the big guns of science now began to point their barrels at him. For many mathematicians there was too much woolly 'yes, but...' biology in the relationship, and to many biologists there was too much maths. In particular, went one of the repeated questions, what were the assumptions behind the variables B and C?

**'Hamilton replaced 'classical fitness' (which took account only of lineal descendents)
by 'inclusive fitness', which is a carefully weighted sum embracing collateral
as well as lineal kin. As far as the Darwinian principle is concerned, sibling care
and parental care are favoured for the same reason: the cared-for
individual contains copies of the genes that programme caring behaviour.'
Richard Dawkins, *The Selfish Gene***

But then arguably the biggest gun of all turned his fire on the doubters. This was one of the great men of theoretical biology, the 'father of biodiversity', a high-profile Harvard professor called EO Wilson who'd devoted his life to ants, and to understanding the behaviour of eusocial insects.

It was largely due to his research that biologists had been exposed to these amazing organisms' crucial importance in Nature, and to the ways in which individual insects cooperate to form colonies of quite staggering numbers. As part of his work, he'd shown that although the incidence of these sorts of group enterprise might be fairly rare, eusociality was an extremely successful behavioural system that accounted for the great majority of all the insect biomass.

'While only 2% of known insect species are eusocial, these species compose most of the insect biomass; in one patch of rainforest assayed near Manaus in Amazonian Brazil, they made up over three-fourths of the insect biomass.'
EO Wilson, *Eusociality: Origins and Consequences*

Now Wilson wrote about kin selection in a hugely influential book called *Sociobiology: The New Synthesis* that was published in 1975. It not only put Hamilton's Rule at the centre of the arguments about what shaped an organism's behaviour, but it made the concept of 'sociobiology' - an explanation of evolution with social behaviour at its core - a new branch of science.

The concept of kin selection now became increasingly accepted, and evolutionary biologists were soon recognising altruism's place as another important behavioural strategy. Just as parasitism could be a genetically profitable approach on the Spectrum, they now saw, so could altruism.

It worked. And it increased cooperative genes, rather than reducing them.

Because these genes were being passed on, it was now plain that, over time, *collaboration would grow - and it would logically become the central factor in evolution.* Kropotkin and others who'd claimed that cooperation was the strongest force in Nature were even more right than they could ever have guessed.

In a theme repeated frequently in this book, with good reason, the natural world doesn't deal in expressions like 'good' or 'bad' - because every behavioural decision an organism makes is simply part of a survival strategy. And these strategies had all evolved as the gene created enough diversity to provide it with as many safety nets as possible to see that something would survive, however much the conditions might change.

'There is nothing either good or bad, but thinking makes it so.'
William Shakespeare, *Hamlet*

The ultimate implication of the conclusion, however, was to dismay a great many people. This was because it now became clear, as Bill Hamilton was to later say, that: *'altruism is just genetic selfishness.'*

Yet again, an understanding of how the 'selfish gene' worked had exposed why everything in evolution came from it 'doing its job'. The gene was behind replication, replication was behind errors, errors were behind mutations, mutations were behind natural selection and natural selection was behind the success of behavioural strategies… and that success was behind why cooperation worked.

It all leads back to seeing how the gene works its magic in arriving at different ways of ensuring that some kind of vehicle is going to survive. Once more, though, one should stress that although the gene may have been the unchanging constant in the long narrative of life, its actions have neither foresight nor inherent consciousness. It simply 'is'.

'Evolution has no long-term goal. There is no long-term target, no final perfection
to serve as a criterion for selection, although human vanity cherishes the absurd
notion that our species is the final goal of evolution.'
Richard Dawkins, *The Blind Watchmaker*

But… aaargh! 'Altruism is just genetic selfishness.'

How awful does that sound? It's strong meat, isn't it? No doubt you'll agree that a lot of the chain of logic in this chapter is understandable, but it's this last bit you're not going to stand for. You probably feel much the same as the American psychiatrist Randolf Nesse did when he described his reaction to hearing this in his book *Why We Get Sick*: 'When I first grasped it, I slept badly for many nights, trying to find some alternative that did not so roughly challenge my sense of good and evil.'

Doubtless as Dr Nesse did, one has to accept that our human version of altruism very rarely occurs without the hope or expectation of some kind of gain. Even if it's simply the best way for us to get to heaven. But equally, it's pretty repulsive to think we could ever be like non-human organisms in having our behaviour driven by a biological selfishness that originates in our genes.

You might agree that this astonishing insight is just about acceptable for the natural world. But not in *us* for heaven's sake… not with our thoughts and sensibilities, not with our morality, our codes of ethics and our instinctive judgements about what's right and wrong. It's exactly these higher qualities, you would say, that make us *human*… that's why we're so different.

Richard Dawkins says that all living things are just vehicles for their genes. But he also says that humans are unique in being able to override the instructions those genes are giving us. So, does that imply that because we've got intelligence and self-criticism and empathy and all the other good stuff… that *our* altruism isn't just a biological imperative?

Can this mean that we truly are separate and superior beings?

George Price in 1973. 'Price came to see what had eluded many before him: whereas others, in the hunt to fathom goodness, pitted different levels of organisation of life against one another - the gene conniving with the individual, the individual subverting the group, one group fighting doggedly against another - this lonely outsider understood that they would all have to be part of the same equation. It was a dramatic flash - a penetration that would forever change our view of the evolution of life. Unknown, untrained, in a foreign country, dejected and alone, he had caught a glimpse of the great canvas of natural selection and seen its splendour and broadness. And, writing the elegant equation, he literally came off the street, anonymous, to present it to the world.' Oren Harman. *The Price of Altruism: George Price and the Search for the Origins of Kindness*

CHAPTER TWENTY

Is the human capacity for altruism just genetic selfishness? If so, does this mean that we're the same as other organisms - or are we really different?

Are you upset by the idea that any goodness, self-sacrifice or concern for other people there might be in us stems from a chain of biological theory? Are you repelled by the thought that these higher human qualities could have their roots in a genetically selfish survival strategy?

If so, you wouldn't be alone in holding these views.

Many people would agree with you, and it was one of them, an 'unemployed American... a very strange character' as Maynard Smith was to later describe him, who had a particular rejection of the logic. Who was he? Well, he was someone called George Price, and I'm afraid what happened to him makes for a pretty horrible story. If it's going to distress you, maybe you should just jump to the end of the chapter?

Born in 1922, Price had been a child of extraordinary promise, but he'd grown up to become a restless, cynical man. He initially majored as a physical chemist, and did important work on the Manhattan Project before he later became a science journalist. He'd married in his mid-twenties and had fathered two daughters, but his difficult nature and absolute commitment to atheism led to him falling out with his staunchly Catholic wife, and they divorced in 1955.

About ten years later he was treated for thyroid cancer, but the operation was botched, and it left him with a paralysed shoulder and a lifelong dependence on thyroxine medication. For his own reasons, he tragically chose to keep the condition a secret and never disclosed his illness to anyone. If he had, things might have turned out differently.

Nonetheless, it was the payout from his medical insurance that allowed him to come to London, and start carrying out private research into the reasons that humans lived in families.

It was while he was doing this that he came across Bill Hamilton's work on altruism. It intrigued him, and he began to play around with the cost and benefit variables in the Rule and started working up what's known as a covariance equation, a mathematical way of measuring the direction of a relationship between the returns on two fluctuating assets. A positive covariance means that asset returns move together, while a negative covariance means that they move inversely.

What he was attempting to show was how the trajectory of a gene could change in frequency over generations. It was breakthrough stuff, and the more he refined the equation, the more fully it seemed to capture the mechanics of how evolution worked by natural selection, meiotic drive and kin selection.

He continued, alone and unfunded, and eventually he developed the basis of a mathematical relationship that would later become famous as the Price Equation.

What was to excite people about this work was its key insight into how increases in fitness can become more prevalent in populations as each new generation appeared. But the equation also showed how the opposite was true, and therefore how fitness could diminish. Even though he'd been constrained by a self-taught knowledge of genetics, Price could see that he had stumbled on something that no one else had arrived at, something that might be of great significance.

And so, one day in September 1968, he turned up off the street, unknown and without an appointment, at the Galton laboratory at UCL (yes, *that* Galton) and asked to see someone. He had no occupation or academic credentials, but he did have an equation. And what it showed, he claimed, was the mechanism that provided the proof for altruism's place in evolution. An hour and a half later he walked out with a job, an honorary title, a salary and an office.

Now that the knowledge and insights of the leading biologists in the field were available to him, George Price continued to improve his mathematical workings by having a better understanding of the factors to input as variables. The results became increasingly informative and, in particular, the equation began to yield insights into what made some traits more likely to be passed on than others.

But as he worked and reworked the biological factors, what kept emerging to his dismay was the degree to which the relatedness of kin was influencing natural selection. No doubt like you and I, Price was offended by this finding, and he persisted in trying to make the equation show that the driver for this direction wasn't individual altruism at all, but the benefits that resulted for 'the group' - a nest, a hive, a colony - when it was in competition with others.

It was this outcome, he was determined to show, that was leading to change. What was good for the group, in other words, was outweighing what was good for the individual. And that it was this collective success that was leading the pathway for evolution.

There were two problems with this theory - what became known among biologists as 'group selection'. The first was that it wasn't the group that was replicating itself in reproduction. It was the genes that were resident in individuals. The second, however, was that it didn't explain how altruism could have evolved in the first place.

Individuals who sacrificed themselves would have been at such a genetic disadvantage, went the argument, that they'd never have been able to breed others like themselves. If you didn't buy Hamilton's arguments, then Darwin had to be right and the altruistic genes would have left the gene pool. The process of cooperation could never, therefore, have taken root.

But there was another side to Hamilton's Rule that was also disturbing Price. As Bill Hamilton had continued to investigate the role of kinship, he'd realised that just as an organism might favour closely related organisms of the same parentage, it was also incentivised, under certain circumstances, to be *harmful* to others that were less related, and therefore would be genetically dilutive.

This cropped up everywhere in Nature, and biologists were now given an explanation for the ruthless behaviour that's intended to wipe out competing genes. This became known as 'Hamiltonian Spite' and it was typified by organisms killing the offspring of competitors, sometimes even their own family, particularly if they were from a new breeding mate. Evil stepmothers, anyone?

> **'On top of all the miseries inflicted by predators and parasites,**
> **the members of a species show no pity to their own kind.'**
> **George Williams, *Adaptation and Natural Selection***

Poor George. Hadn't he done the same thing himself? Hadn't he been spiteful, deserting his children and putting himself first? He put this to one side and worked on. Yet as he did so, the equation seemed to be shouting out still more terrible truths - yes, not only had he been selfish, but now it seemed that any altruistic feelings he might have ever had for others were nothing to do with any goodness in him, but had instead been shaped by his genes.

How he came to loathe the conclusion that Oren Harman was later to summarise in his biography, *The Price of Altruism: George Price and the Search for the Origins of Kindness*: 'What determined whether a living being should act kindly or with malice had nothing to do with 'essence' or 'inner core' - both, after all, reside within us. Instead, if the surrounding creatures were similar, altruism could evolve; if they were different, spite was the solution. Pure unadulterated goodness was a fiction.'

By now George must have been in agony. How the equation's conclusions ate away at him. But he stuck at his work, refining the variables, often baffling his colleagues with its mathematical complexities (as Maynard Smith was later to say in an interview: 'I'm not going to tell you what Price's Theorem says, because I don't actually understand it') but also worrying them deeply with his increasingly erratic behaviour.

In June 1970 the dam broke and Price, the utterly rational atheist, was struck down by a profound religious experience. Perhaps he'd been in a manic period, but for whatever reason he'd stopped taking his medication and was now clearly unwell.

His life began to lurch dramatically adrift. God was talking to him, he began to say, and was telling him that he'd been chosen by divine intervention to discover the equation. When his grant ran out and he had to leave UCL, he took to roaming the corridors shouting that he 'had a hotline to Jesus.' (Maynard Smith was to be heard murmuring: '… yes, just like St Paul.')

What did he think God was saying? Perhaps that the equation had to be wrong? That Hamilton's Rule was limited to non-sentient life forms and that human altruism wasn't genetically based at all - but celestial in its origin. By God's grace we were different, he said, and we could be pure in our motives to help others. Then, in a vision, he heard Jesus whisper to him: 'Give to everyone who asks of you.'

By now, Price was convinced that God had directed our cultural evolution to give the human species alone the capacity for a true, inner-generated and higher concern for others. His vocation was now to live that way, and he began to devote himself to an extreme version of it. Swept along by this conviction, he embarked on a crusade to show that the biological evidence of his discoveries had no place in human behaviour.

First, he gave his savings away to the homeless. Then he invited them to live in his flat, helping them out wherever he could with their alcoholism and mental health issues. The lease soon ran out, and with his money gone, he began taking jobs as an office cleaner to supplement his academic income, sleeping on the floor at the university.

By now his thyroid issues must have been contributing to his deepening depression and he began to suffer from psychotic delusions. His friends tried to help: one advised him not to 'out-God God' and Maynard Smith wrote to say that he had 'less faith in God providing than you do, George', and that he would help in any way he could.

At that time in the early 1970s, lengthy battles were breaking out between property developers and the planners about the future of many of the period buildings around the university. Entire terraces were lying empty and George now moved into the famous squatter city of Tolmers Square by Euston Station.

It was there, one freezing January night in 1975, alone and disillusioned, in despair at the implications of his great work, his beliefs torn apart, his altruism abused and even his clothes given away, he took a final control of his life and decided to end it. His funeral a week later was attended by just five mourners, three of them derelict men. The other two were the world's most distinguished evolutionary theorists, Bill Hamilton and John Maynard Smith.

Price's daughters later arranged for a tombstone to be made for his pauper's grave. Under his name are inscribed the words: 'Father. Altruist. Friend.' And then, under these, cut into the granite, is his equation.

What of the others in the story? What happened to them?

John Haldane, too, became disillusioned. Disappointed by communism and angry with Britain's invasion of Suez, he'd left for India in 1956 to work in statistics. He loved it there, dressing in a traditional dhoti and achieving his sixty-year ambition of not wearing socks. He took Indian citizenship and died in 1964, the year of Bill Hamilton's papers.

What would he have made of Hamilton's breakthrough thinking? One hopes he'd have thought it a worthy outcome to his famous pub quip. And perhaps he'd even have applied his famous dictum on scientific discoveries to it: 'I suppose the process of acceptance will pass through the usual four stages: (i) this is worthless nonsense; (ii) this is an interesting, but perverse, point of view; (iii) this is true, but quite unimportant; (iv) I always said so.'

Bill Hamilton, himself, became increasingly recognised for his work, and was showered with medals and honours, eventually becoming the Royal Society Professor of Zoology at Oxford before spells at Harvard and the University of Michigan. Ideas continued to spill out of him but, as ever, one of his most endearing qualities was that he always let others take the credit.

Reckless about his safety to a terrifying degree, he was eventually felled by a rare strain of malaria that he contracted in the Congo jungle. He returned to England and died in 2000, leaving instructions that his body should be buried in the Brazilian forest to feed his favourite insect, the great *Coprophanaeus* beetle, so that they: '… will enter, will bury, will live on my flesh; and in the shape of their children and mine, I will escape death… so finally, I too will shine like a violet ground beetle under a stone.'

And EO Wilson? He remained at Harvard until his death at the age of 92 in 2021, conducting research into his beloved ants until very nearly the end, and continuing to enjoy his role as teaser-in-chief to the evolutionary biology community. His distinguished career included twenty-four books, two Pulitzer prizes and the authorship of the standard work on ants.

But his views on kin selection had shifted completely in recent years and, in 2010, he announced that he no longer supported the concept. This came to a head with the publication of a new book, *The Social Conquest of Earth*, in which he laid out his belief that natural selection was acting at the level of the colony, and therefore that group selection rather than kin selection was the behavioural mechanism at work in evolution.

This view, he claimed, was supported by mathematical analyses that appeared to prove it was groups that were competing for evolutionary success. He and his supporters now proposed that altruism had evolved for the benefit of the community, rather than for the reproductive benefit of individual genes.

The reason all those kin were working together, he thought, was as a consequence of social behaviour and not as the cause of it. For Wilson, this new thinking was an explanation for why social insects were so successful as life forms, but why such species occurred so rarely.

At this point the balloon went up. Suddenly the embers were blown on an old academic spat, and kin selection versus group selection became 'the Sun round the Earth, or the Earth round the Sun' of our day. In a furious letter to *Nature*, 137 of the world's leading biologists claimed Wilson had not only misunderstood evolution - but that he'd got his sums wrong. Richard Dawkins was particularly strident in his response to Wilson's change of mind, writing: '…the case for inclusive fitness is overwhelming. To say otherwise is simply wrong.'

Oof! What are we mere nobodies to make of it all? Is altruism a cause or an effect?

The kin selection brigade dug in with the argument that group selection could never have evolved because altruistic genes would have left the gene pool.

The group selection howitzers fired back with the question of how related, altruistic individuals would ever identify each other.

The kin boys responded that they were bound to encounter one another in 'viscous' communities in which there'd be pretty well nothing else but relations - as in beehives and termite hills.

And anyway, yah boo, they continued, groups don't replicate, genes do. This led Dawkins to throw a couple of heavy punches in his review of Wilson's book in *Prospect* magazine: 'The essential point to grasp is that the gene… is on its own as a replicator with its own unique status as a unit of Darwinian selection. Genes, but no other units in life's hierarchy, make exact copies of themselves in a pool of such copies… groups or species or ecosystems (do not). None makes copies of themselves. None are replicators. Genes have that unique status.'

But back came a group selection uppercut that there would always be long-term problems with kin selection as it was bound to lead to breeding depression over time - and that this would end up by producing lower overall fitness levels.

Who can be certain? To a dispassionate observer, it does seem that relatedness, altruism and the gene as replicator have to be the key elements at the bottom of all this. However, a body of biologists has even emerged saying 'calm down, calm down, perhaps what's happening is a combination of the two' - what they call 'multilevel selection' - on the grounds that gene frequency change could be correctly arrived at by using either approach.

And so it went, punch and counterpunch, and all the while something has to be going on, because being self-sacrificial would seem to be both contrary to the mechanics of natural selection, and yet, equally clearly, the cornerstone of social communities.

Does that include us? Well, one thing that doesn't seem to be in any doubt is the role self-sacrifice plays in our mate signalling. Countless studies have shown that women find altruistic men more attractive than others. Why would they do that? Presumably because it suggests, at some profound level, that this kind of guy is more likely to share his resources with a woman and their children, rather than thinking only of himself. Poor George, how his wife got that bit wrong.

And, what happened to the Old Orange Tree pub?

Ha, in one of those delicious temporal ironies that could only have been thought up by a committee of heavenly jokers, a genetic revolution was trumped by… a pop music revolution. The Victorian pile was demolished in the year that Hamilton's papers were published, to make way for a new office block. And the rubble of the bar where Haldane had growled out his mathematical workings became the backdrop for one of the iconic early album covers for The Beatles.

The Secrets of Life - Book One

Perhaps the four mop heads are jumping on the remains of all that scientific joke making? It's stretching it to say that the two events are related but, since that time, twisting and shouting just about sums up the 'group selection' versus 'kin selection' tussle. And one wonders whether John Lennon bought his round glasses from the same place as John Maynard Smith?

Which brings us to Maynard Smith himself. What of him?

Well, in the early 1970s he and George Price had begun to collaborate. What interested them both was seeing whether an emerging new branch of mathematics called game theory could have applications for understanding behaviour in the natural world.

What's game theory? It's a mechanism that's used for studying the mathematical processes involved in decision-making. At base, it's a way of looking at all the possible outcomes of a decision event, and then weighing up which choice would best suit something when it's up against an opponent… that's also making decisions. Sounds simple enough, but the trick is to try not to make a decision until one's opponent has made theirs.

Why might this have been significant for their work? It was because what was indisputable was that organisms had been making biological, genetic and behavioural decisions since the first emergence of Luca. And it was the accumulated result of these decisions that had led to the history of life on earth, and to the great diversity of species that have come and gone - and those that survive with us now.

The advances in game theory that were coming out of the US were almost all dealing with how humans made decisions in the fields of social interaction and economic theory. But Maynard Smith began to question whether this same thinking might not have a role to play in understanding evolution. This was because one of the areas that most interested him was looking at whether natural selection favoured organisms that acted aggressively, and led them to fight with other members of their species.

Game theory's findings seemed to be suggesting that uncooperative behaviour was self-defeating. Yet the accepted belief in biology had always been that being strong, and taking command, was a sexual display for showing how great an animal's genes must be.

But was that right? After all, Maynard Smith now began to wonder, wasn't it strange that competing animals often indulged in elaborate displays of combat, and yet they very rarely did each other any lasting harm.

Why were some animals perfectly happy to carry out terrible acts of infanticide in displays of Hamiltonian Spite as a way of limiting competition to their genes - and yet they behaved completely differently when they picked on someone their own size? Maynard Smith and George Price now began to look around at examples of this in the natural world - and they became particularly intrigued by the behaviour of stags.

Stags interested them because they seemed to represent exactly the kind of strutting displays of power that are intended to show females how great their reproductive qualities would be. And yet, for all their aggression and elaborate fighting rituals, these huge beasts never actually risked much. They had enormous and presumably awkward antlers as a mate signally phenotype and they used these to rut with competitive males. It all looked terribly dangerous, but in reality most contests weren't actually spent scrapping, but in roaring loudly at each other.

What they seemed to be doing, Maynard Smith thought, was behaving just like humans do when they're weighing up an opponent, hesitating to see what the other person did before they made their own move. Clearly each stag wanted to 'win' for their hierarchical position in the colony, but it was equally evident that they weren't going to risk their lives for the sake of power. This bellowing therefore seemed to be rather like drunks shouting about how they're going to 'moider da bum' rather than actually getting down to it.

The two researchers now began attaching game theoretic probabilities to the outcomes of injury, survival, loss, stalemate and victory in these contests. And then the penny dropped. Instead of being weapons, Maynard Smith now speculated, evolution had made the vicious-looking antlers into a form of defensive buffers, a deer's version of the puffy leather gloves that protect a boxer's hands.

It was from this realisation that the two men then began to develop the theory that the most successful animals were those that had the most limited aggression strategies.

But what were animals like this trying to achieve with the ritualised conflict fandangos so many of them used?

By giving animals strategies like probing and retaliation, and then setting them against each other as in a game, Maynard Smith and Price ran computer simulations that weighed up the outcomes. Their conclusions would go against all the mythology about the drama of contests that most of us would have thought were going on. Instead, they concluded that it was evolutionarily beneficial for individuals *not* to escalate a fight, or to run the risk of wounding - and only rarely or accidentally to do anything that could lead to death.

Then a whole cash register of pennies dropped. Maynard Smith suddenly saw that if success in life was all about surviving and reproducing, then staying safe and protecting oneself and one's kin was a critical factor. What could wipe a species out were two things: first, environmental change - and there was only so much that could be done about that. Mutations could provide the changes needed to stay out of trouble, but they depended on the roll of the genetic dice and this couldn't be relied on to protect a species.

However the second great unknown arose because organisms were always in danger of a competitor doing what they did, *but doing it better*. From here the two men speculated that what was really going on in these contests was that the scuffling animals were showing each other the degree to which they were superior in the species' survival strategy.

In short, the interests of both fighters were best served if each of them decided to *act out* fights rather than risk real damage. It was hardly surprising, they concluded, that these skirmishes were so often a kind of formalised, pretend combat. They wrote up their findings in a paper entitled *The Logic of Animal Conflict* and sent it off to *Nature*. It made the front cover.

And then a whole amusement arcade of pennies dropped. Now Maynard Smith began to see through to one of the most fundamental of all the evolutionary forces. What organisms want, and indeed what everything in life wants, is to be safe from a competitor invading its niche - a concept that he was to call an 'evolutionary stable strategy' (ESS). This, he said, meant arriving at an unbeatable strategy for a species that *couldn't be bettered by an opponent unless there was a step change in the other's intelligence or physical additions*.

Rather like businessmen looking at competitive brands to see what the threats might be to their own products and development plans, or security forces running mock attacks on themselves to check on their defence procedures, so Maynard Smith now concluded that organisms in the natural world were forever conducting their own research to find out if their phenotypes and behavioural strategies were watertight. It appeared, he thought, that these ritual contests were one of the ways.

Individuals, in other words, were not only 'fighting' for themselves, but they were fighting for the good of their species, and the good of their genes, because they were endlessly making sure that their ESS was still fit for purpose.

Where had all this ended up?

Hamilton had shone a light on how selfishness, altruism, cooperation, and spite could all be explained by mathematical modelling and testing.

He and Maynard Smith had shown there was no argument that altruism could evolve as long as its benefits were shared by a genetically related individual, rather than by random members of a community.

Now Maynard Smith and George Price were saying that related individuals use aggressive behaviour towards each other as a way of ensuring that their life strategies were safe from outside invasion.

These insights were now widening everyone's thinking - and it must have been at around this time that Maynard Smith turned his attention to a more general aspect of the same issue. This arose because if competition and conflict were to be seen everywhere, then how come symbiotic cooperation was such a self-evidently successful strategy in Nature? The difference between the phenomenon and members of the same species working together for the good of their genes was… that the individuals weren't related!

What was going on? Why would *different* things decide to cooperate, let alone display altruistic strategies to each other? The only explanation he could see was that the entire Behavioural Spectrum was an illustration of why species and ecological relationships in the natural world were held *in balance*… and why nothing ever 'won' for long, let alone forever.

In looking at this he was putting his finger on perhaps the most bewildering of all life's mysteries. If there'd been billions and billions of organisms on earth, he was saying - from single-celled creatures to phenomenally complicated mega structures like ourselves and stags - why had nothing ever evolved to be truly secure in life, never mind lording it over its competition?

Why did everything always have weaknesses?

Maynard Smith could see that every species was *trying* to find somewhere ecologically safe so that nothing could invade its niche. An evolutionary stable state.

But now he began to use game theory to find the holy grail of evolutionary biology… and to identify the mechanism that was controlling why creatures and species could coexist, could even live in harmony, in spite of being motivated to steal each other's energy, or to grab one another's niches.

You'd think this never-ending process would lead to chaotic anarchy and mutual destruction. And yet that didn't seem to happen. Most noticeably, there weren't continual collapses. Quite the opposite seemed to be the case, there was evidently a 'balance of nature'.

Competition and conflict clearly weren't leading to chaos at all, but were somehow producing order.

It was from this start point that he went on to develop his great explanation for the way aggressive organisms that were following a 'zero sum' approach to life - trying to win by beating the competition - could coexist in a balanced way with cooperative organisms that won by being part of winning groups. These were termed 'non-zero sum' or simply 'non-zero' and Maynard Smith began to hypothesise that it was the tension and interaction between these two different approaches that held the natural world in equilibrium. This, he was sure, was the mechanism that made certain no organism's strategy was ever consistently superior to its competition over the long run of evolutionary time.

Why not though? Surely some things would win by being more aggressive and wiping out their competitors?

John Maynard Smith plunged once more into game theory for the answers. He reasoned that if the outcomes of contact between species could be mathematically modelled in the same way that he'd applied them to ritual contests, then perhaps he could see why there was no such thing as a single winning strategy.

The problem he faced, however, was the usual one that the results of evolutionary decision-making and behaviour simply take such a colossally long time to reveal themselves. Like most scientists he'd always used the *Drosophila* fruit fly as his test subject because it could produce a new generation every seven days - but even this was too slow to highlight real change.

Now he realised that even better insights, and certainly faster ones, could come from looking at how *humans* behaved, and what the decision-making processes were that they used. Just like other organisms, we sometimes use 'hawkish' strategies in dealing with other people when we try to get an advantage by behaving aggressively and selfishly. On other occasions, we might use more 'dovish' behaviour and cooperate unselfishly to get what we want.

What makes us so completely different from other organisms, however, is that we arrive at these choices quickly, hopping around on the Behavioural Spectrum and changing our approach depending on what the other person does.

Where we match the colonies of the natural world, however, is that our human societies seem to be held in the same balance as they are. Yes, ours fluctuate between order and disorder in the same way as theirs, but taken over the very long run, we tend not to collapse into permanent chaos any more than they do.

Perhaps, Maynard Smith now speculated, the game theoretic insights that were showing how decision-making processes drove our cultural evolution could be a model to illustrate how natural selection had worked everywhere else throughout the history of life. (By the way, if you find it interesting how we and every other organism come to the same behavioural outputs, I expand on this and Maynard Smith's use of the mechanics of game theory in Book Three.)

But if this was to hold water as a theory, how had humans developed cultural evolution? We'd arrived on the planet as a species right at the fag end of the evolution story, nearly four billion years after life kicked off.

So what had we inherited from everything that had come before us?

Maynard Smith had to have been right in saying that we were descendants of the rules and processes that had developed in other organisms to govern decision-making… yet we were also clearly quite different in many other ways.

In which case, what did their history tell us about ourselves - and what did we show about them?

'Think of life as an ocean...'

CHAPTER TWENTY ONE

Geneticists say humans are the only organisms on earth that can override the instructions of their genes, but what are we rebelling against?

The Seeker after the Truth was on the last stage of his journey. He'd spent days in planes and airports, snatching sleep on trains and, for a horribly long time, bouncing around in the back of a vegetable truck. Thirty miles on foot had followed, stumbling along a stony path, until a friendly goatherd had pointed him upwards to where a rocky ledge hung out from the side of a mountain. Up and up, he'd clambered, ignoring his vertigo until now, as he hauled himself over the sharpness of the last stone, he saw the bearded figure that he'd travelled so far to meet.

The Hermit Guru.

The Seeker lay still for a few moments, gathering himself, but his laboured pants soon alerted the guru. With a slight shake, the man emerged from the depths of his meditation.

'Yes?' he said, immediately sensing that the Seeker's handmade Savile Row hiking gear marked him out as English. 'What do you look for?'

'I have come far, O great Guru', the Seeker replied, barely able to contain his excitement, 'to ask you about ourselves. I wish to know if man is simply an intelligent animal… or has he become a different being altogether?'

That was a pause, then the hint of a smile passed over the mystic's wrinkled face.

'Think of life as an ocean…'

Oh dear, groaned the Seeker inwardly, suddenly exhausted. It had been a very long way to come to hear this kind of hippy-dippy nonsense. Then he sighed in resignation; after all, he might as well hear the old boy out.

'An ocean?'

'Yes, indeed. We usually think of oceans only in terms of the part we can see, the waves. But these are just tiny clues about the whole. The surface appearance confuses us with its unpredictability, its powerful swells, its sudden ferocity… waves can change in an instant from being calm to a troubled madness. They can sometimes be inviting, sometimes terrifying, but at all times their behaviour is almost impossible to forecast. Yet they don't tell the whole story.'

'Not the whole story?'

'No. Because beneath these waves is another world. A vast, dark place where the water is sometimes miles deep. Unlike the waves, the sea here seems stable and solid. But it would be a mistake to think that. For in these depths are strong currents that flow in constant, known directions. Scientists can measure their movements and are able to predict their actions.'

The Seeker nodded and the Guru closed his eyes. Then he continued:

'But why are there such currents? The answers are also known to science. It is because of temperature differences around the globe, gravitational pulls, variations in the salinity of different regions, winds and even the forces created by the Earth's rotation.'

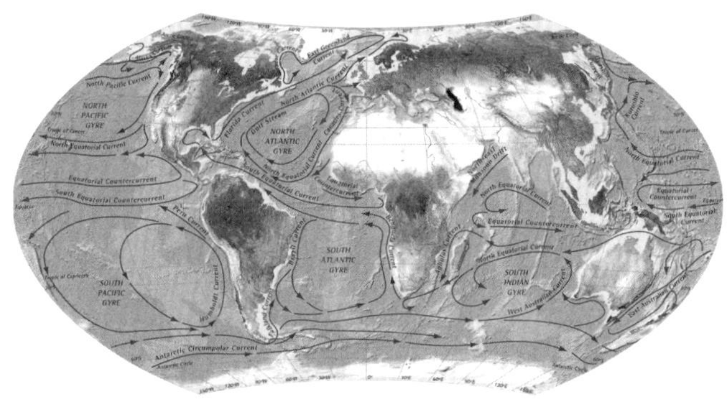

The currents in life are just like the currents in the oceans.

Hmm, thought the Seeker, now impressed. Not much hippy stuff here. But what was the metaphor the Guru was describing? He waited for the old man to speak again.

'In the same way, all life forms have similar reasons for shaping the actions we can see. Just as there are surface appearances, so there are currents beneath them that are like the profound forces at work in evolution. What are they? First, the Laws of Thermodynamics are demanding that living things find strategies to get the energy they need to survive in a world of never-ending decay and change. Then the dedication of the gene - its 'selfishness' - and the brilliance of the way it influences everything in life, means that organisms are forever altering to meet new demands. Only the best adapted win.

'Nothing in life is ever wholly right or wholly wrong, and every action we see is just a part of their strategies for survival. That is why there is such diversity and why, for each catastrophe and extinction, there will always be new species. In spite of this, every organism is programmed to find a place where it can be safe from threats, stable within evolution. But stability is a chimaera, my friend, challenges are everywhere and endless. And nothing is forever.'

'Although evolution may seem, in some vague sense, a 'good thing',
especially since we are the product of it, nothing actually 'wants' to evolve.'
Richard Dawkins, *The Selfish Gene*

There was silence. The Seeker's astonishment could not have been more complete.

'You surprise me, O Wise One,' he said. 'May I ask how you came by such knowledge?'

'Of course. My first degree was in biology at Stanford and I did postgraduate work at Harvard in evolutionary theory. You wonder at my present choice of life? Well, I like it here. It's nice and quiet, the view pleases me and the villagers bring me food.'

The Seeker laughed. 'Go on with your analogy… what are the currents?'

'They are the reasons that life has survived for so long. At every step of the unfolding story of evolution, living things have merged their assets so that the problems that were defeating them as individuals could be solved by pooling their resources. They then share in the benefits. This process brings about new life, and it releases spare energy.

'Humans see differences between good and bad, light and dark, selfishness and sacrifice. And these distinctions form the basic material for religions and philosophies - and even for our own thought processes. But the gene doesn't care about such notions and feelings. Its sole task is to ensure that life survives. To do that it will pursue any strategy it can find to help it succeed. This is why the gene encourages cooperation. It is because cooperation wins… even though any selflessness one sees was born of selfish drives. Altruism is just genetic selfishness.'

'Survive, survive and survive - these are the quintessential laws of Nature.

But survive does not always mean being mean.

Suzanne Palmer, *Finder*

The Guru drew a deep breath, and after pausing to order his thoughts, he began to list out the currents that life had established over its immensely long history. As he did so the Seeker slid a hand into his pocket and quietly pulled out some paper and a pen. Many hours later he would review his scrawled handwriting and read again the Guru's points:

1. Cooperation is the cornerstone of success. All major evolutionary breakthroughs have come from different things combining to exchange their specialisms and assets - so they can make new organisms that are more complex than themselves.

2. In this way, symbiotic alliances have been critical to progress, even if one party will likely gain more from them than the other. There will always be tensions in these relationships, and sometimes these can even undermine the health of the organism itself. However, it does not matter if one party seems to be getting more than the other, only that they are both dependent on the relationship.

3. Evolutionary breakthroughs frequently come when living things outsource a function to something else.

4. Nature appears to avoid ever letting its old survival strategies disappear, even though it is always looking to improve the organism's security by creating adaptations.

5. Natural selection means behavioural strategies work together to produce the fittest winners - this is how successful organisms get more genes out into the world than the competition. The invention of sex led to an explosion of new life forms.

6. Species diversity is critical to creating security for the gene. Its actions may lead to consistency in reproduction, but this same process also produces occasional

errors. These are mutations, and it's because of these that life can eventually lead on to new organisms which might, one day, survive environmental change.

7. All strategies and all evolutionary decisions are only about survival and reproduction - and about the wish to gain an advantage. This is why genes and organisms might appear to be acting selfishly, but their strategies are simply different ways of winning.

8. All living things choose how to behave with the other organisms around them. Some are simply ignored but, where there are interactions, there is a Behavioural Spectrum of these decisions. At one end of this organisms will be parasitic and kill their hosts, while at the other extreme they are altruistic, and live only for the benefit of others. This self-sacrificial strategy shows the genius of the gene at its most subtle. Here it is attracting profitable relationships by dealing with other living things, and sometimes this leads them to even separate out the functions of survival and reproduction with relatives within their own species.

9. Organisms try to win in life either by beating the competition - the so-called zero sum approach - or by cooperating with other things and therefore winning by helping their species and communities win. Zero sum strategies succeed when energy is transferred to meet the 1st Law of Thermodynamics. But non-zero cooperation is the only way to overcome the 2nd Law… because it creates energy surpluses that can challenge the relentless action of entropy. When organisms employ a non-zero strategy, then they are constantly looking for ways to establish trust with the other things they are dealing with.

10. Nature is providing constant challenges - from parasites, from competitors, even from other members of the same species - but these are all forces that can improve the organism.

The Guru had leant forward as he'd come to the end of his explanation for how the currents of evolution ran so deep. Now he stretched out a bony finger to emphasise his final points.

'Behind all these things is the gene. Just chemistry, of course, but nonetheless the great organiser of our collective existence. It is what led life to evolve the creation of the vast diversity of different forms we share the world with, and it has supported and refined each and every one of them. Yet it will accept the constant failure and extinction of these creations as the price of its own success. These vehicles may disappear - but the gene will always find new ways for it to be carried around.

'But why does nothing ever win in life? Why does everything try to survive forever, and yet nothing ever does? Why does every single life form have weaknesses that will bring about its downfall? You'd think this would lead to chaos, wouldn't you? Yet in spite of the constant challenges of other organisms, all of them endlessly trying to exploit the weaknesses of others, why does life result in order? Answer these questions, my young friend, and you will see how it is that the world can be held in balance.'

It was clear that the Guru was coming to the end of his explanation, and was now leaving the Seeker to ponder alone on these final issues. The man put away his notes, still anxious to steer the discussion back to his original question.

'And mankind?' he repeated. 'Does our species follow your currents of existence?'

'Yes, of course we do. People may be offended by comparisons with lower animals, but we're made of exactly the same cells as other things, we have the same biochemistry, we reproduce in the same way, and we react to the same forces. We, also, are selfish and driven to win in life because we, too, wish to survive and attract mates to reproduce with - however little we may want to acknowledge it.

> **'All of today's DNA, strung through all the cells of the Earth,**
> **is simply an extension and elaboration of the first molecule.'**
> **Lewis Thomas, *The Medusa and the Snail***

'Our forebears emerged as a new species only after life had already been evolving for nearly four thousand million years. That is 99.99% of the time that some kind of life form has been around, and we employ exactly the same mechanisms as other creatures. In doing this, we've been relying on billions of years of trial and error to make us the way we are.'

'But we're so obviously different from other living things!' said the Traveller hotly.

'That's because we've followed our own evolutionary path. There have been physical, behavioural and cultural revolutions along the way that have made us unique. If you like my analogy, we have been shaped by the same currents, but our waves are now different.'

'You mean we've been overriding the currents - rebelling against the instructions we get from our genes?'

'Quite. And that, my friend, is why there are such troubled waters in human existence. Our development has given us the ability to see who we are, and frequently to not like it. We make our own decisions about how to live and how to behave. Other organisms don't have our insights, nor our freedom to make changes.

But we pay a high price when we mutiny against these natural forces, and much pain comes from the conflict. This is the 'human condition'. It is little wonder to me that you are here, seeking answers to life. Humans are fixated by trying to understand the waves of our existence, yet they so seldom seem interested in understanding the currents that have made them what they are.'

**'Some people would claim that things like love, joy and beauty belong
to a different category from science and can't be described in scientific terms,
but I think they can now be explained by the theory of evolution.'
Stephen Hawking, *The Theory of Everything***

The old man was beginning to tire, and the Seeker rose to thank him. He began to retrace his steps, and as he descended, he turned the Guru's comments over in his mind, and began to wonder what he'd meant when he spoke of our unique ability to make decisions.

At what point had we departed from the evolutionary path of other organisms? And when in mankind's history had the greatest changes arisen - the crucial decision events at which we'd leapt forward in our development as a species?

The Seeker remembered that anthropologists and evolutionary biologists had often talked about the cultural 'Revolutions' that had shaped *Homo sapiens*, and he now started to list them in his mind as he walked. By the time he was back on the road, a direction had started to take shape in his imagination that allowed him to see the ways the human species had taken to break away from every other living thing.

But where had we come from as a species anyway? And how had we split away from other organisms in such an incredibly short time? What, exactly, were these 'Revolutions' that people spoke of? And how had they made us rebel against the currents of our existence?

In short, he wondered, what had made us who we are?

Acknowledgements

The term 'Acknowledgements' doesn't begin to express the debt I owe to the people whose books and articles I gulped down before and during the writing of this series. I began as a complete outsider, a blank slate, and anything I learnt came from them.

In doing this I structured the four volumes largely as someone who was trying to join the dots - taking the thoughts and findings of countless academics and commentators, and then coming up with insights about what it all might mean. My intention was to arrange things into a chronology of life's story in such a way that it would hopefully illustrate how the same natural forces have been at work from the first instant of creation right down to the present day. It was why and how this happened that most interested me.

Many of the conclusions I came to, however, were my own, and if I've misrepresented any of the specialists who unknowingly passed on their knowledge, then I can only plead ignorance. Nonetheless my anxiety on the issue led to enough non-sleepers to decide on peppering the text with direct quotes.

I figured that if interested readers knew who the experts were, they could then go to the original sources. The writers of these books would doubtless explain things better than I ever could, and I've therefore compiled a list of the ones I found particularly helpful. Many were utterly fascinating. These are the mother lode, and the list I've given here should hopefully cover the four books in the series.

It goes without saying that their authors, together with the people who contributed to the countless articles I read on the internet (and particularly the anonymous altruists behind the non-zero miracle that is Wikipedia) have my deepest gratitude.

Abbey, E. *A Voice Crying In The Wilderness*. Griffin, 1991

Acemoglu, D. and Robinson, JA. *Why Nations Fail: The Origins of Power, Prosperity and Poverty*. Profile Books, 2013

Adams, D. *The Hitchhiker's Guide to the Galaxy*. Macmillan, 2009

Alexander, RD. *The Biology of Moral Systems*. Aldine de Gruyter, 1987

Alexander, RD. *Darwinism and Human Affairs*. Pitman, 1980

Allen, D. *Article in Psychology Today*, 2018

Amadae, SM. *Prisoners of Reason*. Cambridge University Press, 2016

Amis, M. *Inside Story*. Vintage, 2021

Arendt, H. *The Origins of Totalitarianism*. Penguin Classics, 1973/2017

Armstrong, K. *A History of God*. Ballantine Books, 1994

Atwood, M. *Morning in the Burned House*. Virago, 1995

Axelrod, R. *The Evolution of Cooperation*. Penguin Books, 1984

Axelrod, R. and Hamilton, WD. *The Evolution of Cooperation*. Science, 1981

Baechler, J. *Suicides*. Basic Books, 1979

Bailey, R. *The End of Doom. Environmental Renewal in the Twenty-First Century*. Thomas Dunne Books, 2015

Behe, M. *Darwin's Black Box*. Simon and Schuster, 2006

Belton, C. *Putin's People*. William Collins, 2021

Bernstein, W. *A Splendid Exchange: How Trade Shaped The World*. Lampe, Markus, 2009

Biggs, A. and Burke, P. *A Social History of the Media*. Polity, 2020

Biglan, A. *The Nurture Effect: How the Science of Human Behavior Can Improve Our Lives and Our World*. New Harbinger Publications. 2015

Binmore, K. *Game Theory. A Very Short Introduction*. OUP, 2007

Binmore, K. *Playing for Real*. OUP, 2007

Binmore, K. *Game Theory and The Social Contract*. MIT Press, 1994

Birch, J. *The Philosophy of Social Evolution*. OUP, 2017

Blackmore, S. *The Meme Machine*. OUP, 1999

Boltzman, L. *Theoretical Physics and Philosophical Problems*. Springer, 1886/1974

Bond, M. *The Power of Others: Peer Pressure, Groupthink and How the People Around Us Shape Everything We Do*. Oneworld Publications, 2015

Borden, R. *Ecology and Experience*. North Atlantic Books, US, 2014

Boyd, R. *A Different Kind of Animal. How Culture Transformed Our Species*. Princeton University Press, 2018

Boyd, R. and Richerson, PJ. *The Origin and Evolution of Cultures*. OUP, 2005

Boyd, R. and Richerson, PJ. *Culture and the Evolutionary Process*. University of Chicago Press, 1985

Boyd, R. and Richerson, PJ. *Culture and Cooperation. In: Beyond Self-Interest* (ed Mansbridge, JJ) Chicago University Press, 1990

Boyd, R. and Silk, JB. *How Humans Evolved*. WW Norton Books, 2006

Brams, SJ. and Taylor, AD. *Fair Division From Cake-Cutting to Dispute Resolution*. Cambridge University Press, 1996

Bregman, R. *Humankind. A Hopeful History*. Bloomsbury, 2020

Bricker, D. and Ibbitson, J. *Empty Planet: The Shock of Global Population Decline*. Robinson, 2020

Brockman, J. (ed) *The Third Culture: Beyond the Scientific Revolution*. J. Doyne Farmer essay is Chapter 22. Simon and Schuster, 1996

Brockman, J. (ed) *This Idea Is Brilliant:Lost, Overlooked and Underappreciated Scientific Concepts Everyone Should Know*. Harper Perennial, 2018

Bronowski, J. *The Ascent of Man*. BBC Publications, 1973

Brusatte, S. *The Rise and Fall of Dinosaurs*. Picador, 2019

Butler, E. *Adam Smith - A Primer*. Institute of Economic Affairs and Profile Books, 2007

Camerer, C. *Behavioral Game Theory*. Princeton University Press, 2003

Campbell, RH. and Skinner, AS. *Adam Smith*. St Martin's, 1982

Carey, J. William Golding. *The Man Who Wrote Lord of the Flies*. Faber and Faber, 2010

Carlyle, T. *Critical and Miscellaneous Essays*. Arkose Press, 1838/2015

Chalupa, LM. *This Idea Is Brilliant*. See Brockman, J.

Chambers, R. *Vestiges of the Natural History of Creation*. Hard Press, 1844/2018

Chenoweth, E. and Stephan, MJ. *Why Civil Resistance Works: The Strategic Logic of Nonviolent Conflict*. Columbia University Press, 2011

Chomsky, NM. *Syntactic Structures*. Mouton, 1957

Chomsky, NM. *Language and Mind*. Harcourt, Brace and World, 1968

Chomsky, NM and others. *The Mystery of Language Evolution*. Frontiers of Psychology, 2014

Chown, M. *What a Wonderful World. Life: The Universe and Everything in a Nutshell*. Faber and Faber, 2013

Chown, M. *The Magic Furnace*, Vintage, 2000

Churchill, WS. *A History of the English Speaking Peoples*. Three volumes. Bloomsbury, 1956/2015

Clark, G. *A Farewell to Alms*. Princeton University Press, 2007

Conway, A. *Sapienta: The 40 Principles of Wisdom*. 2016-2019

Coyne, JA. *Why Evolution Is True*. Viking Books, 2009

Cressman, R. *Evolutionary Dynamics and Extensive Form Games*. MIT Press, 2003

Crichton, M. *Prey*. Harper Fiction, 2006

Darwin, C. *On The Origin of Species by Means of Natural Selection*. John Murray, 1859

Darwin, C. *The Descent of Man, and Selection in Relation to Sex*. John Murray, 1871

Davis, MD. *Game Theory. A Nontechnical Introduction*. Dover, 1997

Dawkins, R. *The Selfish Gene*. OUP, 1976

Dawkins, R. *The Extended Phenotype: The Gene as the Unit of Selection*. WW Norton, 1982

Dawkins, R. *The Blind Watchmaker*. Longman, 1986

Dawkins, R. *The God Delusion*. Houghton Mifflin, 2006

Dawkins, R. *The Greatest Show on Earth: The Evidence for Evolution*. Bantam Press, 2009

Dawkins, R. *An Appetite for Wonder. The Makings of a Scientist*. Black Swan Press. 2014

Delingpole, J. *How To Be Right*. Headline, 2007

deGrasse Tyson, N. *Universe Down to Earth*. Columbia University Press, 1995

deGrasse Tyson, N. *Astrophysics For People In A Hurry*. WW Norton, 2017

de Waal, F. *Good Natured: The Origins of Right and Wrong in Humans and Other Animals*. Harvard University Press, 1996

de Waal, F. *Primates and Philosophers: How Morality Evolved*. Princeton University Press, 2006

de Waal, F. *The Inner Ape: The Best and Worst of Human Nature*. Granta Books, 2006

Dennett, DC. *Darwin's Dangerous Idea: Evolution and the Meanings of Life*. Simon and Schuster. 1995

Dennett, DC. *Consciousness Explained*. Little, Brown and Company, 1991

Denton, M. *Evolution: A Theory in Crisis*. Adler and Adler, 2996

Deutch, D. *The Beginning of Infinity. Explanations that Transform the World*. Allen Lane, 2011

Diamond, J. *The Rise and Fall of the Third Chimpanzee*. Radius Books. 1991

Diamond, J. *Guns, Germs and Steel: The Fates of Human Societies*. WW Norton, 1999

Diamond, J. *Collapse: How Societies Choose to Fail or Survive*. Allen Lane, 2005

Diamond, J. *Why Is Sex Fun?* Quicklet, 2012

Disraeli, B. *The Vindication of the English Constitution*. HardPress Publishing, 1835/2020

Dixit, A. and Nalebuff, BJ. *Thinking Strategically: The Strategic Edge in Business, Politics and Everyday Life*. WW Norton. 1991

Dobzhansky, T. *Mankind Evolving*. Yale University Press, 1962

Dobzhansky, T. *Genetics and the Origin of Species*. Columbia Classics, Columbia University Press, 1982

Dresher, M. *Games of Strategy: Theory and Applications*. Prentice Hall, 1961

Dronamraju, K. *The Life and Work of JBS Haldane*. OUP, 2017

Dunbar, R. *Grooming, Gossip, and the Evolution of Language*. Cambridge University Press, 1996

Dunbar, R. *How Many Friends Does One Person Need?: Dunbar's Number and Other Evolutionary Quirks*. Faber and Faber. 2011

Dunbar, R., Barrett, L. and Lycett, J. *Evolutionary Psychology. A Beginner's Guide*. Oneworld, 2005

Dyson, F. *Origins of Life*. Cambridge University Press, 2010

Eagleman, D. *Incognito. The Secret Lives of the Brain*. Canongate, 2011

Edelman, S. *Computing the Mind.: How the Mind Really Works*. OUP, 2008

Eisenstein, EL. *The Printing Press as an Agent of Change*. Cambridge University Press, 1980

Eisenstein, EL. *The Printing Revolution in Early Modern Europe*. Cambridge University Press, 1993

Einstein, A. *Living Philosophies*. Creative Company, 1985

Einstein, A. *Ideas and Opinions*. Random House, 1997

Enders, G. *Gut: The Inside Story of Our Body's Most Underrated Organ*. Greystone Books, 2018

Ehrlich, P. *The Population Bomb*. Ballantine, 1968

Everett, D. *Don't Sleep, There Are Snakes. Life and Language in the Amazonian Jungle.* Profile Books, 2008

Everett, D. *How Language Began: The Story of Humanity's Greatest Invention.* Profile Books, 2018

Farmer, JD. See Brockman, J.

Ferguson, N. *The Ascent of Money.* Allen Lane, 2008

Feynman, R. *The Meaning of It All.* Allen Lane, 1998

Fisher, RA. *The Genetical Theory of Natural Selection.* OUP, 1930

Flanders, M. and Swann, D. *The Songs of Michael Flanders and Donald Swann.* Faber Music, 2007

Flynn, JR. *What Is Intelligence?* Cambridge University Press, 2007

Flynn, JR. *Are We Getting Smarter? Rising IQ In The Twentieth-First Century.* Cambridge University Press, 2012

Frank, SA. *Foundations of Social Behavior.* Princeton University Press, 1998

Frankopan, P. *The Silk Roads. A New History of the World.* Bloomsbury, 2015

Freud, S. *The Future of an Illusion.* Pacific Publishing Studio, 2010

Freud, S. *Civilisation and Its Discontents.* Martino Fine Books, 2011

Freud, S. *A General Introduction to Psychoanalysis.* 28 Lectures, published 2018

Friedel, R. *A Culture of Improvement.* MIT Press, 2007

Frisby, D. *Life After the State.* Unbound, 2013

Fry, DP. *The Human Potential for Peace: An Anthropological Challenge to Assumptions About War and Violence.* OUP, 2006

Fukuyama, F. *The End of History and The Last Man.* Free Press, 1992

Gamlin, L. *Evolution.* Dorling Kindersley, 1973

Gates, B. *How to Avoid a Climate Disaster: The Solutions We Have and the Breakthroughs We Need.* Penguin, 2022

Gelb, M. *Innovate Like Edison.* Plume, 2009

Gilbert, DT. *Stumbling on Happiness.* Knopf, 2006

Gladwell, M. *Blink: The Power of Thinking Without Thinking.* Penguin, 2006

Gleick, J. *The Information: A History, A Theory, A Flood.* Fourth Estate, 2012

Goddard, J. and Eccles, T. *Uncommon Sense, Common Nonsense.* Profile, 2012

Godfrey-Smith, P. *Other Minds. The Octopus and the Evolution of Intelligent Life.* William Collins, 2017

Golding, W. *Lord of the Flies*. Faber and Faber, 1997

Gould, SJ. *Ever Since Darwin*. Burnett Books, 1978

Gould, SJ. *The Panda's Thumb*. WW Norton, 1980

Gould, SJ. *Hen's Teeth and Horse's Toes*. WW Norton, 1983

Gould, SJ. *The Mismeasure of Man*. Includes: *Biological Potentiality vs Biological Determinism*. WW Norton, 1996

Gould, SJ. *Full House: The Spread of Excellence from Plato to Darwin*. Harmony Books, 1996

Gould, SJ. *The Structure of Evolutionary Theory*. Harvard University Press, 2002

Gould, SJ. *The Richness of Life*. Vintage, 2007

Gould, SJ. *The Flamingo's Smile*. WW Norton, 2013

Graeber, D. *Debt. The First 5,000 Years*. Grover Gardner, 2015

Green, J. *The Fault in Our Stars*. Penguin, 2013

Greene, G. *The Quiet American*. Vintage Classics, 2004

Greene, J. *Moral Tribes: Emotion, Reason, and the Gap Between Us and Them*. Penguin. 2013

Haeckel, E. *The History of Creation*. Routledge, 1889/2019

Haidt, J. *The Righteous Mind: Why Good People Are Divided by Politics and Religion*. Pantheon, 2012

Haldane, JBS *The Causes of Evolution*. Forgotten Books, 1932/2018

Haldane, JBS. *Population Genetics*. Penguin New Biology, 1955

Haldane, JBS. and Huxley, J. *Animal Biology*. OUP, 1934

Hamilton, WD. *The Evolution of Altruistic Behavior*. American Naturalist, 1963

Hamilton, WD. *The Genetical Evolution of Social Behaviour*. Journal of Theoretical Biology, 1964

Hamilton, WD. *Extraordinary Sex Ratios*. Science, 1967

Hamilton, WD. *Evolution of Social Behaviour: Vol 1 of Narrow Roads of Gene Land*. WH Freeman, 1996

Hamilton, WD. *Evolution of Sex: Vol 2 of Narrow Roads of Gene Land*. OUP, 2001

Hammond, NGL. *Alexander the Great*. Bristol Press, 1989

Harari, YN. *From Animals into Gods*. CreateSpace Independent Publishing, 2012

Harari, YN. *Sapiens. A Brief History of Humankind*. Vintage, 2015

Harari, YN. *Homo Deus. A Brief History of Tomorrow*. HarperCollins, 2017

Harari, YN. *21 Lessons for the 21st Century*. Jonathan Cape, 2018

Hardin, G. *The Tragedy of the Commons.* Science, 1968

Harford, T. *The Undercover Economist*. Abacus Books, 2007

Harford, T. *Adapt: Why Success Always Starts With Failure*. Abacus Books, 2012

Harker, J. (Ed) *The Last Ever Notes & Queries* Guardian Books/Fourth Estate, 1998

Harman, O. *The Price of Altruism: George Price and the Search for the Origins of Kindness.* The Bodley Head, 2010

Harris, M. *Cannibals and Kings: Origins of Culture*. Vintage Books, 1991

Harrison, GP. *At Least Know This: Essential Science to Enhance Your Life*. Prometheus Books, 2018

Hartson, W. *The Things That Nobody Knows*. Atlantic Books, 2011

Hauser, MD. *The Evolution of Communication*. Harvard University Press, 1996

Hawking, S. *The Theory of Everything*. Jaico Publishing House, 2008

Hawking, S. *The Dreams That Stuff Is Made Of: The Most Astounding Papers of Quantum Physics - and How They Shook the Scientific World*. Running Press, 2011

Hayek, FA von. *The Road to Serfdom*. Harper and Brothers, 1944

Hayek, FA von. *The Constitution of Liberty*. Chicago University Press, 1960

Hayflick, L. *The Future of Aging*. Nature, 2000

Hayflick, L. *Biological Aging Is No Longer An Unsolved Problem*. NY Academy of Sciences, 2007

Hazen, R. *The Story of Earth: The First 4.5 Billion Years, From Stardust to Living Planet.* Penguin, 2013

Henrich, J. *The Secret of Our Success: How Culture Is Driving Human Evolution, Domesticating Our Species, and Making Us Smarter*. Princeton University Press, 2016

Henrich, J. *The Weirdest People in the World: How the West Became Psychologically Peculiar and Particularly Prosperous*. Penguin, 2021

Highfield, R. and Coveney, P. *Frontiers of Complexity: The Search for Order in a Chaotic World.* Faber and Faber, 1996

Hill, C. *The World Turned Upside Down: Radical Ideas During The English Revolution.* Penguin, 1971

Hitchens, C. *The Missionary Position: Mother Teresa in Theory and Practice*. Verso, 1995

Hobbes, T. *Leviathan*. OUP, 1651/1957

Hofbauer, J. and Sigmund, K. *Evolutionary Games and Population Dynamics.* Cambridge University Press, 1998

Holland, J. *Emergence: From Chaos to Order.* Basic Books, 1999

Holmes, R. *Acts of War. Behaviour of Men in Battle.* Weidenfeld and Nicolson, 2004

Howard, T. *Dove Descending.* Ignatius Press, 2006

Howes, A. *Arts and Minds: How the Royal Society of Arts Changed a Nation.* Princeton University Press, 2020

Hoyle, F. *The Intelligent Universe: A New View of Creation and Evolution.* Michael Joseph, 1983

Hugo, V. *Les Misérables.* Penguin Classics, 2015

Hume, D. *A Treatise on Human Nature.* OUP, 1739/2000

Hutton, J. *Theory of the Earth; or an Investigation of the Laws Observable in the Composition, Dissolution, and Restoration of Land upon the Globe.* Transactions of the Royal Society of Edinburgh, 1788

Huxley, J. *Evolution: The Modern Synthesis.* MIT Press, 1942/2010

Huxley, T. *Man's Place In Nature.* Ann Arbour Paperbacks, 1863

Huxley, T. *The Struggle for Existence in Human Society.* 1888

James, W. *The Principles of Psychology.* Henry Holt and Co., 1890/2021

Jefferson, T. *Memoirs. American Classics*, 1821/2020

Johnson, MB. *The Angel of Compassion.* TP Press, 2015

Kahneman, D. *Thinking Fast and Slow.* Penguin, 2011

Kahneman, D., Slovic, P. and Tversky, A. *Judgement Under Uncertainty: Heuristics and Biases.* Cambridge University Press, 1982

Kay, J. *The Truth About Markets.* Allen Lane, 2003

Kennedy, P. *Rise and Fall of the Great Powers.* William Collins, 2017

Keynes, JM. *Economic Possibilities for Our Grandchildren.* In *Essays in Persuasion.* Harcourt Brace, 1932

King, ML, Jr. *Why We Can't Wait.* Penguin Classics, 1963/2018

Kipling, R. *The Jungle Book.* Macmillan Collector's Library, 2016

Kropotkin, P. *Mutual Aid: A Factor in Evolution.* Allen Lane, 1902/1972

Krugman, P. *Ricardo's Difficult Idea*. In *Freedom and Trade: The Economics and Politics of International Trade*. Routledge, 1998

Kwarteng, K. *War and Gold: A Five Hundred-Year History of Empires, Adventures and Debt*. Bloomsbury, 2015

Laing, RD. *The Divided Self: An Existential Study in Sanity and Madness*. Penguin Classics, 2010

Lane, N. *Life Ascending: The Ten Great Inventions of Evolution*. Profile, 2010

Lane, N. *The Vital Question: Why Is Life The Way It Is?* Profile, 2016

Larkin, P. *The Complete Poems*, Faber and Faber, 2014

Leadbetter, C. *Up The Down Escalator: Why the Global Pessimists Are Wrong*. Viking, 2002

Leakey, R. *The Origin of Humankind*. Basic Books, 1994

Leakey, R. and Lewin, R. *Origins*. Penguin, 1982

Le Bon, G. *Psychology of Revolution*. SMK Books, 1913/2018

Le Guin, U. *The Dispossessed*. Victor Gollancz, 1999

Lerner, J. *Kin and Kind*. Article in the New Yorker, February, 2012

Levi, M. *This Idea Is Brilliant*. See Brockman, J.

Levin, SA. *Games, Groups and the Global Good*. Springer, 2009

Levitt, SD. and Dubner, SJ. *Freakonomics. A Rogue Economist Explores the Hidden Side of Everything*. William Morrow, 2005

Levitt, SD. and Dubner, SJ. *Think Like A Freak*. Allen Lane, 2014

Lewens, T. *Cultural Evolution*. OUP, 2015

Lewis, M. *The Undoing Project*. Penguin, 2007

Lewis, M. *Boomerang: Travels in the New Third World*. WW Norton, 2011

Lieberman, DE. *The Story of the Human Body: Evolution, Health and Disease*. Penguin, 2014

Ligotti, T. *The Conspiracy Against the Human Race*, Penguin, US, 2018

Lipton, B. *Spontaneous Evolution: Our Positive Future and a Way to Get There from Here*. Hay House, 2011

Locke, J. *An Essay Concerning Human Understanding: Second Treatise of Government*. Wordsworth Editions, 1690/2014

Lockwood, C. *The Human Story*. Sterling, 2008

Lomborg, B. *The Sceptical Environmentalist*. Cambridge University Press, 2001

The Secrets of Life - Book One

Lorenz, K. *On Aggression*. Harcourt Brace, 1966

Losos, J. *Improbable Destinies*. Penguin, 2018

Lovelock, J. *The Vanishing Face of Gaia: A Final Warning*. Allen Lane, 2010

Macaulay, TB. *Review of Southey's Colloquies on Society*. Edinburgh Review, 1830

Macfarlane, A. *The Origins of English Individualism*. Blackwell, 1979

Mackie, J. *Ethics. Inventing Right and Wrong*. Penguin, 1976

Malatesta, E. *Life and Ideas*. PM Press, 2015

Malthus, TR. *An Essay on the Principle of Population as it Affects the Future Improvement of Society*. Macmillan, 1798/1926

Margulis, L. *Origin of Eukaryotic Cells*. Yale University Press, 1970

Margulis, L. *Symbiosis in Cell Evolution*. WH Freeman, 1981

Margolis, H. *Selfishness, Altruism and Rationality*. Cambridge University Press, 1982

Margulis, L. *Origins of Sex: Three BIllion Years of Genetic Recombination*. Yale University Press, 1986

Margulis, L. and Sagan, D. *What Is Life?* Simon and Schuster, 1995

Maugham, WS. *Of Human Bondage*. Vintage Classics, 2000

May, R. *Man's Search for Himself*. WW Norton, 2009

Maynard Smith, J. *Group Selection and Kin Selection*. Nature, 1964

Maynard Smith, J. *The Theory of Games and the Evolution of Animal Conflict*. Journal of Theoretical Biology, 1974

Maynard Smith, J. *The Evolution of Sex*. Cambridge University Press, 1978

Maynard Smith, J. *Evolution and the Theory of Games*. Cambridge University Press, 1982

Maynard Smith, J. *The Problems of Biology*. OUP, 1986

Maynard Smith, J. *Games, Sex and Evolution*. Harvester Wheatsheaf, 1988

Maynard Smith, J. *Evolutionary Genetics*. OUP, 1998

Maynard Smith, J. *The Theory of Evolution*. Cambridge University Press, 2008

Maynard Smith, J. and Price, GR. *The Logic of Animal Behaviour*. Nature, 1973

Maynard Smith, J. and Szathmary, ER. *The Major Transmissions in Evolution*. OUP, 1997

Maynard Smith, J. and Szathmary, ER. *The Origins of Life: From the Birth of Life to the Origin of Language*. OUP, 1999

McAfee, A. *More from Less: The Surprising Story of How We Learnt to Prosper Using Less Resources.* Simon and Schuster, 2020

McCloskey, D. *The Bourgeois Virtues: Ethics for an Age of Commerce.* Chicago University Press, 2006

McCloskey, D. *Bourgeois Dignity: Why Economics Can't Explain the Modern World.* Chicago University Press, 2011

McDougall, C. *Born to Run: The Hidden Tribe, the Ultra-Runners and the Greatest Race The World Has Ever Seen.* Profile Books, 2010

McLean, I. *Adam Smith, Radical and Egalitarian: An Interpretation for the 21st Century.* Edinburgh University Press, 2006

McLuhan, M. *Understanding Media: The Extensions of Man.* Routledge, 1964/2001

Mendel, G. *Experiments in Plant Hybridisation.* Kindle, 1866/2020

Mesoudi, A. *Cultural Evolution: How Darwinian Theory Can Explain Human Culture and Synthesize the Social Sciences.* University of Chicago Press, 2011

Miller, J. *Game Theory at Work. How To Use Game Theory to Outthink and Outmanoeuvre Your Competition.* McGraw-Hill, 2003

Micklethwait, J. and Wooldridge, A. *The Fourth Revolution.* Allen Lane, 2014

Minsky, M. *Society of Mind.* Simon and Schuster, 1986

Mises, L. von. *Liberalism: The Classical Tradition.* Liberty Fund, 2005

Mises, L. von. *Omnipotent Government.* Liberty Fund, 1944/2009

Mises, L. von. *Human Action: A Treatise on Economics.* Martino Fine Books, 1949/2012

Mises, L. von. *The Theory of Money and Credit.* Pacific Publications Studio, 1950/2010

Monod, J. *Chance and Necessity: Essay on the Natural Philosophy of Modern Biology.* HarperCollins, 1972

Montague, PR. *Your Brain is (Almost) Perfect: How We Make Decisions.* Plume, 2008

Morris, D. *The Naked Ape.* Vintage, 2005

Morris, I. *War, What Is It Good For? The Role of Conflict in Civilisation, from Primates to Robots.* Profile Books, 2014

Mukherjee, S. *The Gene. An Intimate History.* Vintage, 2016

Nasar, S. *A Beautiful Mind.* Simon and Schuster, 1998

Nascar, A. *Homo: A Brief History of Consciousness.* CreateSpace Independent Publishing, 2015

Nesse, RM. and Williams, GC. *Evolution and Healing: The New Science of Darwinian Medicine.* Weidenfeld and Nicolson, 1995 (Called *Why We Get Sick* in its US edition)

Neumann, J. von. and Morgenstern, O. *Theory of Games and Economic Behavior.* Princeton University Press, 1944

Norman, J. *Adam Smith: What He Thought, and Why It Matters.* Allen Lane, 2015

Nowak, MA. *Evolutionary Dynamics: Exploring the Equations of Life.* Harvard University Press, 2006

Nowak, MA. and Sigmund, K. *Tit for Tat in Heterogeneous Populations.* Nature, 1992

Nowak, MA. and Sigmund, K. *A Strategy of Win-Stay, Lose-Shift that Outperforms Tit for Tat in Prisoner's Dilemma.* Nature, 1993

Nowak, M., May, RM. and Sigmund, K. *The Arithmetics of Mutual Help.* Scientific American. 1995

Nowak, MA. and Sigmund, K. *Evolution of Indirect Reciprocity.* Nature, 2005

Nowak, M. and Highfield, R. *SuperCooperators. Altruism, Evolution, and Why We Need Each Other To Succeed.* Canongate, 2011

Nye, B. *Undeniable: Evolution and the Science of Creation.* St. Martin's Griffin, 2015

Oakley, B. *Pathological Altruism.* OUP, 1964

O'Rourke, PJ. *Republican Party Reptile.* Avalon Publishing, 1995

O'Rourke, PJ. *On The Wealth of Nations.* Atlantic, 2007

Orwell, G. *All Art Is Propaganda.* Mariner Books, 2009

Ostrom, E. *Governing the Commons: The Evolution of Institutions for Collective Action.* Cambridge University Press, 1990

Ostrom, E. *Coping with Tragedies of the Commons.* Annual Review of Political Science, 1999

Ostrom, E. *Understanding Institutional Diversity.* Princeton University Press, 2005

Ostrom, E., Gardner, R. and Walker, J. *Rules, Games and Common Pool Resources.* Princeton University Press, 1993

Palahniuk, C. *Invisible Monsters.* Vintage, 2000

Paine, T. *Ultimate Collection: Political Works, Philosophical Writings, Speeches, Letters and Biography.* Prague: e-artnow. 1778/2016

Palmer, S. *Finder.* Daw Books, 2019

Paxton, R. *The Anatomy of Fascism.* Vintage, 2005

Perry, G. *Behind the Shock Machine: The Untold Story of the Notorious Milgram Psychology Experiments*. Scribe, 2013

Pfaff, DW. *The Neuroscience of Fair Play: Why We (Usually) Follow The Golden Rule*. Dana Press, 2007

Pfaff, DW. *The Altruistic Brain: How We Are Naturally Good*. OUP, 2015

Pinker, S. *The Language Instinct*. HarperCollins, 1994

Pinker, S. *How The Mind Works*. WW Norton, 1997

Pinker, S. *The Blank Slate: The Modern Denial of Human Nature*. Viking Penguin, 2002

Pinker, S. *The Stuff of Thought: Language As A Window Into Human Nature*. Viking, 2007

Pinker, S. *The Better Angels of Our Nature: Why Violence Has Declined*. Penguin, 2011

Pinker, S. *Enlightenment Now. The Case for Reason, Science, Humanism and Progress*. Allen Lane, 2018

Pinker, S. *This Idea Is Brilliant*. See Brockman, J.

Pinker, S., Ridley, M., de Botton, A. and Gladwell, M. *Do Humankind's Best Days Lie Ahead?* Oneworld Books, 2016

Popper, K. *In Search of a Better World*. Routledge, 1995

Poundstone, W. *Prisoner's Dilemma: John von Neumann, Game Theory and the Puzzle of the Bomb*. Anchor Press, 1993

Poundstone, W. *Rock Breaks Scissors: A Practical Guide To Outguessing and Outwitting Almost Everybody*. Little Brown, 2014

Poundstone, W. *The Hidden Psychology of Value*. Oneworld Publications, 2011

Purkiss, D. *The English Civil War: A People's History*. Perennial, 2007

Raine, A. *The Anatomy of Violence: The Biological Roots of Crime*. Allen Lane, 2013

Rand, A. *Atlas Shrugged*. Random House, 1957

Rand, A. *The Virtue of Selfishness*. Signet, 1961

Rapoport, A. *Fights, Games and Debates*. University of Michigan Press, 1960

Rapoport, A. *Strategy and Conscience*. Harper and Row, 1964

Rapoport, A. *The Origins of Violence*. Paragon Books, 1989

Rapoport, A and Chammah, AM. *Prisoner's Dilemma*. University of Michigan Press, 1965

Rasmussen, DC. *The Infidel and the Professor. David Hume, Adam Smith and the Friendship that Shaped Modern Thought*. Princeton University Press, 2017

Read, L. I, *Pencil*. The Freeman Press, 1958 or on EconLib.org

Restak, R. *The Naked Brain*. Harmony Books, 2006

Ricardo, D. *The Principles of Political Economy and Organisation*. John Murray, 1817

Richardson, MEJ. *Hammurabi's Laws*. Clark International, 2000

Richerson, PJ and Boyd, R. *Not By Genes Alone: How Culture Transformed Human Evolution*. University of Chicago Press, 2005

Ridley, M. *The Problems of Evolution*. OUP, 1986

Ridley, M. *The Red Queen: Sex and The Evolution of Human Nature*. Viking, 1993

Ridley, M. *The Origins of Virtue*. Viking Books, 1995

Ridley, M. *The Rational Optimist: How Prosperity Evolves*. Fourth Estate, 2010

Ridley, M. *The Evolution of Everything. How Small Changes Transform Our World*. Fourth Estate, 2015

Roberts, R. *How Adam Smith Can Change Your Life*. Penguin, 2014

Robespierre, M. *Virtue and Terror*. Verso, 1789/2007

Ronson, J. *The Psychopath Test: A Journey Through the Madness Industry*. Riverhead Books, US, 2012

Rosenthal, EC. *The Complete Idiot's Guide to Game Theory*. Alpha Books, Penguin. 2011

Rosling, H. and Rosling, O. *Factfulness: Ten Reasons We're Wrong About The World - And Why Things Are Better Than You Think*. Sceptre, 2019

Rothman, J. *Why Is It So Hard To Be Rational?* The New Yorker, 2021

Rousseau, J-J. *A Discourse on Inequality*. Penguin, 1775/1984

Rousseau, J-J. *The Social Contract*. Wordsworth, 1762/1998

Rousseau, J-J. *Discourse on the Origin of Inequality*. Dover Publications, 1755/2004

Rucker, R. *Nested Scrolls - A Writer's Life*. PS Publishing, 2011

Ruskin, J. *Unto This Last and Other Writings*. Penguin Classics, 1985

Russel Wallace, A. *Darwinism*. Franklin Classics. 1889/2018

Rutherford, A. *A Brief History of Everyone Who Ever Lived. The Stories in Our Genes*. Weidenfeld and Nicolson. 2011

Sadedin, S. *Biologically Speaking, This Is Why Humans Are Born To Die*. Forbes, 2016

Sagan, C. *Cosmos: The Story of Cosmic Evolution, Science and Civilisation*. Abacus, 1983

Sagan, C. *The Dragons of Eden: Speculations on The Evolution of Human Intelligence.* Ballantine Books, 1989

Sagan, C. *The Daemon-Haunted World: Science as a Candle in the Dark.* Ballantine Books, 1997

Sagan, C. *Billions and Billions: Thoughts on Life and Death at the Brink of the Millennium.* Random House, 1997

Sandel, MJ. *What Money Can't Buy.* Allen Lane, 2012

Schelling, TC. *The Strategy of Conflict.* Harvard University Press. 1960

Schumacher, EF. *Small Is Beautiful: Economics as if People Mattered.* Penguin, 1975

Seeger, P. *Centennial Songbook Melody Line, Lyrics and Chord Symbols.* Hal Leonard, 2019

Semprun, J. *The Cattle Truck.* Serif, 1993

Sen, A. *Identity and Violence: The Illusion of Destiny.* WW Norton, 2006

Service, ER. *Origins of the State and Civilisation: The Process of Cultural Evolution.* WW Norton, 1975

Sharpe, J. *A Fiery and Furious People: A History of Violence in England.* Arrow, 2018

Shellenberger, M. *Apocalypse Never. Why Environmental Alarmism Hurts Us All.* HarperCollins, 2020

Shermer, M. *Why Darwin Matters.* Times Books, 2006

Shubin, N. *Some Assembly Required: Decoding Four Billion Years of Life, from Ancient Fossils to DNA.* Oneworld Books, 2021

Shubin, N. *The Universe Within: A Scientific Adventure.* Allen Lane, 2012

Siegfried, T. *A Beautiful Math: John Nash, Game Theory and the Modern Quest for a Code of Nature.* Joseph Henry Press, 2006

Sigmund, K. *Games of Life: Explorations in Ecology,* Evolution and Behaviour. OUP, 1993

Sigmund, K. *The Calculus of Selfishness.* Princeton University Press, 2010

Sigmund, K. *Moral Assessment in Indirect Reciprocity.* Journal of Theoretical Biology, 2012

Sloan Wilson, D. *Evolution for Everyone: How Darwin's Theory Can Change the Way We Think about Our Lives.* Delacorte, 2007

Sloan Wilson, D. *Does Altruism Exist? Culture, Genes and the Welfare of Others.* Yale University Press, 2015

Sloan Wilson, D. *The Tragedy of the Commons: How Elinor Ostrom Solved One of Life's Greatest Dilemmas.* Essay in David Sloan Wilson's online archive

The Secrets of Life - Book One

Smith, A. *The Theory of Moral Sentiments*. Liberty Classics, 1759/1976

Smith, A. *The Wealth of Nations*. Classic House Books, 1776/2009

Snow, CP. *The Two Cultures and the Scientific Revolution*. Cambridge University Press, 1959

Sober, E. and Wilson, DS. *Unto Others: The Evolution and Psychology of Unselfish Behavior*. Harvard University Press, 1999

Solomon, S. *Future Humans: Inside the Science of Our Continuing Evolution*. Yale University Press, 2016

Sparks, N. *True Believer*. Sphere, 2008

Specter, M. *Denialism: How Irrational Thinking Harms the Planet and Threatens Our Lives*. Penguin, US, 2010

Spencer, H. *The Principles of Biology*. Wentworth Press, 1867/2019

Stent, G. and Dohm, J. *Molecular Biology of Bacterial Viruses*. Literary Licensing, 2012

Stevenson, M. *An Optimist's Tour of the Future*. Profile Books, 2011

Stewart, J. *The Daily Show and Jon Stewart Present EARTH: A Visitor's Guide to the Human Race*. Particular Books, 2010

Strathern, P. *Hume in 90 Minutes*. Constable, 1996

Suarez, D. *Daemon*. Quercus, 2010

Sun Tzu. *The Art of War*, Translation made in 1782, Pax Librorum, 2009

Surowiecki, J. *The Wisdom of Crowds: Why the Many Are Smarter Than the Few*. Abacus, 2005

Sutherland, R. *This Idea Is Brilliant*. See Brockman, J.

Tainter, JA. The *Collapse of Complex Societies*. Cambridge University Press, 1990

Taleb, NN. *The Black Swan: The Impact of the Highly Improbable*. Penguin, 2007

Taleb, NN. *Skin In The Game. Hidden Asymmetries in Daily Life*. Allen Lane, 2018

Thaler, RH. *The Winner's Curse: Paradoxes and Anomalies of Economic Life*. New York: Free Press, 1992

Thaler, RH. *Misbehaving. How Economics Became Behavioural*. Allen Lane, 2015

Thaler, R. and Sunstein, CR. *Nudge: Improving Decisions About Health, Wealth and Happiness*. Yale University Press, 2008

Thomas, C. *Inheritors of the Earth: How Nature Is Thriving in an Age of Extinction*. Penguin, 2018

Thomas, L. *The Lives of a Cell*. Penguin, 1978

Thomas, L. *The Medusa and the Snail*. Penguin 1995

Thompson, H. *This Thing of Darkness*. Tinder Press, 2006

Thoreau, D. *On The Duty of Civil Disobedience*, Book Jungle, 1840/2007

Thoreau, D. *Walden: Or Life in the Woods*. Vintage Classics. 1845/2017

Tippett, K. *Becoming Wise: An Enquiry into the Mystery and the Art of Living*. Corsair, 2017

Tocqueville, A. de. *Democracy in America*. Penguin Classic, 1835/2006

Torday, J. and Rehan, V. *Evolutionary Biology: Cell-Cell Communication and Complex Disease*. Wiley-Blackwell, 2012

Trivers, RL. *The Evolution of Reciprocal Altruism*. Quarterly Review of Biology. 1971

Trivers, RL. *Social Evolution*. Benjamin-Cummins, 1985

Valen, L. van. *A New Evolutionary Law*. Evolutionary Theory, 1973-1976

Vikoulov, A. *The Origins of Us*. In: *The Science and Philosophy of Information* Edition, 2019

Vikoulov, A. *Noogenesis: Computational Biology*. Kindle, 2020

Vonnegut, K. *A Man Without A Country*. Bloomsbury, 2007

Wagner, J. *The Search for Intelligent Life in the Universe*. HarperCollins, 1986

Ward-Perkins, B. *The Fall of Rome: And The End of Civilisation*. OUP, 2006

Watson, J. *The Double Helix*. Mentor, 1969

Watson, J. *Avoid Boring People, and Other Lessons From a Life of Science*. OUP, 2008

Watson, R. *Future Files. A Brief History of the Next 50 Years*. Nicholas Brealey Publishing, 2010

Watts, DJ. *Everything Is Obvious. How Common Sense Fails*. Atlantic Books, 2011

Watts, P. *Blindsight*. Tor Books, 2020

Weatherford. J. *The History of Money*. Crown Publications, 1998

Weibull, JW. *Evolutionary Game Theory*. MIT Press, 1995

Weikart, R. *From Darwin to Hitler: Evolutionary Ethics, Eugenics and Racism in Germany*. Palgrave Macmillan, 2004

Wells, HG. *Ancient Experiments in Cooperation*. Essay of 1892

West, EG. *Adam Smith and Modern Economics*. Edward Elgar. 1990

Whitman, D. *The Optimism Gap: The I'm OK - They're Not Syndrome and the Myth of American Decline*. Walker and Co., 1998

Williams, GC. *Adaptation and Natural Selection*. Princeton University Press, 1966

Williams, GC. *Sex and Evolution*. Princeton University Press, 1975

Williams, JD. *The Compleat Strategyst*. Dover, 1954

Wilson, EO. *The Insect Societies*. Belknap Press,1971

Wilson, EO. *Sociobiology: The New Synthesis*. Harvard University Press, 1975

Wilson, EO. *On Human Nature*. Harvard University Press, 1978

Wilson, EO. *Biophilia*. Harvard University Press, 1984

Wilson, EO. *Naturalist*. Island Press, 1994

Wilson, EO. *Storm Over The Atlantic. A Chapter from The Diversity of Life*. Penguin, 2001

Wilson, EO. *The Future of Life*. Abacus, 2003

Wilson, EO. *The Social Conquest of Earth*. Liveright, 2012

Wilson, EO. *The Meaning of Human Existence*. Liveright, 2015

Wilson, EO and Holldobler, B. *Eusociality: Origins and Consequences. Proceedings of the National Academy of Sciences*, 2005

Wilson, JQ. and Kelling, G. *Broken Windows: The Police and Neighborhood Safety.* Atlantic Monthly, 1982

Winchester, S. *The Map That Changed The World: A Tale of Rocks, Ruin and Redemption.* Penguin, 2002

Wolf, M. *Why Globalisation Works*. Yale University Press, 2004

Wolfe, T. *The Kingdom of Speech*. Jonathan Cape, 2016

Woodcock, G. and Avakumovic, I. *The Anarchist Prince: A Biographical Study of Peter Kropotkin.* Boardman, London. 1950

Wrangham, RW. *Catching Fire: How Cooking Made Us Human*. Basic Books. 2009

Wrangham, RW. *The Goodness Paradox*, Profile Books, 2019

Wright, R. *The Moral Animal: Evolutionary Psychology and Everyday Life*. Pantheon Books, 1994

Wright, R. *Nonzero: The Logic of Human Destiny*. Pantheon, 2000

Wright, R. *The Evolution of God*. Little, Brown, 2009

Wright, R. *Why Buddhism Is True: The Science and Philosophy of Meditation and Enlightenment.* Simon & Schuster, 2017

Yanai, I. and Lercher, M. *The Society of Genes*. Harvard University Press, 2016

Yancey, R. *The Last Star*. Penguin, 2016

Yardeni, E. *In Praise of Profits*. Topical Study, 2021

Yeats, WB. *The Second Coming*. First printed in The Dial, 1919

Yong, E. *I Contain Multitudes*. The Bodley Head, 2016

Zhu, P. *Decision Master: The Art and Science of Decision Making*. Kindle, 2017

Zimmer, C. *Parasite Rex: Inside the Bizarre World of Nature's Most Dangerous Creatures*. Simon and Schuster, 2002

Picture Credits

Cover:	Cover and end papers: Details from Agave Americana by Bruce McLean. Copyright, the artist. Published by CCA Galleries, London and printed by Coriander Studios. Reproduced by kind permission of Bruce McLean and the CCA Galleries, September, 2022
Introduction:	Alamy
Chapter 1:	©Pasquale Bova/Ropi via ZUMA Press, Alamy
Chapter 2:	Alamy
Chapter 3:	Getty Images
Chapter 4:	Alamy/Salvador Dali Museum St. Petersburg Florida, iStock/Getty Images
Chapter 5:	Alamy, Universal History Archive/UIG/Bridgeman Images
Chapter 6:	Both Alamy (Second one posed by model)
Chapter 7:	Both Alamy
Chapter 8:	iStock/Getty Images, Shutterstock
Chapter 9:	iStock/Getty Images (Posed by models), Alamy
Chapter 10:	Shutterstock, Alamy
Chapter 11:	Alamy (Posed by models), CartoonStock
Chapter 12:	Alamy, CartoonStock
Chapter 13:	Alamy
Chapter 14:	Darwin Archive/Cambridge University Library, Chris Madden
Chapter 15:	Source unknown, Alamy
Chapter 16:	Alamy, Don Grant, author's collection
Chapter 17:	Alamy
Chapter 18:	Getty Images, Alamy
Chapter 19:	Alamy, Haldane/Krishna R. Dronamraju/Vicky
Chapter 20:	Source unknown, Alamy
Chapter 21:	www.CartoonStock.com, Getty Images